LITERATURE
AND THE
AMERICAN
COLLEGE

Irving Babbitt

LITERATURE AND THE AMERICAN COLLEGE

Essays in Defense of the Humanities

INTRODUCTION BY RUSSELL KIRK

NATIONAL HUMANITIES INSTITUTE
WASHINGTON, D.C.

ISBN 0-932783-01-5

Library of Congress Catalog Card No. 86-062218

"There are two laws discrete
  Not reconciled,—
  Law for man, and law for thing;
  The last builds town and fleet,
  But it runs wild,
  And doth the man unking."

—EMERSON

Contents

Foreword

IN PUBLISHING THIS NEW EDITION of Irving Babbitt's *Literature and the American College*, with the extensive introduction written by Russell Kirk exclusively for this volume, the NATIONAL HUMANITIES INSTITUTE addresses one of the most significant questions of this or any age: the role of education.

It would be unwise—and certainly contrary to American tradition—to prescribe a rigid, centralized curriculum for this nation's elementary and secondary schools. But equally dangerous is the tendency, all too prevalent in recent years, to move away from any common body of educational content, any coherence of educational purpose. As Secretary of Education William J. Bennett has noted: "We shift and change in what we ask our students to learn from year to year. There seems to be a new educational fad for every freshman high school class."

Given the infinite multiplicity of "facts" in the world, it is impossible to master all of them, nor is this desirable. What is needed, as Secretary Bennett has indicated, is to identify standards of selection that can be used by educators in developing curricula so that those things which are truly important to all Americans—as persons and as citizens—are included. From such standards of selection, a common body of educational content will emerge that embodies the best that the long history and tradition of mankind has to offer. It is particularly essential, Secretary Bennett has added, to identify standards that will help to develop the character of American students: to enable them to distinguish between right and wrong and to act on that knowledge.

Babbitt's *Literature and the American College*, first published in 1908, anticipates Secretary Bennett's recognition that the development of the intellect and moral character are intimately related. This new edition, published under a grant from the U.S. Department of Education, can give educators a renewed appreciation of the role that the humanities—history and literature especially—must play if education is to be effective.

According to Babbitt, attempts by modern philosophy to solve the problem of knowledge rest on a vain belief in abstract rationality as the way to truth. These attempts, he argues, signify a failure to understand that in the end man will attach himself only to a standard of reality that has immediacy and concreteness—one that is firmly established in experience. Far more than by abstract argument, Babbitt writes, man learns by example and by concrete action or experience. To a greater extent than has been acknowledged in recent years, the quality of a society depends upon the quality of the examples it chooses to follow. It is better to follow the "wisdom of the ages" than the "wisdom of the hour." Questions regarding reality are best answered by those who have let their own experience be enriched, ordered and interpreted by that sense of the universal that emerges from the human heritage of literature, art, and tradition. As Babbitt's student Walter Lippmann was to observe, it is the "history of the community"—the "great deeds and the high purposes of the great predecessors"—that inspire the rising generation to add new acts of nobility to life's unfinished story.

For Babbitt, then, teachers—if they are doing their job correctly—form the great link in the chain of civilization without which it cannot hold. They are both the conservators and the transmitters of culture. It is from them that future generations come to appreciate the ideals of their country and the wider civilization of which it is a part: justice, for example, and equality, and ordered liberty. It is by the difficult work of assimilating and embodying in their very lives and deeds the hard-won lessons of many generations that teachers earn the right to be heard respectfully by the students encharged to their care. If teachers recently have lost much of the honor that they were accorded traditionally by their communities, it is largely because they are perceived as having betrayed this sacred trust.

The inversion of the educator's traditional role is well illustrated by recent trends in "values education," which seek the answers to moral development in mere abstract intellection. According to contemporary theories, the children are to develop their "own" values through classroom discussion, dialogues, games, and so forth. In marked contrast with his traditional role as a transmitter of culture, the teacher, according to these theories, is strictly admonished not to allow his own values or those of the traditional culture to "interfere" with this process. The students, accordingly, are left with little more guidance than their own momentary "feelings" and those of their peers. Values are chosen in an historical and cultural vacuum. The result, predictably, is moral relativism.

For Babbitt, this is to miss the most essential meaning of education—as if, in what is most crucial to human life and happiness, each generation had to invent the wheel anew. Prevalent trends in American education tend to associate the ethical life with sentimental sympathy and unrestrained impulse. By contrast, Babbitt holds, a proper understanding of history and the classics leads to a quite opposite concept of morality: one based on restraint and self-discipline, "a sense of proportion and pervading law." He insists on an all-important distinction between genuine morality, which is an exercise of will based on moral character, and a pseudo-moralistic "virtue" of the emotions.

Babbitt points to Rousseau as among the most influential of those who have tried to redefine moral virtue in terms of emotion. The subtle attraction of this new "morality" is that it liberates men and women from the painful effort of actual improvement of character. It does not require of man that he should ceaselessly criticize his own moral failings and undertake a continuous and difficult reform of self, as in the classical and Judaeo–Christian traditions in ethics. Man is essentially good and need only give free vent to a natural feeling of brotherhood.

Unlike Christian love, which begins with love of neighbor and consists first of all of caring *actions* toward concrete living human beings close at hand, Rousseauistic sentimental "virtue" consists of merely emotional benevolence toward nobody in particular. Its object is a distant and abstract "mankind." Sentimental "morality" places no burdensome obligations on the bearer; it conveniently transfers duties to some agency other than self, such as government.

Americans in overwhelming numbers see this new "morality" as largely responsible for many contemporary social ills among the nation's young population, including the explosion in teen-age pregnancies, the rampant use of abortion, drug and alcohol abuse, and the alarming number of teen-age suicides. They are demanding that the schools impart to our young people a respect for traditional Western beliefs about what is important, and especially the difference between right and wrong. A sense that the public schools in many jurisdictions have been failing to meet this standard is one reason that many parents have been opting to send their children to private schools, despite the considerable financial burden that entails. Recently there have been encouraging signs that the educational community is beginning to respond to these concerns, and that there is a new search among teachers for ways to improve their curricula accordingly. *Literature and the American College*, the book in which Babbitt most directly expresses a philosophy of education, offers much that is useful to those engaged in that quest.

Joseph Baldacchino
President
NATIONAL HUMANITIES INSTITUTE

Introduction

Babbitt and the Ethical Purpose of Literary Studies

by Russell Kirk

I. The Stature of Irving Babbitt

IT IS IN HISTORIES OF LITERARY CRITICISM that one encounters the name of Irving Babbitt, rather than in treatises on American schooling. Yet his influence as a champion of humane learning has been enduring, if subtle. On Babbitt's death in 1933, T. S. Eliot wrote of him, "After a life of indefatigable, and for many years almost solitary intellectual struggle, he had secured for his views, if not full appreciation, at least wide recognition; he had established a great and beneficial influence, of a kind which has less show than substance, through the many pupils who left him to become teachers throughout America; and he had established a strong counter-current in education."

Eliot had studied under Babbitt at Harvard, a quarter of a century earlier, as did a good many other young men who would

1

rise to some considerable intellectual and moral influence. For thirty-eight years Babbitt taught French literature—and, informally, much else besides—at Harvard. "I think that the point at which Babbitt's ideas converged with the greatest force was the subject of Education..." Eliot continued. "In America, where education has for two or three generations responded to the whim of any modern theory, where a single man of character and conviction can impose his views, from time to time, upon the methods of the whole nation, and where the divergent tastes and ideals of scholars variously trained in Germany, France or England, have been a source of weakness and instability, every vagary has had its opportunity, and successive scholastic generations have only suffered from successive experiments.... Thirty years ago Babbitt was a young tutor of insecure position, when he began almost single-handed (though perhaps under the approving eye of Charles Norton) to attack the system which Charles Eliot of Harvard had built up and popularized through the country; to the end of his life he opposed the heresies of the school of John Dewey. These facts deserve to be recorded in his honour...." [1]

Literature and the American College, published in 1908—though several of its constituent essays had appeared in periodicals earlier, and one of them had been a lecture in 1895—was Babbitt's first book. It would be followed by *The New Laokoon: An Essay on the Confusion of the Arts* (1910); *The Masters of Modern French Criticism* (1912); *Rousseau and Romanticism* (1919); *Democracy and Leadership* (1924); *On Being Creative and Other Essays* (1932); a translation of *The Dhammapada*, with an essay on the Buddha (1936); and *Spanish Character and other Essays* (1940). [2]

1. Eliot, "Commentary," *The Criterion*, Vol. XIII (October 1933–July 1934), pp. 115–19.

2. Several of Babbitt's books have been reprinted, with introductions by other hands, in recent years: *The Masters of Modern French Criticism*, with introduction by Milton Hindus (New York, 1963); *Rousseau and Romanticism*, with foreword by Harry Levin (Austin, Texas, 1977); *Democracy and Leadership*, with introduction by Russell Kirk (Indianapolis, 1979); *Literature and the American College*, with introductions by Russell Kirk (Chicago, 1956, and the present new edition). See also *Irving Babbitt: Representative Writings*, edited, with an introduction, by George Panichas (Lincoln, Nebraska, 1981).

Far more clearly than his pedagogical adversary John Dewey, Irving Babbitt foresaw the difficulties of the dawning era. Without having intended it, Babbitt soon found himself (with his ally Paul Elmer More) the leader of a movement of sorts—critical, educational, political—called the New Humanism or American Humanism, which for three decades packed the serious journals of the United States, and even of Britain, with friendly or hostile criticism, and which remains a living intellectual force in any American educational institution worthy of the name, although everywhere in a minority. Quite conceivably Babbitt's Humanism, drawing its strength from ancient roots, may continue to be discussed long after various intellectual fads detested by Babbitt have gone down to dusty death.[3]

Born at Dayton, Ohio, in 1865, Irving Babbitt — late in life sometimes accused of being an obdurate survivor of the Genteel Tradition, and so still tagged by Arthur Schlesinger Jr. in the 1950s—was a little newsboy on the streets of New York, a youthful farmhand near Cincinnati, a cowboy in Wyoming, and a newspaper reporter covering the police court in Cincinnati, before he was enrolled at Harvard College. The rest of his life, spent almost wholly at Harvard, was unadventurous in the ordinary sense of that word, but intellectually exciting, especially at the height of the controversy over the New Humanism, with its public debates—even over radio—and its vehement animosities.

Babbitt's books and lectures provoked the men of the Left—though not of the Left merely, for Allen Tate set his face against Humanism and T. S. Eliot had his differences with his old

3. Although a considerable body of periodical writing about Babbitt's ideas has accumulated, curiously few book-length studies have been published as yet. See the following: Francis E. McMahon, *The Humanism of Irving Babbitt* (Washington, D.C., 1931); Folke Leander, *Humanism and Naturalism: A Comparative Study of Ernest Seillière, Irving Babbitt, and Paul Elmer More* (Göteborg, Sweden, 1937); *Irving Babbitt: Man and Teacher*, edited by Frederick Manchester and Odell Shepard, containing thirty-nine memoirs by various writers (New York, 1941); and Thomas R. Nevin, *Irving Babbitt: An Intellectual Study* (Chapel Hill, North Carolina, 1984).

professor.[4] The less civil of his adversaries denounced Babbitt as a Brahman and, almost in the same breath, as a vulgarian. In truth, Babbitt was a big likeable man who, like Samuel Johnson, read nearly every book he came upon—but, unlike Johnson, read some of them to the last page. He lived with a high dignity reflected in his very dress, and loved and hated with a prophetic vehemence, disdaining easy success and the popularity of the academic neoterist.

Ernest Hemingway inquired brutally, in his *Death in the Afternoon* (1932), whether Humanists would be dignified as they died: "So now I want to see the death of any self-called Humanist because a persevering traveller like Mungo Park or me lives on and maybe yet will live to see the actual death of members of this literary sect. . . . I hope to see the finish of a few, and speculate how worms will try that long-preserved sterility; with their quaint pamphlets gone to bust and into foot-notes all their lust. . . ." Hemingway did live well beyond the year of Babbitt's death. It was of a most painful disease, ulcerative colitis, that Babbitt died; almost to the end, Professor Babbitt continued to meet his Harvard class. A member of that class published in *The New Yorker*, seven years later, some account of Babbitt's final months, pointing out that indeed Babbitt died with dignity and high courage — "definitely heroic" was the phrase a physician used. Hemingway, when old age settled upon him, killed himself with a shotgun.[5]

Yes, Babbitt died manfully, as he had lived. "His life was a doubly concentrated one; he not only centered his life upon scholarship, teaching and writing, but also steadily pursued a single aim and preached an unvarying faith. . . ." So Hoffman Nickerson, the military historian, wrote of Babbitt. "Humanism was his god, and to its service he devoted a great, virile

---

4. See Allen Tate, "The Fallacy of Humanism," *The Criterion*, Vol. VIII (September 1928–July 1929), pp. 661–81; and T. S. Eliot, "The Humanism of Irving Babbitt," in Eliot's *Selected Essays, 1917–1932* (New York, 1932).

5. See John A. Yunck, "The Natural History of a Dead Quarrel: Hemingway and the Humanists," *The South Atlantic Quarterly*, Vol. LXII, No. 1 (winter, 1963), pp. 29–42; also Russell Maloney, "A Footnote to a Footnote," *The New Yorker*, July 15, 1939.

personality, a solid and sober eloquence set off with dry, cutting wit, and a learning of astonishing accuracy and vastness.'' [6]

Eliot, powerfully influenced in many ways by Babbitt and repeatedly acknowledging that beneficent guidance, was Professor Babbitt's most distinguished disciple—which sufficiently suggests the absurdity of Harold Laski's assertion that Babbitt had no disciples. Among Babbitt's allies and intellectual followers were such scholars as Paul Elmer More, Warner Rice, G. R. Elliot, Louis Mercier, Austin Warren, Gordon Chalmers, Harry Hayden Clark, James Luther Adams, Theodore Spencer, John Livingston Lowes, Harold Lynn Hough, Ernest Seillière, Stuart P. Sherman, Norman Foerster, Nathan Pusey—not that all these men always agreed with Babbitt on every point, but rather that they were roused and strengthened by Babbitt's seminal mind. Fifty years after Babbitt's death, a later generation of writers and scholars rallied to his standard. [7]

Contemptuous of a sentimental internationalism, Babbitt nevertheless was an intellectual universalist. ''He was American in his restless energy,'' G. R. Elliott writes. ''His was a restless campaign against American restlessness—a battling effort to turn our thinking towards the Supreme Peace. That paradox was vital, since fire when it is bad enough has to be fought with fire. Hence his unfailing devotion to Harvard University, even the modern Harvard, our leading American factory for mental mass-production. He himself was a distinguished product of that mill; distinguished, because from the outset the Buddha, instead of President Eliot, had played the dominant part in the shaping process. Babbitt once pointed out to me, with a mien of gratitude to fate, an avenue in the outskirts

6. Hoffman Nickerson, ''Irving Babbitt,'' *The Criterion*, Vol. XIII (October 1933–July 1934), pp. 179–95.

7. See an important early examination of Babbitt's influence and Eliot's partial dissent: G. R. Elliott, ''T. S. Eliot and Irving Babbitt,'' *The American Review*, Vol. VII (April–October, 1936), pp. 442–54. The most recent collection of essays on Babbitt, with contributions by several scholars, is *Irving Babbitt in Our Time* (Washington, 1986), edited by Claes Ryn and George Panichas.

of Cambridge where as a young undergraduate he had been wont to trot back and forth holding a Pâli text to his eyes, learning its language and absorbing lore while exercising his legs." Babbitt held that, in Elliott's words, "America, now inundated with contemporaneity, must rediscover the noblest heights of thought in the past, the whole long past, Occidental and Oriental, of which she is the inheritor." [8]

The personality of this remarkable scholar and man of letters deserves a fuller examination; but in this new edition of Babbitt's first book we are concerned with his educational ideas, rather than his character and milieu; and that is just as Babbitt, not a proud man, would have had us do. Babbitt's educational insights, eight decades after *Literature and the American College* first was published (in Boston, by Houghton Mifflin), in some ways seem more pertinent to our own time than to his.

For the subtitle of Babbitt's first book is *Essays in Defense of the Humanities*; and in these closing years of the twentieth century, humane studies have a hearing once more. Why are the humane disciplines important to the person and the republic? What is this "humanism" and how is it related to humanitarianism? Does literature have an ethical function, so to form good character among the rising generation? Is the literary discipline meant to support a moral order? Are there perils in academic specialization? How is continuity of culture maintained? Is it possible for humane studies to provide in public schools a satisfactory alternative to either dogmatic religious instruction or to the civil religion of "secular humanism"? Literary studies neglected, does there remain any cement to make a curriculum cohere? What should a tolerable literary curriculum provide? All these are some of the questions being asked nowadays about the humanities. Babbitt's forceful little book is concerned with just such difficulties and aspirations.

"What Is Humanism?" That title of the first chapter is enlarged upon by all the rest of Babbitt's books. We will

---

8. G. R. Elliott, "Irving Babbitt as I Knew Him," *The American Review*, Vol. VIII (November, 1936–March, 1937), pp. 36–60; reprinted in Manchester and Shepard, *Irving Babbitt: Man and Teacher, op. cit.,* pp. 144–64.

consider that question soberly a little later in this Introduction. Just now, putting matters very briefly, we may define Babbitt's humanism as the belief that man is a distinct being, governed by laws peculiar to his nature: there is law for man, and law for thing. Man stands higher than the beasts that perish because he recognizes and obeys this law of his nature. The disciplinary arts of *humanitas* teach man to put checks upon his will and his appetite. Those checks are approved by reason—not the private rationality of the Enlightenment, but the higher reason which grows out of a respect for the wisdom of our ancestors and out of the endeavor to apprehend that transcendent order which gives us our nature. The sentimentalist, who would subject man to the rule of impulse and passion; the pragmatic naturalist, who would treat man as a mere edified ape; the levelling enthusiast, who would reduce human differences to a collective mediocrity —these are the enemies of true human nature. Against them Babbitt directed this book and all his other books.

For Babbitt, the great end of education is ethical. In the college, as at all other levels of the educational process, the student comes to apprehend the differences between good and evil. It is this humane tradition and discipline which makes us true human persons and sustains a decent civil social order.

Irving Babbitt saw about him a civilization intellectually devoting itself to the study of subhuman relationships, which it mistook for the whole of life; that civilization was sinking into a meaningless aestheticism, an arid specialization, and a mean vocationalism. Babbitt's attempted renewal of an understanding of true humanism was intended to return his generation to the real aim of education, the study of the greatness and the limitations of human nature.

Against the humanist, Babbitt set the humanitarian. The humanist struggles to develop, by an act of will, the higher nature in man; the humanitarian, for his part, believes in "outer working and inner *laissez faire*," material gain and emancipation from ethical checks. What the humanist desires is a working in the soul of man; what the humanitarian seeks is the gratification of appetites. Francis Bacon symbolized for Babbitt the utilitarian aspect of humanitarianism, the lust for power

over society and physical nature; Rousseau symbolized for him
the sentimental aspect of humanitarianism, the treacherous
impulse to break what Burke had called "the contract of eternal
society" and to substitute for moral obligation the worship of a
reckless egoism.

To egoism and appetite, which so oppress our time, Babbitt
opposed humanism, the study of man's essential nature, with its
strict ethical disciplines. Humane studies are those that teach
human beings their dignity and their duties. They teach that
man is a little lower than the angels, but infinitely higher than
the beasts.

This theme is examined by Babbitt in a variety of ways. His
observations on leisure, on originality, on the classics, on the
doctoral degree, and on the study of literature, remain witty and
urbane as they were in 1908. It scarcely is necessary to remark
that America is eighty years closer to that total collapse of
humane disciplines which Babbitt, in his era of optimism,
already discerned as a grim possibility. Will and appetite have
had their way little checked in a great part of the world, and here
in America humanism seemingly fights a rear-guard action; like
the Celts of the twilight, humane scholars have gone forth often
to battle, but not to victory. Whether we can restore order in
education, in personality, and in society depends now, in some
part, on whether there survives among Americans a remnant
sufficiently educated to understand Babbitt's sentences and
sufficiently resolute to act upon Babbitt's admonitions.

In this Introduction we take up Babbitt's educational principles in the light of changes that have occurred during the past
eight decades. First we consider the distinctions between
humanism and humanitarianism, with remarks on the ideology
called Secular Humanism. Then we turn to the degradation of
the democratic dogma on the campus. Next we examine Babbitt
on literary pedantry, literary frivolity, and academic degrees.
We discuss the intellectual attitudes called classicism, romanticism, and nihilism, and analyze three types of imagination.
We present some reflections on originality, perversity, and regeneration. Concluding, we contrast what might be in the
American college with what is.

The dead alone give us energy, said Le Bon; and surely, when we think of educational renewal and reform, Irving Babbitt looms tall among the energetic dead. Those fallacies in education that Babbitt assailed so strenuously during his time now are perceived as ruinous errors by many Americans, from the Secretary of Education and the members of the National Commission on Excellence in Education to teachers in the most bucolic schools and parents in the most affluent suburbs. The wise man is a lover of distinctions, Babbitt said more than once: so we turn to distinguishing between humanism and humanitarianism.

II. Humanists and Humanitarians

THE TERMS "HUMANIST" AND "HUMANISM," much employed in *Literature and the American College*, have an intricate and confused history. Babbitt traces the etymology of these terms, through Aulus Gellius, back to Cicero and beyond, and then down the centuries again to Castiglione and Sir Philip Sidney; many readers may be left at a loss. Our author discusses the words from time to time in other writings of his, most notably in his "Humanism: an Essay at Definition," in *Humanism and America*, edited by Norman Foerster (New York, 1930). There he defines humanists as "those who, in any age, aim at proportionateness through a cultivation of the law of measure." The true humanist, he argues, is mindful of the Hellenic admonition "nothing too much"; the humanist exercises an "inner check" upon his will and his appetites.

In *Literature and the American College*, Babbitt assumes that his readers are familiar with the conventional definitions of "humanist" and allied terms generally accepted at the beginning of the twentieth century — for instance, this definition of "humanist" in the ten-volume *Century Dictionary*, edition of 1904: "One accomplished in literary and classical culture; especially, in the fourteenth, fifteenth, and sixteenth centuries, one of the scholars who, following the impulse of Petrarch, pursued and disseminated the study and a truer understanding of classical, and particularly of Greek, literature.''

Although Babbitt does not happen to mention Pico della Mirandola, Babbitt's humanism is nearly identical with the argument of Pico's famous *Oration on the Dignity of Man* (1486). (Possibly the magical side of Pico made Babbitt uneasy.) The Christian humanism of Erasmus and of Sir Thomas More clearly is a source of Babbitt's twentieth-century humanism, although Babbitt himself was as much a Buddhist as a Christian, and avoided references to the divine. There are strong links between the New Humanism and classical and medieval doctrines of natural law.

Babbitt's educated humanists, then, are those persons, in bygone times or in the twentieth century, whose understanding of the virtues, and whose very manners, are formed in some degree by instruction in the ''ancients'' — the books of the ancient world, the writings of the Greek dramatists, of Plato and Aristotle, of Cicero and Horace and Vergil and Livy, of Plutarch, of the whole corpus of a classical education. Also he implies, when referring to humanism, the large body of works of literature in Italian, French, English, Spanish, and other languages that are derived in part from this venerable classical tradition of thought and style. He is lamenting the decay of this humane schooling during his own lifetime of less than forty years; and he is distinguishing this sort of education from the training in the physical sciences and in utilitarian disciplines and skills that even then had begun to thrust humane schooling out the door. Harvard, too, was giving sociology and the natural sciences pride of place over humane disciplines.

The purpose of studying humane letters was to seek after the Platonic ends of wisdom and virtue: that is, to develop right reason and sound character. The purpose of the rival utilitarian disciplines was to acquire power and wealth. In the long run and perhaps in the short run, Babbitt is demanding, what will become of college graduates who know the price of everything and the value of nothing? And what will become of a nation led by men adept at grasping power and money, but who never have acquired that moral discipline and that power of imagination which a humane schooling is meant to confer? Whether reared in the utilitarian school of Bacon or the sentimental school of Rousseau, such people are not to be trusted.

The American colleges, like the colleges of Oxford and Cambridge, had been founded to enable the better minds among the rising generation to study certain great works of literature, in the expectation that intellectual and moral elevation would be gained thereby, to the benefit of the student and of the nation. That is what is signified by the term "the humanities": those studies, in a number of languages, which nurture mind and conscience through serious introduction to literary productions that have endured the test of time. Of such studies Babbitt became the most formidable champion, in the early years of this century.[9]

But there were other claimants to the concept or word "humanism"—the philanthropists, the enthusiasts for an indiscriminate benevolence, sternly opposed by Aulus Gellius in the second century of the Christian era and by Irving Babbitt in the twentieth. Such folk Babbitt styled humanitarians; one definition in the *Century Dictionary* of 1904 comes close to his meaning: "One who adopts the doctrine or theory that man's sphere of duty is limited to a benevolent interest in and practical

9. The numerous different significations of the words "humanist," "humanism," etc., are ably summed up by Vito R. Guistiniani in "Homo, Humanus, and the Meanings of 'Humanism,'" *Journal of the History of Ideas*, Vol. XLVI (April–June 1985), pp. 167–95. A considerable number of books arose out of the American Humanist controversies, discussing the interpretation of these terms. See particularly, in addition to earlier references, Louis J. A. Mercier, *American Humanism and the New Age* (Milwaukee, 1948); Lawrence Hyde, *The Learned Knife: an Essay on Science and Human Values* (London, 1928); Jacques Maritain, *True Humanism* (Westport, Connecticut, 1941); Hough, Harold Lynn, *Vital Control* (New York, 1934); G. R. Elliott, *Humanism and Imagination* (Chapel Hill, North Carolina, 1938); J. David Hoeveler, Jr., *The New Humanism: a Critique of Modern America, 1900–1940* (Charlottesville, Virginia, 1977); George A. Panichas, "The Critical Mission of Irving Babbitt," in his collection *The Courage of Judgment* (Knoxville, Tennessee, 1982); William Van O'Connor, "The New Humanism," in his *An Age of Criticism, 1900–1950* (Chicago, 1952). Other studies are listed in the bibliographies of Panichas, *Babbitt: Representative Writings, op. cit.*, and Nevin, *Babbitt, op. cit.*

promotion of the welfare of the human race, apart from all considerations of religion."

As Babbitt puts it, "A person who has sympathy for mankind in the lump, faith in its future progress, and desire to serve the great cause of this progress, should be called not a humanist, but a humanitarian. From the present tendency to regard humanism as an abbreviated and convenient form of humanitarianism there must arise every manner of confusion. The humanitarian lays stress almost solely upon breadth of knowledge and sympathy. The poet Schiller, for instance, speaks as a humanitarian and not as a humanist when he would 'clasp the millions to his bosom,' and bestow 'a kiss upon the whole world.' The humanist is more selective in his caresses."

It may be said without much exaggeration that in education the humanist thinks of that great well of wisdom called the past; while the humanitarian thinks of current awareness, the passing moment. In politics, the humanist tends to think of permanence; the humanitarian, of change. Humanitarians of this description were ready to dispute definitions with Babbitt, More, and other New Humanists—because somehow there lies an advantage in holding possession of this tag "humanism."

For even as Babbitt wrote the essays that make up *Literature and the American College*, there was taking form an intellectual movement—calling itself American Humanism—that by 1933 would issue the Humanist Manifesto (sometimes, rather oddly, called the Religious Humanist Manifesto). John Dewey was the principal author of that document, and the other leaders in this movement, most of them, were Dewey's friends and disciples; also they were socialists of a sort, although not ordinarily Marxists; Instrumentalists in education, nearly all; hostile toward churches; rationalistic; progressivists, shrugging their shoulders at the past, or else condemning earlier ages. In short, they were extreme humanitarians who preferred to be styled humanists. The New Humanists or original American Humanists had been making an intellectual stir for a quarter of a century, when these militantly secularistic rivals sprang up.

"The Humanist Manifesto (somewhat reminiscent in its title of Marx's *Kommunistisches Manifest* of 1848) is an effort to replace traditional religious beliefs by stalwart confidence in our capacity to achieve moral perfection and happiness along the lines and within the limits of our earthly nature," Vito Giustiniani writes. "The 15 articles of the Manifesto are a blend of old tenets of 18th-century Enlightenment and worship of reason, of utilitarianism à la Bentham, of positivism and Darwinism, of 19th-century absolute faith in the power of science and so on, not without a considerable touch of American pragmatism. For the *Manifesto* 'the universe is self-existing and not created'; 'religion consists of those actions, purposes, and experiences which are humanly significant. Nothing human is alien to the religious. It includes labor, art, science, philosophy, love, friendship, recreation—all that is in its degree expressive and intelligently satisfying human living.' A person's relation to society is no less vaguely outlined: 'the humanist finds his religious emotions expressed in a heightened sense of personal life and in a co-operative effort to promote social well-being,' and 'the goal of humanism is a free and universal society in which people voluntarily and intelligently co-operate for the common good.'

"The all-out negation of everything supernatural and transcendental," Giustiniani remarks, "makes this *Manifesto* opposed to what Revelation preaches.... Its church, if such a word can be used here, is the American Humanist Association, with its branch in Britain (British Humanist Association)." [10] In 1973 the remaining original signers of this Humanist Manifesto, together with later recruits, issued a still more radical Manifesto.

To Irving Babbitt, dying by inches in 1933, the abduction of the word "humanist" by John Dewey's circle must have seemed an abomination worse than the assault of the philanthropists upon true humanism in Aulus Gellius' era. Ever since Dewey and his colleagues of the American Humanist Association established a headquarters (long at Yellow Springs, Ohio; latterly at Amherst, New York), and began mailing the magazine *The Humanist* throughout the land, previous popular confusion about humanism and humanitarianism, and about

10. Vito Giustiniani, *op. cit.*, pp. 178-79.

those two very different groups, both called in newspapers "The American Humanists," has been worse confounded.

There exist yet other groups calling themselves "humanists": Scientific Humanists, swearing by evolutionary doctrines; Sartre's Existential Humanists; even Rosenberg's Biological Humanists of the Third Reich. But ordinarily, when "humanism" is discussed in connection with American education, there is meant either the atheist-leaning and militantly socialistic creed of the Deweyites, or else the teachings of Babbitt, More, and other New Humanists. These two bodies of opinion are at opposite poles.

In recent years many parents and various churches have expressed alarm at the intrusions of "humanism" into public schools. The term Secular Humanism is employed to describe this intellectual or ideological program, militantly secularistic; federal courts have recognized Secular Humanism as a body of doctrines—in effect, an ideology—equivalent to a religion. The American Humanist Association and allied Secular Humanist groups have made headway in introducing "sex education" courses into schools, promoting "values clarification" school programs that recognize no religious norms, opposing any school ceremonies of a religious cast, and in general nudging public schools in directions approved by the American Humanist Association, which is quite unrelated to either classical or Christian humanism.

To Irving Babbitt and the New Humanists generally, this Secular Humanism and its positivistic or humanitarian forerunners were detestable. It is not that Babbitt was a religious man; but neither was he an atheist. An ethical philosopher—or, more strictly speaking, a sage — Babbitt much reminds one of Confucius in this. Babbitt judged it prudent to keep ethical discussion on the mundane level, so far as possible, in the hope of obtaining practical consensus without unanimity in dogmata. He never freed himself from uneasiness with churches visible. Yet he could imagine circumstances in which the Roman Catholic Church might be the last defense of civilization; and many of his close associates, Paul Elmer More especially, were men of religious faith. The progressivism and radicalism of the

American Humanist Association seemed to Babbitt absurd and malign.

James Hitchcock, historical scholar and editor of the theological journal *Communio*, endeavors to distinguish among the several types of humanists, present or past, in a little book intended for a popular readership, *What Is Secular Humanism?* He remarks the gulf fixed between Secular Humanists and Christian humanists, and in one paragraph happens to express the limited sense in which Babbitt uses the word "humanist" in *Literature and the American College*:

"In the narrowest sense, a humanist is someone who is interested, often in a professional way, in those intellectual and academic disciplines called the humanities — so called because they deal with human nature in its fullness, the non-rational side of man as well as the rational. These have traditionally included literature, history, the fine arts, philosophy, and sometimes theology. Alexander Pope's dictum that 'the proper study of mankind is man' is a watchword of the discipline. The humanities tend to be somewhat intuitive and do not make man an object of properly scientific scrutiny." [11]

Babbitt would have been uneasy at Hitchcock's mention of the irrational, and would have emphasized more strongly than did Hitchcock the ethical purpose of humane learning. Otherwise, Hitchcock's succinct description is useful in helping a reader to apprehend the humanism advocated in *Literature and the American College*. [12]

Nowadays the need for some form of moral instruction in

11. James Hitchcock, *What Is Secular Humanism?* (Ann Arbor, Michigan, 1982), pp. 8–9.

12. The relationship of humanism and religion, and the assertedly equivocal views of Babbitt, More, and others in such concerns, were the subject of much and sometimes heated discussion in serious periodicals of the 'Twenties and 'Thirties. See, for instance, Herbert Read, "Humanism and the Absolute," *The Criterion*, Vol. VIII (September 1928–July 1929), pp. 270–76; Norman Foerster, "Humanism and Religion," *The Criterion*, Vol. IX (October 1929–July 1930), pp. 23–32; G. R. Elliott, "The Religious Dissension of Babbitt and More," *The American Review*, Vol. IX (April–October 1937), pp. 252–65.

public schools is recognized widely. Teaching of any religious creed has been prevented by the federal courts, and indeed dogmatic instruction never did prevail in public schools of the present sort. What can be done to remedy this deficiency? Perhaps the humanistic spirit of education so warmly described by Babbitt may come into its own again. Humane literature— the poem, the novel, and the play particularly—is the school discipline best calculated to wake the moral imagination, at every age-level. An obsession with contemporaneity in school readers and anthologies has worked to enfeeble the imagination of American students over several decades. Thus the reintroduction of really great imaginative literature, redeeming young people from what T. S. Eliot called "the provincialism of time," could be a more effective educational reform than all the salary-increases and computer-innovations and certification-requirements put together. Such a shift would be an escape from a boring humanitarianism in the classroom and the textbook, back to a proliferating humanism.

III. The Collegiate Degradation of the Democratic Dogma

HARVARD, AS THE TWENTIETH CENTURY BEGAN, and American colleges generally, were afflicted by a Rousseauistic humanitarianism: so Irving Babbitt declared boldly. Humanitarian sentimentality lay back of the elective system, installed by President Charles W. Eliot of the Five-Foot Shelf of Books. Rousseau's exaltation of sympathy encouraged a lowering of academic standards so that the slack and the dull might not be left behind: in Babbitt's sentences, "As formerly conceived, the college might have been defined as a careful selection of studies for the creation of a social elite. In its present tendency, it might be defined as something of everything for everybody."

The Baconian or scientific version of humanitarianism

worked in a fashion no less malign. It neglected quality for the sake of quantity; it thrust aside the Greek and Roman classics as useless in the production of goods and services. Jeremy Bentham, "the great subversive" (John Stuart Mill's description), had come to advocate the democratic cause so that Parliament might be compelled to enact his Utilitarian measures; now at American colleges the scientific humanitarianism of Bentham combined with the sentimental humanitarianism of Rousseau (whose works Bentham had detested) in a democratic spirit of rebellion against the humane tradition.[13]

Might it be possible to develop in the American college a democracy of elevation, not of degradation? Babbitt's college humanism is equivalent to John Henry Newman's concept of liberal education, as described in *The Idea of a University* and *The Office and Work of Universities*. By a liberal discipline, Newman wrote, there is formed a habit of mind "which lasts through life, of which the attributes are, freedom, equitableness, calmness, moderation, and wisdom, or what...I have ventured to call the philosophical habit." [14] That was precisely what Babbitt hoped to restore in the American college, through a reinvigorated humanism — except that Newman meant to educate Christian gentlemen, and Babbitt would have been content "in a quantitative age to produce men of quality." Himself a child of the American democracy, Babbitt (rather like John Adams in this) asked for nothing more oligarchic than a body of college-educated persons who might exert some check upon the American drift toward pure democracy; here he had Tocqueville to cite. Humanitarian policies might have a large place in the lower schools; but in colleges, careful selection of studies,

13. Although he wrote next to nothing about Bentham, Babbitt analyzed J. J. Rousseau in a whole volume of mordant criticism: *Rousseau and Romanticism* (Boston, 1919). The dullness of Bentham's prose, and the reflection that ultimately a utilitarian materialism bores nearly everybody, doubtless persuaded Irving Babbitt to fire his heavy guns at Rousseau, whose "idyllic imagination" (fully examined in *Rousseau and Romanticism*) made revolutions by providing a sham spirituality for the discontented and obscure.

14. John Henry Newman, Discourse V, *The Idea of a University Defined and Illustrated* (London, 1853).

with firm standards of quality, is essential. "If our definition of humanism has any value, what is needed is not democracy alone, nor again an unmixed aristocracy, but a blending of the two — an aristocratic and selective democracy.... The democratic spirit that the college needs is a fair field and no favors, and then the more severe and selective it is in its requirements the better." [15]

Those sentences were written more than eighty years ago, at a time when some eminent educators talked of consolidating America's liberal-arts colleges—the better colleges, that is—under the domination of universities and closing the rest. Other people recommended that the colleges be converted into high schools. No such sweeping changes, disagreeable to Babbitt, actually occurred: until the end of the Second World War, the majority of young Americans continued to attend independent colleges and universities, not state institutions; and despite lamentations and Cassandra-like predictions about the dwindling of independent colleges, their total number has not much decreased.

But as for the maintenance of standards — why, some of the better colleges held out stoutly down to the Second World War, in part because of the exhortations of gentlemen and scholars of Babbitt's mold. The normal schools (later teachers' colleges, still later transmuted into state universities), the land-grant agricultural and technical colleges, and proprietary business schools might accept most applicants; still, pressures for the deliberate lowering of standards at the better-reputed state universities and liberal-arts colleges were exerted only gradually and piecemeal. The dykes of quality, on such campuses, would not be ruinously breached until the end of World War II.

The curricula of even the better institutions, nevertheless, as the years passed, increasingly reflected the commercial and industrial interests of the American Republic, at the cost of humane studies. The size and influence of departments of

15. For an examination of Babbitt's politics, see Chapter XII of Russell Kirk's *The Conservative Mind, from Burke to Eliot* (seventh edition, Chicago, 1986).

classics and of philosophy diminished; these relics of the old intellectual order might find themselves lodged in the most decrepit buildings on a campus.

For how many entering freshmen, and how many of their parents (most of whom had not attended college), desired humane learning? President Eliot's elective system, emulated almost everywhere in the United States (even when modified somewhat from what it had been in the 'Eighties and 'Nineties), gave freedom of choice to young people unprepared to choose wisely. In what were they and their parents interested, where the higher learning was in question? By the 1960s, Christopher Jencks would suggest that the majority of undergraduates had no real purpose in being enrolled at a college. Perhaps twenty per cent desired technical training; another twenty per cent, certification as potential employees; five per cent, a general introduction to middle-brow culture and middle-class conviviality; possibly two per cent, a tolerable general education; but one per cent, a serious intellectual discipline of any sort. To this the "democratic spirit" had descended intellectually, six decades after *Literature and the American College*. Both utilitarian humanitarianism and sentimental humanitarianism had put down humanism on all campuses but a very few. And even at those few, the curricula were confused and confusing usually, requiring little vigor of mind.

At the end of the Second World War, passage of the "G.I. Bill" by Congress sent tremendous crowds of discharged soldiers into the colleges and universities—some of those veterans desirous of intellectual discipline, most not. When this supply of students ran dry after a few years, the colleges deliberately lowered their standards to attract boys and girls to fill the half-empty dormitories and justify the salaries of the ranks of postwar instructors and professors. There occurred a frenzy of educational imperialism and indiscriminate expansion that might have left speechless even the voluble Babbitt.

The doubling, tripling, and quadrupling of college enrollment did not lack for apologists, most of whom knew on what side their bread was buttered. Powerful social forces approved such instant enlargement of the higher learning, as part of the "knowledge explosion." President Dwight Eisenhower beamed upon it, and the expansion was defended at every point, and praised to the skies, by his brother, Dr. Milton Eisenhower, himself a university president. Walter Reuther, president of the United Automobile Workers, demanded that the children of every UAW member be given a college education; it remained unclear as to who, in the long run, would be left to turn out automobiles.

In Babbitt's undergraduate years, some had enrolled at college out of snobbery, as he remarked in *Literature and the American College*; but most students had assumed that they had some serious purpose in their studies. It had begun to be otherwise by the time Babbitt obtained a Harvard appointment. By the 1960s, collegiate snobbery attained tremendous proportions: every mother's son and daughter was urged to exercise "the right to attend the college of your choice." Why go there? Because the neighbors' kids were going: it had become the thing to do, and a sneering pity was the lot of young people unable or unwilling to conform by enrollment on a mass campus. By the 'Sixties, about half the young people in America enrolled for at least one year of some form of education allegedly higher, and about half of that multitude—a quarter of the rising generation, that is—eventually would obtain some sort of diploma or certificate. It did not follow that they would have been educated.

Colleges had been founded for the study of abstractions, not as schools to supply entertainment and job-certification for boys and girls. College curricula, even the softened curricula that Babbitt frowned upon at Harvard, had not been designed to satisfy the tastes of this new multitude of young folk uninterested in abstractions. Who wants the humanities? What kind of job will the humanities get you? Who needs philosophy when he's got acid rock?

A large proportion of the new crowd of undergraduates having rejected the higher culture that colleges had endeavored to confer, there arose the famous Counter Culture of the 'Sixties —which persists, though diminished, to the present. That Counter Culture, frantically radical, denying the possibility of objective consciousness, drug-intoxicated, moved by impulses obscene and destructive, rapidly swept through the Rousseauistic phase of what Babbitt called "the idyllic imagination" into the sadistic phase that T. S. Eliot called "the diabolic imagination." [16]

Throughout the western world, the boredom of masses of "students" who cared to study nothing became a 'Sixties phenomenon — worse in much of Europe than in North America. Weakening of religious convictions, of families, of communities —these forms of social disintegration furnished crowds of recruits to the Counter Culture. It required only the catalyst of the prolonged war in Indo-China to bring about explosions of violence on most American campuses. "It is not good to be educated in a crowd," Lord Percy of Newcastle had written. A campus crowd readily is converted by a few ideologues into a campus mob, sometimes not reluctant to put the torch to the campus library. [17]

There is not space in this Introduction for an analysis of the college disorders of the late 'Sixties and early 'Seventies. Few of the students who shouted down visiting speakers, imprisoned college presidents in their offices, burned professors' typescripts, conducted fanatic "teach-ins," destroyed university buildings, and made impossible for long periods of time the routines of instruction—why, few of these students or the young assistants and instructors who led them (instructors in philosophy or literature, often!) had read Jean-Jacques Rousseau. Nevertheless, they had absorbed Rousseau at third hand or fourth hand, through the books, pamphlets, and speeches of the radical intellectuals of the Counter Culture. Often the radical doctrinaires mingled Marx with Rousseau; yet the dominant assumptions of the Counter Culture clearly went back to the

16. A principal champion and apologist of the Counter Culture was Theodore Roszak; see his book *The Making of a Counter Culture: Reflections on the Technocratic Society and Its Youthful Opposition* (Garden City, New York, 1969).

17. The decline of academic standards, the growth of the ills of the mass campus, and other troubles of college and university after World War II are traced year by year by Russell Kirk in *Decadence and Renewal in the Higher Learning: an Episodic History of University and College since 1953* (South Bend, Indiana, 1978).

eccentric man of letters whom Burke had called "the insane Socrates of the National Assembly"; an interesting large book might be written about Rousseau's resurrection in the 'Sixties by the enemies of social and moral order.[18]

By the middle of the 1970s, campuses everywhere were quiet again. But during the previous decade they had been most thoroughly democratized by the students. "Open admissions" had been forced upon the colleges of the City of New York by militant "minorities": anyone could get into a City college, and nearly anybody could stay there so long as he might like; elsewhere, a great many colleges adopted policies of open admissions, or virtually open, under no compulsion except budgetary difficulties. Honors programs within universities also were opened to all comers, however little qualified for serious study: that was the democratic way. As for the elective system — why, on a great many campuses virtually any specific requirements for graduation were abolished, so that students might be enabled to browse as they listed through the offerings of every department. (With this abolition of the vestiges of a fixed curriculum, enrollment in departments of history fell off catastrophically, and enrollment in programs of photography increased famously: both offered credit toward graduation and certification as a potentially employable young person.) Cohabitation of the sexes in certain dormitories, or all dormitories, triumphed on most campuses. Extensive boondoggle programs in "black studies," "women's studies," "global studies,"

18. For studies of the course and the causes of radical movements in college and university during the 1960s and 1970s, see Klaus Mehnert, *Twilight of the Young: the Radical Movements of the 1960s and Their Legacy* (New York, 1977); William P. Gerberding and Duane E. Smith (editors), *The Radical Left: The Abuse of Discontent* (Boston, 1970); Edward E. Ericson, Jr., *Radicals in the University* (Stanford, California, 1975); Sidney Hook, *Academic Freedom and Academic Anarchy* (New York, 1970); L. G. Heller, *The Death of the University, With Special Reference to the Collapse of City College of New York* (New Rochelle, New York, 1973); Geoffrey Wagner, *The End of Education* (South Brunswick and New York, 1976); Russell Kirk, *The Intemperate Professor and Other Cultural Splenetics* (Baton Rouge, 1965); Matthew Hodgart, *A Voyage to the Country of the Houyhnhnms, Being the Fifth Part of the Travels...by Lemuel Gulliver, Wherein the Author Returns and Finds a New State of Liberal Horses and Revolting Yahoos* (New York, 1970).

"peace studies," and a diversity of nonexistent academic disciplines were added to the college catalogues, often at the mutter of that magical phrase "non-negotiable demands" and the menace of massive student demonstrations. But it would be wearisome to prolong this litany of the academic fads and foibles of the 'Sixties and 'Seventies.

On the typical American campus, in short, by the 'Sixties there remained next to nothing of the humane learning beloved by Irving Babbitt. Here and there a veteran professor of English literature might hold a seminar on Ben Jonson or Samuel Johnson for a half-dozen graduate students; or an elderly gentleman might tutor two young men in New Testament Greek; or mediaeval architecture might be discussed within some special endowed institute on a large campus. With three hundred classmates, however, the representative undergraduate might doze in a lecture-hall, nominally being instructed in "basic history of world civilization" or "general science." At what had been liberal-arts colleges, often "business administration majors" made up the majority of the student body.

In the 'Seventies, colleges timidly resumed some of their old functions. At Harvard, birthplace of the elective system, a core curriculum (rather an imperfect one) actually was drawn up and adopted. Even departments of classics survived, here and there gaining a little ground. It became possible once more for reactionaries on college staffs, or the more intrepid among their number, to suggest that some minimum standards, however merciful, might be set for students' performance. It was said with relief that the new set of undergraduates were indifferent on political questions; they were interested simply in being certified as future salary-recipients or industrial managers. Utilitarian notions had succeeded sentimental notions.

In the first paragraph of his essay on "The College and the Democratic Spirit," Babbitt had quoted Edmund Burke to the effect that liberty and restraint must be held in a tension, for the achieving of free government. Had Babbitt been able to see the American college sixty years later, or eighty years later, presumably he would have been tempted to quote Burke's more famous sentences, so reproached by Tom Paine, in his *Reflections on the Revolution in France*—his reference to the seventh chapter of the Gospel according to Saint Matthew: if Jacobin democracy should triumph, "Along with its natural protectors and guardians, learning will be cast into the mire, and trodden down under the hoofs of a swinish multitude." Jacobin democracy had triumphed in the American college.

Had Babbitt been transported from Purgatory to Harvard in Anno Domini 1978, say, he might have regretted his translation back to the world of the flesh. In Harvard Yard or on Tory Row, he might have enjoyed a few glimpses of the university life he had known; but the new Harvard University would have been thoroughly abhorrent to him. In the opinion of many in Cambridge, the University's principal problem was where to park automobiles. Desperately crowded, noisy, encircled and penetrated by crowds of Counter Culture beardies (this scruffy class of pseudo-students having become a fringe around every sizeable university), Harvard seemed swollen and distorted to those who had known it in their youth. Scores of specialized programs, mostly Baconian in character, were lodged and subsidized there; but humane studies cowered in holes and corners, at best tolerated, fearful of banishment. Presidents of Harvard competed with presidents of Yale in absurdity of utterance, usually in the "liberal" vein of humanitarianism. Youngish Marxists on the faculty found the democratic spirit of latter-day Harvard, nevertheless, not yet democratic enough. Snobbery was worse in 1978 than it had been in 1908, for a Harvard degree—an M.B.A. especially, or better still a degree from the Law School—was assumed to guarantee lucrative and agreeable connections lifelong. The Harvard of Professor Irving Babbitt had been chucked down the memory-hole.

Then how are we to profit nowadays from Babbitt's observations on the workings of the democratic spirit in the shadow of the ivory tower? Why, it was Babbitt who first recognized in Rousseau's idyllic imagination the principal menace to intellectual and moral standards in the American college—this sort of imagination combined, that is, with American circumstances and prejudices. And Babbitt it was who foresaw the lengths to which the impulse toward pure democracy might be carried in the college, and who advocated a prudent restraint upon humanitarian impulses that college presidents and trustees thoroughly ignored. Babbitt's book is not obsolete.

As Heraclitus instructs us, we never step in the same river twice. We are not to expect the colleges of 1988, say, to resemble closely the colleges of 1908. As Babbitt's poet-disciple mused, "We cannot restore old policies/Or follow an antique drum."

To renew some elements of humane studies, for all that, remains quite possible on many campuses — particularly if the better-reputed universities and colleges will lead the way in this. To temper enthusiasm for using colleges to turn the world upside down is no impractical ambition, and the counsels of Babbitt might hearten some college presidents. To affirm anew that colleges are something more than training-grounds for commerce and industry, or centers to provide techniques and personnel for the apparatus of the state, might wake some public approval. To inform the rising generation that the Constitution of the United States owes nothing to Rousseau can be a worthy undertaking. The humanistic sense of moderation and balance still may be applied, in some degree, to the affairs of colleges. Just authority and a responsible freedom for students need not be forever adversaries, and the reading of Babbitt may help us to understand that. The American Republic is not going to cease to be a democracy, and the American college will not close its doors to young men and women whose interests are not purely intellectual. But it is quite as clear now as it was in 1808, or in 1908, that for a democracy to endure and prosper, it must retain elements of aristocracy. That is as true in a college as it is in the federal government. The chaos of the 'Sixties and the 'Seventies sufficiently demonstrated what an attempt at pure democracy does to the higher learning; and so Babbitt is vindicated by the event, and his plea for humanism takes on urgent meaning, for those who encounter it. As Babbitt remarked, intelligence will tell in the long run, even in a university.

IV. Pedantry, Frivolity, and Academic Degrees

THE PRIMARY FUNCTION OF THE COLLEGE—as distinguished from
secondary education and from the graduate school—is the
teaching of a body of important literature. It was long a require-
ment at Oxford and Cambridge that whenever the establishment of a new chair in some discipline was proposed, the question must be put, "To what body of literature does the proposed
chair appertain?" If the dons determined that there did not exist
enough important books in that particular field or discipline, the
proposed chair was not accepted. Within the twentieth century,
a proposal for an Oxford chair of education was rejected, when
first advanced, it being decided that the literature of the subject
was insufficient in quality and volume.

So it is that Babbitt centers his criticism of the American college upon the teaching of literature. Of his chapters "Literature
and the College" and "Literature and the Doctor's Degree,"
some portions are of antiquarian interest chiefly: nowadays
nobody proposes reducing college education in America to three
years rather than four (although the three-year schedule
functions well in Scotland); and nobody now hopes that poetry
may become more biological—the promise of Harvard's commencement speaker.

But most of what Babbit has to say about philologists,
dilettantes, and the doctoral degree—all as related to the effective teaching of literature—is highly relevant to present dis-
putes. Babbitt's general argument passes easily enough from
the subject of educational democracy to the topic of how
literature should be taught: for the character and quality of the
teaching will determine, in part, the kind of people its graduates
become. What sort of men are needed? Men of quality,
prepared for the several forms of leadership. In one of Babbitt's
more memorable passages — "Even though the whole world
seem bent on living the quantitative life, the college should
remember that its business is to make of its graduates men of
quality in the real and not the conventional meaning of the
term. In this way it will do its share toward creating that
aristocracy of character and intelligence that is needed in a

community like ours to take the place of an aristocracy of birth, and to counteract the tendency of an aristocracy of money.''

If the American democracy is to be led by an aristocracy, let it be an aristocracy of humanists, people of moral imagination, sound learning, strong character — not a class the members of which are born to rank and power (an unlikely development in the United States) or an oligarchy of financiers and industrialists (a very real possibility, it seemed, in Babbitt's day, what with the Rockefellers and Harrimans whom he drubbed in his books). In this, Babbitt is in agreement with his British contemporary and counterpart Sir Arthur Quiller-Couch, at Cambridge University.

''I believe that Humanism is, or should be, no decorative appanage, purchased late in the process of education, within the means of a few: but a quality, rather, which should, and can, condition all teaching, from a child's first lesson in Reading: that its unmistakable hall-mark can be impressed upon the earliest task set in an Elementary School.'' So Quiller-Couch said in a lecture of 1920.[19]

Babbitt suspected that perhaps the humane studies of English public schools were more concerned with conventional values than with real ones; but it was otherwise with Quiller-Couch, a scholar and writer wide-ranging and witty as Babbitt.

Both Quiller-Couch and Babbitt were masterly university teachers; and both of them dealt shrewd knocks to philologists. This may seem eccentric and cruel: for in the root sense of the term, a philologist is a lover of literature and learning. But Babbitt and Quiller-Couch looked for lively and eloquent university lecturers, scholars deeply moved by the ethical and dramatic qualities of great books; and such the eminent philologists of their time were not.

During the first two decades of the twentieth century, the domination of the natural sciences within universities had grown so overwhelming — the popularity of Herbert Spencer's

19. Sir Arthur Quiller-Couch, *On the Art of Reading* (Cambridge, England, 1920), p. 195. For his achievements as King Edward VII Professor, see F. Brittain, *Arthur Quiller-Couch: a Biographical Study of Q* (Cambridge and New York, 1948).

writings having something to do with this—that humane disciplines felt themselves under some compulsion to prove how
they too were "scientific." Philology, with its painstaking
search after roots and links, could advance some claim to
pursuing scientific methods; indeed philologists had been
notorious for their singleminded pedantry for three centuries; in
Cowper's lines —

> *Learned philologists, who chase*
> *A panting syllable through time and space.*

But for Quiller-Couch, as for Babbitt, the trouble with the
grave scientific philologists was their lack of imagination, their
neglect of the intellectual and moral content of literature, and
their failure to attract students of high promise to the humanist
camp. At Cambridge University, Quiller-Couch soon succeeded in making English a far more humane study than it had
been previously, so that candidates might sit for an examination
in literature without being required to prepare themselves in
philology, Anglo-Saxon, and Middle English. 'Q' and his
colleagues introduced the new subjects of literary criticism and
comparative literature.

At Harvard, Babbitt confessed that some commendable
philologists existed, their labors akin to the historians'; but in
general the breed were ganging the wrong road. "It is by their
definite contribution to knowledge that our modern linguistic
Baconians would wish to be esteemed; provided they can get at
the precise facts in their study of language, and then disengage
from these facts the laws that are supposed to govern them, they
are content to turn the human values over to the Rousseauist
and to the vagabondage of intellect and sensibility in which the
Rousseauist delights." Thus the dominant school of philologists, usually controlling departments of literature in those
days, deserted the humanist cause in the fond hope of being
admitted to the scientific fraternity on the ground of their simu-
lacrum of the methods of the natural sciences. They had come to
venerate the law for thing, not the law for man.

Today Babbitt's campaign against the pedantic philologists
may seem somewhat odd—today, when learned philologists no

longer often preside over university departments of literature and language, approving or preventing promotions and prescribing curricula. With the triumph of utilitarianism on nearly every campus and the demolition of required curricula, philologists have shrunk to a forlorn remnant, quite powerless in university deliberations, with few exceptions; generally philological scholars now seem rather attractive if abstract gentlemen, happily exempt from the general politicizing of college faculties. This writer recalls one such, a pleasant mild-mannered thin man who lectured at Michigan State University, tracing the history of such English words as "goose." After the lecture he was invited to the residence of the local Marxist couple, Mr. and Mrs. Fagan; and there, all unaware of his hosts' politics, he continued his interesting discourse on the roots and development of words.

Mrs. Fagan's burning eyes were fixed most earnestly upon him; she was sure that these philological explanations somehow veiled profound social significance, for clearly this visiting lecturer was an Intellectual, and were not all Intellectuals, according to Marx, gnawing at the foundations of capitalist society? At length she could not restrain herself, hostess though she was:

"Yes, yes, Professor," she cried, all eagerness for revelation. (The amiable innocent philologist had been in the midst of a digression upon Gothic and Old Norse roots.) "Yes, yes, Professor, you know so much! But tell me, explain to me—how does this relate to the class struggle?"

The philologist fled in company with this writer. Nowadays more learned Marxists abide at Michigan State, but none so entertaining as Mrs. Fagan. In Babbitt's time, before the Russian Revolution, Marxists were not to be found at Harvard; had there been any such, doubtless Babbitt would have spared the philologists and scourged the ideologues with whips of scorpions.

No less reprehensible than the philologist, with respect to the humanist cause, was the academic dilettante, who reduced the teaching of literature to a mere diversion, regarding humane letters as "polite letters," amusing, sentimental, sometimes sweet. "One already sees the time," Babbitt comments grimly, "when the typical teacher of literature will be some young dilettante who will interpret Keats and Shelley to a class of girls."

Babbitt most decidedly did not offer courses in the poetry of Keats and Shelley. Truly humane literature, he knew, had its footing in reason, not in temperament; and its aim was ethical, not sensational. It was from Babbitt that T. S. Eliot acquired his classicism, and from Babbitt his aversion to ungoverned emotionalism in letters.

The dilettante teacher of literature is with us still, eighty years later, with more wide-eyed girl auditors in the front row of chairs. But nowadays he is bullied by the ideologue teacher of literature—usually, but not necessarily, the Marxist variety of ideologue—who thinks it his function to lead the rising generation to a materialist Zion, and who often prefers sermonizing in the classroom on the evils of multinational corporations, or the sins of white South Africans, to dissecting the poetry of Keats and Shelley. The dilettante holding no strong convictions about anything, and the philologist confining himself to what Scottish undergraduates call "Old Gorse," the ideologue frequently obtains a free hand in departments of literature — to the diminishing of the liberties of the mind among both students and professors.

Babbitt, in 1908, was not much vexed by the ideologue colleague; for the notions of ideologues, those folk whom Burckhardt calls "the terrible simplifiers," did not flourish in the American academy until the end of the First World War and the coming of the Russian Revolution. Indeed the Marxist ideologue obtained no secure foothold until the alliance with the Soviet Union, during the Second World War, seemed to provide an apology for professorial sympathy with totalists of the Left. Teachers of literature might subscribe to the *Nation* and to journals more radical; but generally they found it imprudent to declare openly their political inclinations.

Not until the campus radicalism and violence of the late 1960s and early 1970s, then, did the collegiate ideologues obtain an ascendancy in their academic departments, at many universities and colleges. By clever tactics the ideologues took control of several large national scholarly associations, those concerned with literature and language among them; and domination of the learned societies brought domination of the learned journals. A frequent ploy in this conquest of the learned societies was for the radicals to turn up in large numbers at the annual or semi-annual business meeting of the association, which relatively few members of a society trouble themselves to attend; and at that meeting to execute a coup, electing officers from among their own number and altering the whole course of the learned society in question. In a number of national scholarly associations, the ideologues have contrived to remain in control to the present writing; or sometimes the original ideologues have been supplemented or supplanted by ideologues of a different stamp — feminist ideologues or "Gay Liberation" zealots, for instance. A mad world, my masters.

During the Truman and Eisenhower administrations, numerous college presidents declared emphatically that their faculties included no Marxist ideologues — not one; or at least no professed Communists. But such protestations of innocence ceased during the later 'Sixties, there being a great many radical instructors and graduate assistants who instantly would have thrown the lie back in the presidents' teeth. By the early 'Eighties, the Marxists proclaimed their own strength on campuses boastfully, in books published by reputable general publishers.[20]

Babbitt's strictures upon philologists and dilettantes, then, may seem somewhat irrelevant to present dominations and powers in the American college. Yet one reflects that the radicalism of the American campus, over the past twenty years, has been an admixture of the Baconian search for power with the Rousseauistic sentimentality and social primitivism: the two

20. See particularly a book edited by two professed Marxists, Bertell Ollman and Edward Vernoff, *The Left Academy: Marxist Scholarship on American Campuses* (New York, 1982). A principal publication of men and women of a radical cast in the realm of humane letters is George Abbott White and Charles Newman (editors), *Literature in Revolution* (New York, 1972), with contributions by twenty-one writers. See also the lengthy review-essay about this book by Russell Kirk, "Humane Letters and the Clutch of Ideology," in *The Political Science Reviewer*, Vol. III (fall, 1973), pp. 164–82.

sources of academic humanitarianism discerned by Babbitt
eighty years ago.[21]

Present-day campus radicalism being an abstract thing,
running contrary to the general tendency of American public
opinion and of events outside the United States, it seems im-
probable that it will endure for a great while, at least in the form
of conventional Marxist ideology; the professed Marxists dom-
inating certain academic departments, across the country, are
nearly all persons who obtained academic tenure during the
turbulent 'Sixties and early 'Seventies, and will begin to retire
from professorships about twenty years from now. It is even
conceivable that the fashionable Marxism may give way to a
renewed humanism of sorts.

But we turn from the grisly subject of ideology to the farcical
topic of the doctoral degree. Babbitt makes the case against
Herr Professor Doktor without any exaggeration. Imported
from Germany a century ago, the doctorate was meant as certification that a man had accomplished some piece of scholarly
research and was capable of more such. But how valuable was
much of that research, really? And had it to be Dr. Dryasdust
who was needed to instruct undergraduates? Would it not have
been better to engage a man of broad reading and reflection,
more interested in transmitting the meaning of great literature
to the rising generation than in grinding out a pedantic paper on
an obscure—and perhaps justly obscure—point in literature or
history? The university, indeed, should make large provision
for specialized scholarship; but in this little book Babbitt was
concerned with the mission of the American *college*.

Often beneath the doctoral gown is an abstract specialist
gifted neither with a philosophical habit of mind nor with talent

---

21. The infatuation of literary people with revolutionary movements is discussed by Renee Winegarten in her *Writers and Revolution: the Fatal Lure of Action*
(New York, 1974). Several books examining the nature of ideology have been
published in recent years; see Raymond Aron, *The Opium of the Intellectuals*
(New York, 1957); Thomas Molnar, *Utopia, the Perennial Heresy* (New York,
1957); Lewis Feuer, *Ideology and the Ideologists* (New York, 1975); Hans Barth,
Truth and Ideology (Berkeley, California, 1976; originally published in Switzer-
land, 1945); Kenneth Minogue, *Alien Powers: the Pure Theory of Ideology* (New
York, 1985).

for teaching. Loose standards in graduate schools have resulted in the production of an interesting diversity of doctoral charlatans. To put lively young intellects through several years of the American doctoral discipline is to subject them, too often, to the domination of academic dull dogs, and in effect to dishearten aspiring talents — not to mention the monetary cost of so prolonged an apprenticeship. Would not a sound master's degree suffice for the most part, as it did then, and did for long later, in Britain? Surely the professors of Oxford and Cambridge, of Edinburgh and St. Andrews, with their masters' degrees, were not inferior in learning to the younger professors of Yale and Columbia, Harvard and Princeton, with their American doctoral degrees. This prolonged servitude to the graduate-school pedagogues reminds one of Tocqueville's observation that democracies keep people of talent subject to fixed requirements, compelled to surmount artificial barriers to advancement, until the really able grow tired with the passing of the years, resign their early aspirations, and cease to challenge the prevalence of mediocrity. Was it necessary to bow and scrape before the philologist and the dilettante, term upon term, year upon year, before being permitted to teach in a college? "The humanist who at present enters college teaching should not underestimate the difficulties he is likely to encounter. He will find a literature ancient and modern controlled by a philological syndicate, a history dehumanized by the abuse of scientific method, and a political economy that has never been humane. Under these circumstances the humanist will have to undertake the task that Wordsworth so modestly proposed to himself, that of creating the taste by which he is to be enjoyed." So Babbitt, in 1908. In graduate schools today, this sort of servitude is not more mild and humane, and the relatively unpolitical philologist and dilettante have been supplanted as masters of the graduate-school syndicate, at many universities, by arrogant and intemperate ideologues.

Babbitt did not expect American universities to resign their conferring of the degree of Ph.D. But he proposed the creation of a new doctoral degree, or at least revision, most radically, of existing requirements for the Ph.D. What he advocated was "a degree that would lay due stress on aesthetic appreciativeness and linguistic accuracy, but would insist above all on wide reading and the power to relate this reading so as to form the foundation for a disciplined judgment.''

Few other voices in Babbitt's day were raised in advocacy of such a reform; and the Ph.D. discipline became less meaningful and more oppressive with the passing of every decade; yet at the same time the degree became less respected because so widely conferred upon people of scant imagination or intellectual power, but denied to those aspiring talents that refused to submit themselves to the boredom of prolonged Ph.D. candidacy. In Babbitt's words, ''I have known first-class men in both the ancient and modern field who have been literally driven away in disgust by the present requirements for the Ph.D. I have known others who have accepted these requirements, but in bitterness of spirit.''

During one of America's recurrent moods of educational reform, in the middle 'Fifties, a leading light among the reformers, Dr. Arthur Bestor, pointed out the increasing weakness of the Ph.D. program throughout the country, and recommended two improvements. One of these was the appointment for each doctoral candidate of an external examiner from another university; the other was the appointment of one (or preferably two) external professorial readers for each dissertation, whose criticisms must be met satisfactorily before the degree might be conferred. Some universities did adopt such reforms — this writer has served as such a reader and such an examiner more than once at Drew University, and there the doctoral discipline is reasonably humane — but nothing more startling was done by way of improvement.[22]

On the contrary, Behemoth University and Brummagem University conferred doctoral degrees almost indiscriminately and in startling numbers, especially after the Second World War; and for candidates who could not satisfy the Ph.D. requirements, the degree of Ed.D. was devised. (Some persons

22. See Arthur Bestor, *The Restoration of Learning* (New York, 1955), pp. 352–53.

took the doctor-of-education road out of a prudent expediency; but the large majority of men and women upon whom the distinction of Ed.D. was conferred could not or should not have been created Ph.D.'s.)

By the 1960s, athletic coaches were seeking the Ph.D.—provided that they would not be expected to think very hard to obtain this reward for their scholarship. After all, coaches very commonly became high-school superintendents and principals, and aspired to college and university presidencies. Why not style themselves doctors?

If one turns to *Dissertation Abstracts*, May 1961, interesting examples of the liberalized doctoral program may be found—two cases at Michigan State University, a land-grant institution that had expanded immensely under the domination of President John Hannah, whose highest earned degree was a bachelor's in poultry husbandry. In 1960, MSU had conferred earned doctorates upon two candidates in the field of physical education; doctoral dissertations had been submitted by both candidates, and approved. One was the product of a scholar named John Francis Alexander, and the subject of his learned researches was *An Evaluation of Thirteen Brands of Football Helmets on the Basis of Certain Impact Measures*. This valuable work, in photocopy, could be purchased for $6.80. ''The helmets were ranked according to the lower values for each evaluating measure at each velocity and position. Graphs depicted the mean responses of acceleration, deceleration, and rate of acceleration for all velocities and positions.'' Welcome, Dr. Alexander, to the company of the Schoolmen!

A worthy colleague of Dr. Alexander was one Richard Carroll Nelson, also diligent at educational studies in football. He was awarded his MSU doctorate, also in physical education, for a curiously similar contribution to the higher learning: *An Investigation of Various Measures Used in Football Helmet Evaluation*. ''Thirty-nine football helmets were impacted by a pendulum striker at four velocities.'' Dr. Nelson even went so far in modern scholarship as to photograph the impacts with a Polaroid camera. Yes, there was something at MSU for every head—so long as one fretted about the *physical* impact only.

These Ph.D. follies at Michigan State woke the contempt of Dr. Robert Hutchins, of the Center for the Study of Democratic Institutions, and of President Griswold of Yale. No general fuss about the low estate and low esteem of the latter-day Ph.D. resulted from this passing scandal, nevertheless. Some reformers, during those 1950s and 1960s, did recommend that the doctoral degree be divided into two: a degree for persons who intended to teach, and another for persons who intended to engage in research primarily. Separate programs would be drawn up for the two degrees. Nothing, or next to nothing, came of this remarkably sensible argument.

Dr. Jacques Barzun, no warm admirer of Babbitt's writings, had criticized Ph.D. programs much in Babbitt's terms in Barzun's early book *Teacher in America*. By 1968, Barzun, then provost of Columbia University, was inquiring, "Why more and more Ph.D.'s? Why Ph.D.'s at all?" After William James, Barzun called the Ph.D. empire an octopus:

"Universities by the dozen now offer the Ph.D., some genuine, some travesties, because the college market wants the label on its faculty members, even the junior colleges. Even in the leading universities, which have somewhat rationalized and humanized the system, the obtention of the doctorate is still an ordeal. It is costly and time-consuming. The demands are still artificial: a contribution to knowledge of book length, and written to satisfy from three to five unknown judges; written and rewritten; 'researched' abroad (except in American subjects or in science); buttressed by competence in two foreign tongues (what about English for one?); produced while adjusting to married life and babynursing on little or no money; and all this to get a teaching job without ever being taught how a faculty member should think and behave — the whole rigmarole is as wasteful and ineffectual as it was when James first deplored it." [23]

William James had heaped his coals of fire upon the Ph.D in 1903, about the time Babbitt was flaying the Ph.D. in the pages

23. Jacques Barzun, *The American University: How It Runs, Where It Is Going* (New York, 1968), pp. 91–95, 261–64.

of the *Nation*, then edited by his friend Paul Elmer More.[24] Sixty-five years of such criticism of the degree by well-known scholars had accomplished nothing worth mentioning; Barzun's 1968 description of the Ph.D. program is not at all immoderate. Barzun recommended certain practical measures for diminishing the inhumanity of the Ph.D. program, and opening the way for young people who happen to have ideas in their heads. But he declared that the best device would be to "give every native-born American a Ph.D. at birth and start from there." This radical demand, by no means original with Barzun, first had been voiced by Robert Hutchins; and to it, some years before Barzun published *The American University*, Russell Kirk had appended this codicil: if a young person insists upon being graduated from high school, deprive him of his Ph.D.; if he spends four years at a college, take away the M.A. that had been awarded to him at birth; if he proceeds to graduate school, strip him of his B.A. that was his birthright. Thus would degree-snobbery be ended, and the young person would go forth into the sensual world naked of honorific distinctions, but possibly wise. Let learning be its own reward.

If the trustees of some famous and richly-endowed university should choose as that university's president a scholar and gentleman possessed of most of the high old Roman virtues, and also of remarkable intelligence — why, it might be possible for such a president, supposing his will to be very strong, to reform one university as an example to the others. Should he be successful, emulation would follow. Among his first reforms— although doubtless it would be resisted by many professors in the graduate schools—should be the thorough reconstitution of the doctoral degree. Here our imaginary president would do well to commence by meditating on Babbitt's excoriation of the Ph.D. in *Literature and the American College*, and reviewing other strong recommendations by Babbitt in this book, and indeed paying some serious attention to all of Babbitt's books. But among the reasons why today's typical college president does

24. See William James, "The Ph.D. Octopus," *The Harvard Monthly*, March, 1903; also in James, *Memories and Studies* (New York, 1911), p. 329 ff.

not think imaginatively of reform is this: he, too, ordinarily had been subjected to the dreary Ph.D. discipline; and that servitude deprived him, during the years when he should have been reading broadly in that humane literature which Babbitt commends, of opportunity to quicken his intellect; to escape for a while from the provincialism of time and the twilight of academic circumstance.

It is a distasteful spectacle nowadays: hundreds of thousands of people in their twenties, only half educated in their undergraduate years, slaving away year after year across the United States—in the hope of obtaining, eventually, a diploma certifying that they have completed some piece of research. Then they may be entitled to set foot on the first lap of the notorious tenure track — and to begin to perpetuate the absurd system under which they had suffered hitherto.

Just how inhumane this doctoral system has become may be suggested by the following passage from a lengthy manual, brought out by a reputable publisher, which is intended to guide graduate students through the Ph.D. labyrinth. The section of the book from which this passage has been extracted is entitled "The Dissertation Incest Taboo." It is *not* written as a bit of waggery:

"It is most inadvisable for a candidate to go to bed with his or her adviser, or even to allow that possibility to hang temptingly in the air.... There is little reason to doubt that *both* faculty member and student are 'getting something' from the relationship. If the student could be reasonably sure that such an intimate relationship would promote her/his dissertation, fine.... Unfortunately love and passion don't generally yield such critical increments. Totally contrary to the stereotype, an adviser who loves you may do more damage to your dissertation than an indifferent one; he or she will be pushing just those kinds of romantically disorganized and nonroutine concerns that you have determined...to postpone and avoid." [25]

25. David Sternberg, *How to Complete and Survive a Doctoral Dissertation* (New York, 1981), pp. 86–87.

A far cry from Mark Hopkins on one end of a log and a student on the other, this; aye, and a far cry from Irving Babbitt's humane learning.

V. Classicism, Romanticism, and Nihilism

BABBITT'S CHAPTERS "The Rational Study of the Classics" and "Ancients and Moderns" were written when the majority of college students still were enrolled in humane studies—although the pattern was changing then, most notoriously at Stanford University, where, as Babbitt notes, "a student may enter, not only without Latin and Greek, but without any language or nonscientific subject whatsoever except English composition, and then receive his Bachelor of Arts degree on completing a certain number of hours' work in mechanical engineering."

The decline of study of the humanities had commenced. Late in 1984, there reported the Study Group on the State of Learning in the Humanities in Higher Education, appointed by the chairman of the National Endowment for the Humanities, Dr. William J. Bennett, who wrote the report. It was found that "the number of students choosing majors in the humanities has plummeted. Since 1970 the number of majors in English has declined by 57 per cent, in philosophy by 41 per cent, in history by 62 per cent, and in modern languages by 50 per cent." Three out of four colleges would grant bachelors' degrees that did not require the study of European history; seventy-two per cent of the colleges did not require American history or literature for graduation; eighty-six per cent did not require graduates to have studied Greek or Roman civilization.[26]

Foreseeing this descent, Babbitt subtitled his book *Essays in Defense of the Humanities*. In the 1930s it was fashionable in New

26. "To Reclaim a Legacy," report to the National Endowment for the Humanities, printed in *The Chronicle of Higher Education*, November 28, 1984, pp. 16–21.

York's literary circles to ridicule the New Humanists' forebodings as to the future of American civilization. But by the 1980s, the triumph of utilitarianism over humane studies was so nearly complete that men and women of diverse first principles took alarm.

In Babbitt's time, the term "humanities" was less amorphous than it has since become, though far less limited than when it had been applied only to the study of Greek and Latin literature. As employed in *Literature and the American College*, the humanities consist of the disciplines of the classical languages, English literature, the principal European literatures (and sometimes Indic and Chinese literatures), philosophy, and history. It is Babbitt's argument that the whole body of humane studies rests upon the footing of Greek and Latin literature.

Thus Babbitt's case for classicism, as opposed to romanticism, is essential to all his writings. "Classical literature, at its best, does not so much tend to induce in us a certain state of feelings, much less a certain state of the nerves; it appeals rather to our higher reason and imagination—to those faculties which afford us an avenue of escape from ourselves, and enable us to become participants in the universal life." Classical studies develop a power of restraint; the man who writes in the classical tradition employs the snaffle and the curb. Romanticism is all excitement, expansion, emotionalism; with it there comes the peril of personal and social explosion.

If "classicism" signifies Greek and Roman literature, and those works of a high standard in latter national literatures that are strongly influenced by ancient models, the term "romanticism" refers to literary productions having some relationship to the ideas and institutions of mediaeval times. The romantic movement, commencing in Germany during the latter half of the eighteenth century, spread to France and Britain. It is French Romantic ideas, more particularly the school of Rousseau, that Babbitt assails so vehemently, he being a professor of French literature; but he does not spare the Germans or the English. As he writes very truly, "Even for the student of English literature an acquaintance with the Middle Ages before Chaucer is vastly less important than an acquaintance with the classics. The best avenue of approach to the great English poets, for example, is not through Caedmon and Beowulf, as some misguided moderns would have us believe, but through Homer and Virgil.''

To understand thoroughly Babbitt's employment of the term ''romanticism,'' it is well to read his *Rousseau and Romanticism*, published eleven years after *Literature and the American College*.[27] T. S. Eliot, though very strongly influenced in his earlier essays by Babbitt's categories of classicism and romanticism, by 1933 was of a different mind: ''It is true that from time to time writers have labelled themselves 'romanticists' or 'classicists', just as they have from time to time banded themselves together under other names. These names which groups of writers and artists give themselves are the delight of professors and historians of literature, but should not be taken very seriously; their chief value is temporary and political — that, simply, of helping to make the authors known to a contemporary public. . . .'' [28] Truly words are tools that break in the hand, as James Fitzjames Stephen wrote; and Babbitt falls into certain difficulties because of the surprising range of authors whom literary historians classify as romantics.

The romantic writer with the broadest influence in Britain was Sir Walter Scott, a Tory and a champion of custom and convention, popularizing the political principles of Burke. How is it possible to lump Scott together with Shelley or Godwin, say, or with French revolutionaries, when either morals or politics are in question? Or how can Samuel Taylor Coleridge, defender of church and state, demolisher of philosophical absurdities, be classified as an adversary of the ancients? Perhaps Babbitt should have chosen some other word with which to label the literary and artistic enthusiasts for overthrowing the established order — political, moral, economic, and cultural — in order to shape the world nearer to their hearts' desire. The radical

27. See particularly Chapters I and III, *Rousseau and Romanticism* (Boston, 1919).

28. Eliot, *After Strange Gods: a Primer of Modern Heresy* (London, 1934), pp. 25–26.

romantics, after all, were not generally admirers of mediaeval thought or institutions. But Babbitt took a word ready to hand, and perhaps no better was to be found at the time.[29] In the Introduction to *Rousseau and Romanticism*, Babbitt does make it clear that he is dealing with only one of three types of romanticism: that is, with "emotional naturalism," or "the attempt to erect on naturalistic foundations a complete philosophy of life." In *Literature and the American College* his use of the word "romanticism" commonly signifies the preference for mediaeval studies over classical studies. (He does acknowledge that "The average student of modern languages should have a general grounding in the Middle Ages, and should have above all the knowledge of mediaeval life that comes from a careful study of Dante and Chaucer.")

Yet it is not merely a quarrel over precedence between the classical tradition and the mediaeval tradition that Babbitt touches upon in *Literature and the American College*. He is concerned quite as much with a contest between, or among, different types of imagination—although he develops that discussion more fully in *Rousseau and Romanticism* and *Democracy and Leadership*, and T. S. Eliot enlarges the analysis in *After Strange Gods*. These three types are the moral imagination, the idyllic imagination, and the diabolic imagination.

Edmund Burke originated the phrase "moral imagination," today increasingly employed in ethical discussions, sometimes with interpretations that would have surprised Burke.[30] In *Reflections on the Revolution in France*, praising the chivalric spirit and the unbought grace of life, Burke contrasts with such old loyalties the presumptuous rationalism of the French Enlightenment and the new morality of the French revolutionaries:

"But now all is to be changed. All the pleasing illusions,

29. Besides Babbitt, several other important critics of the time drew the same sharp distinctions between classicists and romantics. See, for instance, the English writer T. E. Hulme, *Speculations: Essays on Humanism and the Philosophy of Art*, edited by Sir Herbert Read (London, 1936).

30. See, for example, Chapter 4, "The Meaning and Purpose of Moral Imagination," in Philip S. Keane, S.S., *Christian Ethics and Imagination: a Theological Inquiry* (New York, 1984).

which made power gentle, and obedience liberal, which harmonized the different shades of life, and which, by a bland assimilation, incorporated into politics the sentiments which beautify and soften private society, are to be dissolved by this new conquering empire of light and reason. All the decent drapery of life is to be rudely torn off. All the superadded ideas, furnished from the wardrobe of a moral imagination, which the heart owns, and the understanding ratifies, as necessary to cover the defects of our naked shivering nature, and to raise it to dignity in our own estimation, are to be exploded as a ridiculous, absurd, and antiquated fashion." [31]

This moral imagination is the power to conceive of men and women as moral beings — something more than creatures with animal wants. Burke's moral imagination draws upon the insights into the human condition obtained from Homer, Plato, Aristotle, Cicero, Vergil, Horace, and the classical heritage of literature generally; also upon the great Christian books. This moral imagination looks to the past for guidance. The moral order is perceived to be something larger than the circumstances of one's time or private experience; one is aware of membership in a community of souls, and learns that man is better than a naked ape; out of such imagination arose the knowledge of the dignity of man. Irving Babbitt's humanism, and his love of the classics, are bound up with this moral imagination; and in *Democracy and Leadership* (1924) he gives a whole chapter to "Burke and the Moral Imagination."

A second type of imagination, that of Rousseau, is the idyllic or Arcadian imagination. *"Et in Arcadia ego..."* the broken monumental inscription runs, in a painting of a classical landscape; but the inscribed stone is surmounted by a human skull. This idyllic imagination, criticized acutely if unsparingly by Babbitt in the third chapter of *Rousseau and Romanticism*, longs for the land of heart's desire; it is utopian, fancying that man and society may be perfected by the abolishing of institutions; it is primitivistic, eagerly embracing the notion of the Noble

---

31. Burke, *Reflections on the Revolution in France*, in E. J. Payne, editor, *Burke: Select Works* (Oxford, 1898), Vol. I, p. 90.

Savage. (European discovery of the South Seas, where life seemed simple and labor unnecessary, had much to do with the growth of the idyllic imagination in the latter half of the eighteenth century.) To escape from duties into some charming rural setting, there to indulge the flesh without penalties: that is the dream of many folk in every age, and that was one important aspect of the Rousseauistic revolt of young people in the 'Sixties. Babbitt describes the visionary world of Rousseau:

"Thus alongside the real world and in more or less sharp opposition to it, Rousseau builds up a fictitious world, that *pays de chimères*, which is alone, as he tells us, worthy of habitation. . . . To wander through the world as though it were an Arcadia or enchanted vision contrived for one's especial benefit is an attitude of childhood—especially of imaginative childhood. . . . The striking fact about Rousseau is that, far more than Wordsworth, he held fast to his vision. He refused to adjust it to an unpalatable reality." [32]

There exist limits to the exercise of the idyllic imagination. When those limits are reached — by which time the dreamer may find himself in the clutch of a policeman — the visionary commonly grows indignant and experiences the pangs of frustration. If it is a multitude that suffers such disappointment, that crowd may seek out fancied betrayers or malign opponents. Then there strides upon the scene the humanitarian with the guillotine. This humanitarian drama has been played out in country after country, ever since 1789, taking on a Communist cast after 1917.

The moral imagination Babbitt borrowed from Burke; the idyllic imagination he discerned and described at some length. But the diabolic imagination, unmentioned in Babbitt's books, received its tardy recognition in 1933, the year Babbitt died. For T. S. Eliot chose for the subject of his concluding Page-Barbour Lecture at the University of Virginia "the intrusion of the *diabolic* into modern literature." Eliot doubted whether his auditors would apprehend what he was talking about; he might have added that his old mentor Babbitt never had ventured to

---

32. Babbitt, *Rousseau and Romanticism* (Boston, 1919), pp. 73–74.

mention Satan. "I am afraid that even if you can entertain the notion of a positive power for evil working through human agency," Eliot said at Charlottesville, "you may still have a very inaccurate notion of what Evil is, and will find it difficult to believe that it may operate through men of genius of the most excellent character. I doubt whether what I am saying can convey very much to anyone for whom the doctrine of Original Sin is not a very real and tremendous thing." [33]

In one sense, this diabolic imagination is produced by disillusion: that is, persons who have embraced the idyllic imagination, and in the end have found that they were pursuing a will-o'-the-wisp or a corpse candle, may shift abruptly from utopianism to diabolism; from vain pursuit of a fancied perfection to exulting in the pleasures of evil. In another sense, this diabolic imagination lies latent within the hearts of all of us, an impulse to defy, to befoul, to destroy; it is the legacy of what is called, theologically, Original Sin; and when both the external check of authority (which may be either submission to doctrine or submission to superior power) and the "inner check" of Humanism are removed, the imagination is perverted.

Although Babbitt has nothing to say about the diabolic imagination, keeping clear of the supernatural as was always his way, there lies implicit in his classicism the menacing shape of an imagination worse than the merely idyllic:

> *Tamen ad mores natura recurrit*
> *Damnatos fixa et mutari nescia.*

One may call that diabolic imagination "nihilism," the denial of meaning in existence, the yearning for general extinction; but often that sort of imagination is more than passive, and psychologists call it sadism, after that eminent man of letters the Comte de Sade. Eliot called it the operation of the Evil Spirit, and declared that "the Inner Light, the most untrustworthy and deceitful guide that ever offered itself to wan-

---

33. Eliot, *After Strange Gods, op. cit.*, pp. 56–57.

dering humanity,'' could not suffice to restrain that annihilating impulse of a writer's imagination.[34]

Literature and the American College was published six years before the First World War began, and a decade before the Bolshevik Revolution offered a practical illustration of the idyllic imagination's consequences. Worse was to follow, horror piled upon horror, so long as Babbitt lived and Eliot lived; and events yet more ghastly, in Africa and Asia, came after Eliot's death. The diabolical imagination was applied practically to the destruction of whole peoples.

If the moral imagination, nurtured by the study of classical literature, should be thrust aside by the college's humanitarians, what sort of literature would supplant the great works of Greece and Rome, and the major books in English or French written in the ancient tradition? In 1908, television and radio could not substitute for books, and even films were in their infancy; nor did students have automobiles; so the rising generation doubtless would read something or other. What would it be? Babbitt gives the answer in a series of asides in his first book:

"It would appear, from a comparison of the catalogues of one of our Eastern universities, that its undergraduates now have an opportunity to read 'La Débâcle' of Emile Zola, where twenty years ago they would have been required to read the 'Antigone' of Sophocles. . . . To transform into a Greek scholar the average young man of to-day, whose power of attention has been dissipated in the pages of the American newspaper, whose mind has been relaxed by reading the modern erotic novel, — this, to borrow one of Phillips Brooks' phrases, would sometimes seem about as promising an enterprise as to make a lancehead out of putty. . . . From the lists of books read in schools and colleges

34. Babbitt's understanding of the imagination, and his philosophical assumptions generally, are carefully discussed by Claes Ryn in *Will, Imagination and Reason: Irving Babbitt and the Problem of Reality* (Chicago, 1986). An account of Babbitt and More on imagination is given by J. David Hoeveler, Jr., in *The New Humanism: a Critique of Modern America, 1900–1940* (Charlottesville, Virginia, 1977). On Babbitt's and More's principle of self-restraint, see Folke Leander, *The Inner Check: a Concept of Paul Elmer More, with reference to Benedetto Croce*; foreword by Russell Kirk (London, 1974).

and from publishers' catalogues one might infer that what is now taking the place of the masterpieces of Greece and Rome is a hodge-podge of second-rate French and German novels.''

Eight decades later, undergraduates so talented and scholarly as to read Zola, or second-rate French and German novels, or the more pretentious sort of erotic novel (now usually published in the United States, rather than in France) — why, they would be awarded scholarships and counselled to proceed to graduate school.

VI. Originality, Perversity, and Regeneration

WITH EVERY YEAR THAT PASSES, in our era of transition near the end of the twentieth century of the Christian era, the number of titles of new books published in the United States much exceeds the number published in the preceding year. Yet we live in a time when popular interest in humane literature steadily declines. Of the books that will be written or published in the year of our Lord 1986, few will be read in 1996 or the year 2000; and possibly none of them at all by the year 2086.

As this writer put it fifteen years ago, in his book on Eliot, ''Though here and there some stalwart Gerontion still writes, or some hopeful new talent starts up, for the most part we encounter literary ephemera, or else the prickly pears and Dead Sea fruit of literary decadence.'' [35]

Over the past thirty years, several books about the decadence of ''creative'' writing in our time have been published. Three of them are cited below.

In 1958, Edmund Fuller, a very experienced critic widely respected, published *Man in Modern Fiction: Some Minority Opinions on Contemporary Writing*. He entitled his second chapter ''The Revival of Total Depravity.'' ''What some writers have lost is not an external framework of values,'' he wrote in a later

---

35. Russell Kirk, *Eliot and His Age* (La Salle, Illinois, 1984), p. 3.

chapter, "not just this or that set of value concepts. They have lost the basic vision of the nature of their own kind. They not only do not know *who* they are, which is problem enough; they also do not know *what* they are — and that is the ultimate tragedy; for man not to know the nature of man. Indeed, if he knows not what he is, is he any longer man, until he has re-learned himself?" [36]

Twenty years later, a successful novelist and a Chaucerian scholar, John Gardner, published *On Moral Fiction*. He found that the writings of the most talked-about "serious" novelists of the day failed to be moral in the sense of seeking to find out how human nature may be fulfilled. (Many of those "talked about" writers of only eight years ago already have been forgotten by the public.) He meant to sound an alarm, although not to censor:

"Real art creates myths a society can live instead of die by, and clearly our society is in need of such myths. What I claim is that such myths are not mere hopeful fairy tales but the products of careful and disciplined thought; that a properly built myth is worthy of belief, at least tentatively; that work at art is a moral act; that a work of art is a moral example; and that false art can be known for what it is if one remembers the rules. The black abyss stirs a certain fascination, admittedly, or we would not pay so many artists so much money to keep staring at it. But the black abyss is merely life as it is or as it soon may become, and staring at it does nothing, merely confirms that it is there. It seems to me time that artists start taking that fact as pretty thoroughly established." [37]

During the minor fuss that Professor Gardner's book stirred up, there wrote to this writer James T. Farrell, the famous naturalistic novelist of Chicago life, expressing some disgust at the extremes to which the sensational novel had proceeded; this letter of his was the last piece by Farrell ever published. Should the present tendency of "doing your own thing, acting out, playing out, living nakedly in public your own fantasy"—

36. Fuller, *Man in Modern Fiction* (New York, 1958), p. 52.
37. Gardner, *On Moral Fiction* (New York, 1978), p. 126.

stimulated by fiction, plays, films, poems—prevail and become irreversible, Farrell concluded, we would enter upon a period that "might be described by the slogan *Every man his own Caligula!*" [38]

In 1983, Bryan Griffin, a skillful writer whose articles in *Harper's* two years earlier had ruffled the dovecotes of the American cultural establishment, published *Panic among the Philistines*, a book exposing nearly all America's best-known writers—those praised to the skies in the mass media of book-reviewing, that is, and often in more sensible quarters—as unscrupulous money-grubbers who buttered up one another and took pride in their defiance of decencies, public or private. There had begun, he wrote, a battle "between those who would be governed by the moral instinct, and those who would deny that instinct." He perceived some healthy reaction already working:

"It is the everlasting battle in which there are no truces, the battle between the smile and the leer, between innocence and sophistication, beauty and lust, truth and cynicism, love and pornography; it is the conflict between Dickens and Mailer, Michelangelo and Picasso, Augustine and Updike, Thomas Mann and *Garp*. It is the battle between substance and display, integrity and materialism, good cheer and quiet desperation, duty and hedonism; between earnestness and flippancy, the absolute and the expedient, the eternal and the ephemeral, the moral imperative and the passing whim. It is the ancient fight between the gentleman and the mob, the mother and the barbarian, the immaculate child and the old roué, the monk and the thug, the spirit and the brute: it is the war between the human and the anti-human." [39]

Such judgments as those of these four writers are evidence that Babbitt's humanism has not yet been totally extirpated. There survive at most colleges some good scholars in literature and allied disciplines who continue to offer courses—if to a

---

38. James T. Farrell to Russell Kirk: letter published in *The University Bookman* (Vol. XX, No. 1), autumn, 1979, pp. 22–23.

39. Griffin, *Panic among the Philistines* (Chicago, 1983), pp. 248–49.

handful of undergraduates—in the great authors. After attaining nadir a quarter of a century ago, the study of Latin has been regaining some ground recently in colleges, although Greek cannot be said to experience any such restoration.

But most students entering college are wretchedly unprepared for the study of serious literature, having been offered little in primary or secondary schools except dull anthologies stuffed with "contemporary relevance." A great part of the freshmen, at nearly all colleges, are promptly diverted to such disciplines as "computer science" (the latest foible), leaving no time for literary studies; what literature, if any, they are required to consider in a "survey" class is taught at the lowest level. And at many colleges, the staff indulge or create classes in the most faddish "contemporary literature" or "relevant writing": whole semesters or academic years devoted to such authors as those upon whom Edmund Fuller, John Gardner, and Bryan Griffin have passed sentence. If the choice must be made, it is preferable to read nothing at all than to read the books of the false image of man. What has produced our literary decadence, in the college and out of it? Is it possible to conceive of a regeneration of humane letters?

The first necessity in any reform is to ascertain the causes of abuse or decay. What brings on the sneering, snarling defiance of so many well-known writers of the past several decades? Why do they give us scenes of ghastly torture and cruelty, page after page of obscene descriptions, acts of depravity, characters from the abyss? Why is such unpleasant rubbish cried up to the skies, in book-review media and often in college classes, as the achievement of innovating literary genius?

Several causes are at work here, surely; but one of the more conspicuous is what Samuel Johnson called "the lust of innovation." There comes to mind a sentence from Eliot's famous essay "Tradition and the Individual Talent" (1917): "One error, in fact, of eccentricity in poetry is to seek for new human emotions to express; and in this search for novelty in the wrong place it discovers the perverse." [40]

40. Eliot, *Selected Essays, 1917–1932, op. cit.*, p. 10.

That sagacious sentence may be applied to more than verse. Even theological schools nowadays are afflicted, for a variety of reasons—not the least of them the loss of faith in dogmata—, by the lust of innovation. If one desires notoriety and preferment in such reverend circles, the thing to undertake today is to search for novelty in the wrong place, so discovering the perverse in new aspects of an alleged theology: liberation theology, black theology, chicano theology, feminist theology, ecological theology, theology of animals, gay theology, deconstructive theology, rock theology, Lord knows what else. Often the trumpet-blast proclaiming these new discoveries in the god-science begins with a denial of the dogmata upon which the old theology was founded. The perverse offers its rewards, for a time—although presently yet other and more startling shapes of the perverse must be unveiled, Dinos of the insatiable appetites seizing the throne when Zeus has been expelled.

So it is with the writing of books in our bent world. Many people aspire to the condition of authors, both for emoluments—or fancied emoluments—and for celebrity. Whole departments —nay, schools—of "creative writing" proliferate; writers' workshops and colonies provide supplementary pay to college instructors in "How to Write the Novel" and "Writing Articles for Profit," for the edification and presumptive material advantage of housewives and ambitious tool-and-die makers. Meanwhile it becomes increasingly difficult to discover any publisher who will bring out an author's first novel; probably the novel itself is a dying form of the literary art.

So what is the would-be writer to do? Why, devise some literary novelty. To impress a publisher and sell books, take up a fresh form of perversity—although such innovations increasingly are difficult to fancy, the changes already having been rung on the bells of politics and morals by well-paid literary persons still in the land of the living. In this connection, we turn again to T. S. Eliot, writing in 1933 about the attractions of Marxism for a New York writer:

"The literary profession is not only, in all countries, over-crowded and underpaid (the few overpaid being chiefly persons who have outlived their influence, if they ever had any); it is embarrassed by such a number of ill-trained people doing such a number of unnecessary jobs; and writing so many unnecessary books and unnecessary reviews of unnecessary books, that it has much ado to maintain its dignity as a profession at all. One is almost tempted to form the opinion that the world is at a stage at which men of letters are a superfluity. To be able therefore to envisage literature under a new aspect, to take part in the creation of a new art and new standards of literary criticism, to be provided with a whole stock of ideas and words, that is for a writer in such circumstances to be given a new lease of life. It is not always easy, of course, in the ebullitions of a new movement, to distinguish the man who has received the living word from the man whose access of energy is the result of being relieved of the necessity of thinking for himself. Men who have stopped thinking make a powerful force." [41]

Marxism, or some other ideology, occasionally may serve as well as does erotic salacity to attract notice to a rising would-be luminary of the cosmos of letters; but in America, a non-ideological land, description of sexual perversity or of unbearable physical suffering is a surer road to greatness. Eliot wrote that *Criterion* commentary of his more than half a century ago; the public that used to be called "the common reader" has diminished since then, and employment for persons with literary aptitudes is confined more and more to editorial labors for trade journals, "dumbing down" already dull manuals for school textbook publishers, and copy-writing for advertising agencies. Under such circumstances, the inducements to prostitution of literary skills loom larger.

It is not writers only who abandon real literature in favor of subliterary ephemera. A few years ago this writer gave the dedicatory address at the opening of a new public-library building in a prosperous Michigan town. That structure was handsomely equipped with the newest gadgets of Library Science. Just inside the entrance, close to the circulation desk, stood racks of paperbacks, hot off the press, hundreds of them in their

---

41. Eliot, "A Commentary," *The Criterion*, Vol. XII, No. XLVII (January, 1933), pp. 244–49.

glossy multicolored stridency. It was clear that many of them were pornographic; others pretended to salacity. They were placed in this conspicuous situation that "young adults"—that is, teenagers—might be attracted to them. "The great thing is to get the kids reading: it doesn't matter so much what they read." So apologists tell us. If the kids didn't read, where would graduates of library schools find employment?

At our airport newsracks, scarcely any paperback can be got today except impossibly nasty or impossibly dull productions of Grub Street. Everybody has been compelled to attend school; next to nobody who passes through airports troubles himself to read anything decent, one must assume. The small number of "English majors" who still are required to read Chaucer and Spenser and Shakespeare and Pope and such worthies, and who even may be expected to read superficially in some foreign tongue, scarcely will suffice to leaven the lump of the American college, let alone the American nation.

"The number of people in possession of any criteria for discriminating between good and evil is very small," Eliot said at the University of Virginia, in the year of Babbitt's death; "the number of the half-alive hungry for any form of spiritual experience, or what offers itself as spiritual experience, high or low, good or bad, is considerable. My own generation has not served them very well. Never has the printing-press been so busy, and never have such varieties of buncombe and false doctrine come from it." [42]

What are we to make of the writers who serve up to the half-alive gobbets of sham spirituality—inverted spirituality, that is, in the service of D. H. Lawrence's Dark God? Some of them earnestly desire to degrade, to pull down, to destroy. Once people begin to call themselves intellectuals and cease to believe in the existence of the Evil Spirit, the power of the Dark draws in about them. Lawrence desired to venerate ritually his Dark

---

42. Eliot, *After Strange Gods, op. cit.*, p. 61.

God, sensual passion; his eroticism was mad but genuine.[43] What the "liberated" writers of recent years thrust upon their readers is pseudo-eroticism: in their fiction one encounters clinical sexuality, sexual violation instead of fulfillment, sniggering descriptions at great length of cruelties and the perverse. The genuinely erotic impulse is bound up with love of life; but what we find in the fiction dissected by Fuller, Gardner, and Griffin is appetite for gory death. Like the learned researches of Alfred Kinsey, these stories might convert Casanova into a Puritan: they make sexuality seem totally repellent.

A depraved literature reflects a growing depravity in society generally; but also it nurtures that larger depravity and defiantly attempts to justify it. Sir Thomas Gresham instructs us that bad money drives out good. So it is, more and more, with books in our time; and in part that occurs because at every level of schooling the literary discipline has been enfeebled, and the humane has given ground before the mechanistic and the bestial.

This critic was a sophomore in high school, outside Detroit, in the year when Babbitt died and Eliot delivered the lectures that make up *After Strange Gods*. As the years passed, this writer came to know a diversity of able men and women of letters, and some great ones: Eliot himself, Wyndham Lewis, Roy Campbell, Robert Speaight, George Scott-Moncrieff, Max Picard, Robert Graves, Donald Davidson, Bernard Iddings Bell, Albert Jay Nock, Richard Weaver, Flannery O'Conner, Malcolm Muggeridge, Compton Mackenzie, Andrew Lytle, Julián Marías, Cleanth Brooks, Eliseo Vivas, others. Few of these still are in the land of the living, and the vacant places have not been filled. There have emerged no dominant figures in the drama, poetry, the novel, although the latter half of the twentieth century has benefited by some good critics and some seminal historians.

---

43. See Eliseo Vivas, *D. H. Lawrence: the Failure and the Triumph of Art* (Evanston, Illinois, 1960), Chapter Five particularly; and Russell Kirk, "Vivas, Lawrence, Eliot, and the Demon," in Henry Regnery (editor), *¡Viva Vivas!* (Indianapolis, 1976), pp. 225–50.

Little or no pattern of literary development may be discerned in this literary interregnum.

Or is this age of ours an interregnum, a pause, an interval between one era of high literary attainment and another era of different character but comparable worth? Cultures do suffer from fatigue and cease to rouse the imagination; or they sometimes are ruined utterly by great changes, not necessarily military. There came a time, in the fifth century of the Christian era, when polite literature in the Latin language ceased to be written—ceased totally, although writing continued in church Latin on Christian subjects. There had come a time, three centuries earlier, when imaginative and original literature in classical Greek had dried up. Is it conceivable that after eight centuries of achievement the English language may cease to be the instrument of great poetry and great prose? It comes to mind that Italian, which rose to influence throughout Europe during the Renaissance, has lost the dominion it enjoyed in the times of Dante, Ariosto, and Tasso. Yet what language might supplant English—now the commercial and diplomatic tongue internationally, having supplanted French — as the chief body of literature, during the twenty-first century? Or is it conceivable that the literatures of all nations may be flung into the dust-bin, humane culture being overwhelmed by materialism, the total state, and the fell intellectual affliction that Robert Graves, in *Seven Days in New Crete*, denominated Logicalism? May getting and spending usurp the whole of life, or nearly the whole; and may "literature" be reduced to mere diversion during an idle hour — on a beach, say, when television is unavailable — and that diversion of rather a nasty character, suitable to *Brave New World*?

Irving Babbitt, in 1908, published certain melancholy vaticinations, but wrote nothing so gloomy as the prospect suggested above. Humanitarianism, in its two aspects, has not ceased to undermine the old literary culture in our time. And since Babbitt died, humanism has been assailed by forces peculiar to our time.

Much of the audience for genuine literature has fallen away. People read good authors when there were not more tempting things to do. The coming of films, radio, television, cassettes, video — together with the cost of paying for all these gadgets — has made it unnecessary for a large part of the population of every civilized country ever to open a serious book. That majority of the population has ceased to read, except occasionally in search of such sensations as may not be obtained from films or television.

Not long after television came in, the popular magazine went out, its advertising revenues snatched away: the oldfangled popular magazine that was part of a widespread literary culture a century and a half old. Once upon a time, the novels of William Faulkner and J. P. Marquand appeared as serials in *The Saturday Evening Post*. Now middlebrow culture is prisoner to the television.

The marked reduction, *per capita*, in the number of serious readers, cumulative for the past sixty years or more — from the causes mentioned above and from other causes, among them the feebleminded "look-see" method of instruction in reading — might not in itself adversely affect the quality of new books published; it might have done no more than tend to form a more select body of readers. But intellectual and moral tendencies in publishing — or, in the view of humanists, anti-intellectual and immoral tendencies — worked at the same time to affect adversely the quality of publishing.

Centralization of the publishing trade in New York City has done mischief; the hegemony of Manhattan publishing firms and critical circles has become nearly absolute. T. S. Eliot mentions somewhere that the worst form of expatriation for an American writer is residence in New York City. Early in this century, Hamlin Garland, speaking at the Cliffdwellers' Club in Chicago, predicted that soon Chicago would be America's literary capital. But authors and publishers are not encountered in the Cliffdwellers' Club today, and at this writing Chicago's only general publisher is shifting to Washington. Political perversity is only one of the vices of Madison Avenue's publishers, taken as a species; yet it is New York's book reviews that fix the fate of most new books published in the United States. As Bryan Griffin tells us with much vivid detail, New York book-review media fairly consistently puff up books and authors possessed by what Eliot called the diabolic imagination.

Yet there is a deeper cause than technological change, the decline of middlebrow culture, diminished popular literacy, or centralized publishing and reviewing: a cause of nihilism or diabolism among writers, a cause of depraved taste among much of the reading public. That cause is discussed by T. S. Eliot in his Charlottesville lectures and more fully in later writings of his; and in *After Strange Gods*, Eliot severely criticized Irving Babbitt on this very point.

"I trust that I shall not be taken as speaking in a spirit of bigotry," Eliot said to his audience at the University of Virginia, "when I assert that the chief clue to the understanding of most contemporary Anglo-Saxon literature is to be found in the decay of Protestantism." Most writers in English had come to reject Protestant Christianity, he declared; therefore their imaginations had suffered. And he did not spare Babbitt, though expressing his "highest respect and admiration" for his teacher, who had died earlier in the year.

"It is significant to observe that Babbitt was saturated with French culture; in his thought and in his intercourse he was thoroughly cosmopolitan," Eliot went on. "He believed in tradition; for many years he stood almost alone in maintaining against the strong tendency of the time a right theory of education; and such effects of decadence as are manifest in Lawrence's work he held in abomination. And yet to my mind the very width of his culture, his intelligent eclecticism, are themselves symptoms of a narrowness of tradition, in their extreme reaction against that narrowness. His attitude towards Christianity seems to me that of a man who had no *emotional* acquaintance with any but some debased and uncultured form: I judge entirely on his public pronouncements and not at all on any information about his upbringing. It would be exaggeration to say that he wore his cosmopolitanism like a man who had lost his *complet bourgeois* and had to go about in fancy dress. But he seemed to be trying to compensate for the lack of living tradition by a herculean, but purely intellectual and individual effort. His addiction to the philosophy of Confucius is evidence: the popularity of Confucius among our contemporaries is significant. Just as I do not see how anyone can expect really to understand Kant and Hegel without knowing the German language and without such an understanding of the German mind as can only be acquired in the society of living Germans, so *a fortiori* I do not see how anyone can understand Confucius without some knowledge of Chinese and a long frequentation of the best Chinese society. . . . I do not believe that I, for one, could ever come to understand it well enough to make Confucius a mainstay. . . .

"China is—or was until the missionaries initiated her into Western thought, and so blazed a path for John Dewey—a country of tradition; Confucius was not born into a vacuum; and a network of rites and customs, even if regarded by philosophers in a spirit of benignant skepticism, make a world of difference. But Confucius has become the philosopher of the rebellious Protestant. And I cannot but feel that in some respects Irving Babbitt, with the noblest intentions, has merely made matters worse instead of better." [44]

Here Eliot's argument is that Babbitt, like nearly all twentieth-century writers of Protestant or even Protestant-agnostic background, has rejected the religion of his childhood but has not acquired other theological and moral premises for his writings. The ethical philosophy of Confucius—and Babbitt, though accomplished in Indic studies, knew no Chinese—could not suffice in some attenuated Harvard version of Oriental wisdom; nor could even the Greek and Roman classics. Below there is set down briefly Eliot's case for the Christian foundation of literature — derived in part from the scholarly conclusions of his friend Christopher Dawson, the historian.

The underlying cause of decadence, in any society, has been the decay of religious belief and the religious imagination. Culture arises out of the cult; and when the cult's belief has evaporated almost altogether, the society begins to disintegrate. (This thesis is advanced, in one fashion or another, by such

44. *After Strange Gods, op. cit.*, pp. 38–41.

recent historians as Dawson, Eric Voegelin, and Arnold Toynbee.)

"Decadence" is the loss of an object, an end, in existence.[45] Literary decadence commonly is bound up with a general intellectual and moral disorder in a society—resulting, presently, in violent social disorder. The decay of literature appears often to result from a rejection of the ancient human endeavor to apprehend a transcendent order in the universe and to live in harmony with that order; for when the myths (symbolic truths) and the dogmata are discarded, the religious imagination withers. So it had come to pass with twentieth-century Protestantism, Eliot believed. The rejection of the transcendent is conspicuous among the writers of our day.

Religious assumptions about the human condition having been abandoned by the writer, the moral imagination starves. And presently the moral imagination gives way, among many people, to the idyllic imagination; and after they have become disillusioned with Arcadia, they turn to the diabolic imagination, which afflicts both the best-educated and the worst-schooled classes in Western society today. Upon this corrupted imagination the clever charlatan and the nihilistic writer can prey. Unscrupulous originality thus terminates in a universal boring nihilism—or, yet more catastrophic than the listlessness of nihilism, the common collapse of all standards, of all authority visible or invisible: the ruin of culture, the ruin of life.[46]

Is this criticism of Babbitt's position just? Yes, for the most part. Irving Babbitt avoided the appeal to a revealed religion; he said that economics moves upward into politics, and politics upward into ethics; but on whether ethics moves upwards into theology, he was equivocal—in part because he hoped to obtain some consensus upon moral and educational standards among people of widely diverse religious and philosophical persuasions. Babbitt refused to proceed beyond "tradition" to the

45. See C. E. M. Joad, *Decadence: a Philosophical Inquiry* (London, 1948).

46. For the substance of this argument in Eliot's later writings, see Eliot, *The Idea of a Christian Society* (London, 1939), and *Notes towards the Definition of Culture* (London, 1948).

religious sources of tradition. (In its original signification, "tradition" meant knowledge of Christian truths not derived directly from Scripture, but passed down by word of mouth from generation to generation.) As Babbitt wrote in *Literature and the American College*, "The modern does not, like the Greek, hope to become original by assimilating tradition, but rather by ignoring it, or, if he is a scholar, by trying to prove that it is mistaken." Eliot's own understanding of tradition and of originality was drawn directly from Babbitt; so in pointing out a certain feebleness in Babbitt's refusal to deal with the sources of tradition, Eliot was apologizing, after a fashion, for his confession in 1928 that he was a classicist in literature, a royalist in politics, and an Anglo-Catholic in religion.

Classicism, at least, Babbitt and Eliot shared wholeheartedly. Could study of the Greek and Roman classics, and of the literary tradition derived from those classics, suffice to reinvigorate the American college—or at least suffice to avert the college's degeneration and collapse? More, could the classical spirit possibly withstand the naturalism and utilitarianism of the twentieth century, which, Babbitt feared, would convert society into "a perpetual devil's sabbath of whirling machinery" under the name of progress? To make a stand against the disciples of Bacon and the disciples of Rousseau, must not the friends of the permanent things transcend classicism (the acquisition of a few) to find the authority of religion (the consolation of the many)? Babbitt, skeptical of Revelation, was too honest to make that endeavor.

At the end of his life, Babbitt was not cheerful about prospects for the regenerating of the moral imagination; and Eliot, so early as 1931, had foreseen the coming of dark ages through which the Faith must be preserved alive.[47] Yet the classical humanism of Babbitt and the Christian humanism of Eliot may be renewed.

For civilizations commonly pass through alternating periods of decay and renewal, in the course of their history. One may

47. T. S. Eliot, "Thoughts after Lambeth," in *Selected Essays, 1917–1932, op. cit.*, p. 332.

trace this process in most literatures that have a continuity extending over several centuries. It is not unreasonable to hope for a general renewal of the civilization that is vaguely called "Western"—from causes as yet not possible to specify, perhaps — and a concomitant reinvigoration of the influence of the moral imagination in literature. If it is true that a literature decays when the religious understanding of life is lost — why, there may be observed nowadays certain phenomena of green shoots springing up in the Waste Land.

All life is an allegory, and we can understand it only in parable, G. K. Chesterton instructs us. Increasingly the rising generation turns to fable and fantasy for its reading; one has but to glance at the paperback racks of any popular bookshop. Something other than the diabolical imagination is being sought after.

As the political inclinations of the present college generation are notably different from the frantic politics of students twenty years ago, so literary preferences among the young seem to be shifting. And the young do not stay young: they become dominant adults within a few years. As Disraeli put it, prevailing opinions generally are the opinions of the generation that is passing. When it becomes clear that the public's taste has altered greatly, even Manhattan publishers make changes in their lists; why, even New York book-review media, after some uneasy interval, condescend to review books they would prefer to ignore.

In the dawning era of the twenty-first century, it may be an ancient orthodoxy, or the great works of Greece and Rome, that come to seem original. It may be that the recovery of norms will seem more exciting than surrender to the perverse. It may be that the third century of the American Republic will grow into a regenerate Augustan age. It may be that chastened modes of thought will produce a fresh literature. (John Lukacs believes that "the future of Western thought will be historical . . . a more mature achievement of the human mind than even the mastering of certain forces of nature through the scientific method, and certainly more mature than the simplistic conception of causalities.'') [48] Already civilization may be emerging from the Time of Troubles that commenced in 1914.

Eugène Ionesco, one of the more nearly original dramatists of the twentieth century, received the Eliot Award of the Ingersoll Prizes in 1985. It was Ionesco who created the theater of the absurd. In accepting the prize, the aged playwright expressed clearly for the first time his purpose in having pranced absurdities across the stage. ''If I have shown men to be ridiculous, ludicrous, it was in no way out of any desire for comic effect, but rather, difficult as this is during these times of universal spiritual decay, to proclaim the truth. . . . I have tried to portray the abyss that is the absence of faith, the absence of a spiritual life. If I have consequently at times been comic, it was with the intention to teach. The comic is only the other side of the tragic; absence is only a form of the call of the presence of Him who waits behind the door for someone to open it for Him.''

That is the voice of the moral imagination, reaffirming the humane tradition in the age of ideology. [49]

VII. The College's Enduring Ends

WHAT THE AMERICAN COLLEGE REALLY CAN DO, and ought to do, was well expressed by Irving Babbitt: ''The best of the small colleges will render a service to American education if they decide to make a sturdy defense of the humane tradition instead of trying to rival the great universities in displaying a full line of educational novelties. In the latter case, they may become third-rate and badly equipped scientific schools, and so reenact the fable of the frog that tried to swell itself to the size of an ox. . . . Even though the whole world seems bent upon living the

48. John A. Lukacs, *Historical Consciousness, or the Remembered Past* (New York, 1968), pp. 114–27.

49. Eugène Ionesco, ''Realism and the Spirit'' (address at 1985 Ingersoll Prizes Banquet), *Chronicles of Culture*, Vol. 10, No. 2 (February, 1986), pp. 24, 26.

quantitative life, the college should remember that its business is to make of its graduates men of quality in the real and not the conventional meaning of the term."

Although the American college derives its purposes and disciplines from a very old European scheme of education, and though in its beginnings it was particularly influenced by the colleges of Oxford and Cambridge and of the Scottish universities, as it developed the American college became a unique educational institution. Small, sometimes secluded, and primarily a foundation for teaching rather than for the maintenance of finished scholars, it soon affected the whole tone and temper of American life; the direct influence of Harvard or William and Mary or Yale or the other early colleges scarcely can be paralleled in any other country or era. When, in the latter part of the nineteenth century, the universities began to grow, they took the German system for their model, in considerable part; but the social influence of the college remained larger than that of the university, at least until very recent decades. Should the independent college cease to exist, the root of much in American culture would be grubbed up.

The aim of the oldfangled college education was ethical, the development of moral understanding and humane leadership; but the method was intellectual, the training of mind and conscience through well-defined literary disciplines. A college was an establishment for the study of literature: it was nearly so simple as that. Through an apprehension of great literature young men were expected to fit themselves for leadership in the churches, in politics, in law, in the principal positions of leadership in their communities.

This amounted to what Sir Thomas Elyot, in the sixteenth century, had called "the education of governors." Whatever the shortcomings of this system, it did produce a body of high-principled and literate young men to be the leaders of the American democracy. They learned to govern themselves and to serve the republic, through strict attention to great literature: they were expected to learn the poetry, philosophy, and history of Greece and Rome, especially; the Bible, with Hebrew history; something of modern thought and languages; the art of rhetoric; and something of the literature of science. The subjects of study were few, and the course of study was uniform. The intention of the college was not to confer upon its students a smattering of every branch of knowledge, but instead to teach them the fundamental disciplines of thought, provide them with a taste and a critical faculty for reading, and send them into the world with a cast of character and mind fitting them for ethical and intellectual leadership. If these young men remembered from college little more than something of sacred history, precepts from Cicero, and episodes from Plutarch—some young men retained a great deal besides—still that acquisition prepared them better for life, the life of their age or ours, than does the cafeteria-curriculum of universities and colleges nowadays, whose graduates may not read a single important book after they have snatched their diplomas — if, indeed, they read anything but dull textbooks while undergraduates.

If American institutions of higher learning could impart to their students generally the sort of liberal education described by John Henry Newman, many of our difficulties in the order of the soul and the order of the commonwealth would be much diminished. But in this day and age, to expect such an achievement in mass education would be to set our sights impossibly high. We will be fortunate if we contrive to restore in our time a standard of achievement roughly equivalent to that attained by the oldfangled American college, which doubtless fell short of Newman's ideal.

Since Babbitt's time, most American colleges have failed to reach the fairly modest goal of early American college endeavor because they have tried to be all things to all men. They have promised to teach adjustment to the group, and sociability, and trades, and salesmanship, and business acumen, and the art of worldly wisdom. They have aped the functions of the universities and the technical schools. With murmured apology and shamefacedness they have consigned their old disciplines to a dusty corner of the curriculum—when they have not abolished altogether the classics, polite letters, languages, moral philosophy, and even speculative science. "Business science," "communications skills," "pre-law," "pre-medicine," and all that sort of thing displace the disciplines that teach what it is to be fully human. Most of the colleges have abandoned their ethical end and forgotten their intellectual means. When function ceases, form atrophies.

Certain things a good college can do very well. It can give the student the tools for educating himself thoughout his life. It can present to him certain general principles for the governance of personality and community. It can help him to see what makes life worth living. It can teach him basic disciplines which will be of infinite value in professional specialization at a university, or in his subsequent apprenticeship to any commercial or industrial occupation.

And certain things no honest college can pretend to do at all. It cannot teach him directly how to win friends and influence people. It cannot make him a successful captain of industry or engineer or specialized scientist. It cannot guarantee him worldly prosperity. It cannot simply enroll him in a survey-course in "world culture" and pour wisdom into him, as milk is poured into a bottle.

The good to be got from a college is what Albert Jay Nock called the "useless knowledge" absorbed there—a body of knowledge commonly forgotten in detail for the most part, but precious as discipline and residue. The useful knowledge, the practical instruction, is obsolete almost before the student enters the practical world; so a college is wasting its students' time, and its own resources, when it pretends to teach what really can be taught only in workaday life, in the graduate school, or in the trade school.

Throughout the twentieth century, most colleges have come to disregard Babbitt's admonitions, pleading that the college must give the public whatever the public seems to demand. But nowadays it is the college which can boast of its high standards, its demands upon students' minds, that will attract the better students and the benefactions of industry, the foundations, and the private patrons. The college can survive not by imitating the mass-education methods of Behemoth State University and Brummagem University, but by offering a discipline of intellect, ethical in purpose, that mass education neglects.

Even a good many of today's students have grown aware of the college's deficiencies as an ethical agency. Not a few undergraduates complain that their college offers them no first principles of morality, no ethical direction, no aspiration after enduring truth. Such laments may sound strange enough, coming often from students who rejoice in their defiance of bourgeois conformity, and whose private lives distinctly are not modelled upon the precepts of Jeremy Taylor. Nevertheless it remains true that the hungry sheep—or goats, perhaps—have looked up on occasion, and have not been fed.

At best, what the typical college has offered its undergraduates, in recent decades, has been defecated rationality: that is, a narrow rationalism or Benthamite logicalism, purged of theology, moral philosophy, and the wisdom of our ancestors. This defecated rationality exalts private judgment and gratification of the senses at the expense of the inner order of the soul and the outer order of the republic. On many a campus, this defecated and desiccated logicalism is the best that is offered to the more intelligent students; as alternatives, they can pursue a program of fun and games, or else a program of "social commitment" of a baneful or silly character, wondrously unintellectual.

If we forget the primacy of moral worth in our scheme of education, we will establish no Arcadia of unchecked personal liberty, but instead bring upon ourselves a congeries of warring ideologies and fierce private appetites. Take away from the scholar his rights and duties as a member of what Coleridge called the clerisy, and he is left an intellectual in the root sense of that Marxist term: an adventurer, an ideologue, alienated from society and gnawing at society's roots. Take away from the student his patrimony of moral imagination and ethical knowledge, and we are confronted, perhaps, by the secularized Pharisee, ignorantly denouncing as "immoral" the imperfect but tolerable order to which he owes his existence.

The purpose of the American college defended by Irving Babbitt never was that of the sophist, to teach the ways, often dark enough, to worldly power and wealth; nor that of the humanitarian, bestowing a kiss upon the universe. The high function of the college, in Babbitt's eyes, was to unite wisdom and virtue in the rising generation, and to leaven a democratic nation by raising up a body of humanely-schooled leaders in many walks of life.

To discern a consciousness of such ends in the colleges of 1986 sometimes is difficult. America's higher education has been afflicted by ills that have increased monstrously since Babbitt touched upon them in *Literature and the American College*. It must suffice here to name four of them.

First, purposelessness: the swelling of college and university as a major industry, employing hundreds of thousands of folk at good salaries, and serving as an aging-vat for a Lonely Crowd of young people—but offering little enough for the mind and less for the conscience. This system seems to exist chiefly for the end of its own perpetuation.

Second, intellectual disorder: the cafeteria-style curriculum collapsing into an "open" curriculum, with integration of knowledge abandoned; the prevalence of a vague "career-oriented" chaos of specialized programs; a sharp reduction in the number of courses requiring intellectual exertion; the vanishing, on many campuses, of the humane disciplines (in any rigorous sense) that Babbitt knew to be the essence of liberal learning.

Third, gigantism in scale: a mockery of Babbitt's "atmosphere of leisure and reflection," the inhumane scale of Behemoth State University, with forty thousand students, say, collectivism rather than community, lodged in barren dormitories, with television sets and hi-fis blaring; teen-age ghettos, in which a great many students never become acquainted with a genuine professor, and utilitarian "output" of graduates is the boast of educational administrators.

Fourth, the clutch of ideology, to which many professors and students have surrendered, so that sour professions of resentment against everything inherited from the past or representing authority become a college's dominant mood; and political fanaticism drives out that temperate discourse supposed to be the justification and the reward of academic freedom.

If intellectually we linger smug and apathetic in a bent world, leaving the works of the mind to molder, as a people we will come to know the consequences of personal and public decadence. The alternative to a humane education, Babbitt persisted in saying, is an inhumane servility of the mind. And when the flood-waters of the world are out, even in the America of 1986 it will not suffice to be borne along by the current, singing hallelujah to the river god. Sensing this hard truth, a fair number of men and women now seek for the real ends of the higher learning; and some of them will be instructed and moved by Babbitt's plea for the permanent things of civilization.

At the very end of his little book, Babbitt rebukes humanitarian hustlers and exhorts us to think. "Of action we shall have plenty in any case," he tells us sagaciously, "but it is only by a more humane reflection that we can escape from the penalties sure to be exacted from any country that tries to dispense in its national life with the principle of leisure." That is a humane insight borrowed, with acknowledgement, from Aristotle.[50]

Perhaps more men and women will heed his counsel in 1986 than paid serious attention to it in 1908. For faith in an automatic Progress, the illusion of the humanitarian, no longer dominates American politics or American education so sorely as it did in 1908. Some bold souls even whisper that the ends of a true college, as indeed the ends of all true education, are wisdom and virtue—a very oldfangled Platonic insight. And in "Little Gidding" Eliot reminds us—perhaps with Irving Babbitt, among others, in his memory—that the communication of the dead is tongued with fire beyond the language of the living. So did Babbitt teach his students lifelong; and now he speaks himself in that burning fashion, from these pages.

---

50. For a moving defense of leisure, in the spirit of Babbitt, see Joseph Pieper's *Leisure, the Basis of Culture*, with a preface by T. S. Eliot (London, 1952); also Sebastian de Grazia, *Of Time, Work, and Leisure* (New York, 1962).

Preface

NEARLY HALF THE MATTER in this volume has been printed elsewhere. "The Rational Study of the Classics," "Literature and the College," and "On Being Original" are reproduced with immaterial changes from the "Atlantic Monthly." Two papers in the "Nation" are combined with a great deal of new material in the essay on "Literature and the Doctor's Degree." Portions of the essays on "Ancients and Moderns" and "Academic Leisure" are taken from two articles in the "Harvard Graduates' Magazine." I wish to thank the publishers of these periodicals for permission to reprint.

I have often been forced in these essays to tread on burning ground, at the risk of giving offense to some of my readers. I may at least say that my aim has been to define types and tendencies, and not to satirize or even label individuals. Individuals are usually not easy to label, especially at a time like the present. A highly unified age may offer examples of highly unified personalities; but there is likely to exist in the individual of to-day the same confused conflict of tendencies that we see in the larger world. What I try to show is, not that our contemporary scholars are lacking in humanistic traits, but that the scholars in whom these traits predominate are few (*rari nantes in gurgite vasto*).

I would also remind the reader that my treatment of certain eminent persons of the past and present is limited by my subject, and makes no claim to completeness. It was, for example, inevitable in dealing with college education that I should discuss the role of President Eliot. It was also inevitable, in the case of one who has exercised so many-sided an influence on his time, that I should fall very far short of a rounded estimate.

I desire to take this opportunity of expressing my sense of obligation to Professor Charles Eliot Norton. Those who during the past generation have felt the need of a more humane scholarship are indebted to him, many for direct aid and encouragement, and all for an example. To Mr. Paul E. More, literary editor of the New York "Evening Post" and the "Nation," who read several of these essays in manuscript, acknowledgments are due for various criticisms and suggestions.

I. B.

Holderness, N.H., December, 1907.

I

What Is Humanism?

ONE OF OUR FEDERAL JUDGES SAID, not long ago, that what the American people need is ten per cent of thought and ninety per cent of action. In that case we ought all to be happy, for that is about what we have already. One is reminded by contrast of an accusation brought by a recent historian of Greek philosophy against Socrates, who, according to this historian, exaggerates the reasonableness of human nature. Only think rightly, Socrates seems to say, and right acting may be counted on to follow. The English and American temper is in this respect almost the reverse of Socratic. Act strenuously, would appear to be our faith, and right thinking will take care of itself. We feel that we can afford to "muddle along" in theory if only we attain to practical efficiency.

This comparative indifference to clearness and consistency of thought is visible even in that chief object of our national concern, education. The firmness of the American's faith in the blessings of education is equalled only by the vagueness of his ideas as to the kind of education to which these blessings are annexed. One can scarcely consider the tremendous stir we have been making for the past thirty years or more about education, the time and energy and enthusiasm we are ready to

lavish on educational undertakings, the libraries and laboratories and endowments, without being reminded of the words of
Sir Joshua Reynolds: "A provision of endless apparatus, a
bustle of infinite inquiry and research, may be employed to
evade and shuffle off real labor—the real labor of thinking." We
live so fast, as the saying is, that we have no time to think. The
task of organizing and operating a huge and complex educational machinery has left us scant leisure for calm reflection.
Evidently a little less eagerness for action and a little more of the
Socratic spirit would do no harm. We are likely, however, to be
arrested at the very outset of any attempt to clarify our notions
about education, as Socrates was in dealing with the problems of
his own time, by the need of accurate definition. The Socratic
method is, indeed, in its very essence a process of right defining.
It divides and subdivides and distinguishes between the diverse
and sometimes contradictory concepts that lurk beneath one
word; it is a perpetual protest, in short, against the confusion that
arises from the careless use of general terms, especially when
they have become popular catchwords. If Socrates were here today, we can picture to ourselves how he would go around
"cross-examining" those of us (there are some college presidents in the number) who repeat so glibly the current platitudes
about liberty and progress, democracy, service, and the like;
and he would no doubt get himself set down as a public nuisance
for his pains, as he was by his fellow Athenians.

A good example of the confusion rising from general terms is
the term that is more important than any other, perhaps, for our
present argument. To make a plea for humanism without
explaining the word would give rise to endless misunderstanding. It is equally on the lips of the socialistic dreamer and the
exponent of the latest philosophical fad. In an age of happy
liberty like the present, when any one can employ almost any
general term very much as he pleases, it is perhaps inevitable
that the term humanism, which still has certain gracious associations lingering about it, should be appropriated by various
theorists, in the hope, apparently, that the benefit of the associations may accrue to an entirely different order of ideas. Thus
the Oxford philosopher, Mr. F. C. S. Schiller, claims to be a

humanist, and in the name of humanism threatens to "do strange deeds upon the clouds." Renan says that the religion of the future will be a "true humanism." The utopists who have described their vision of the future as "humanism" or the "new humanism" are too numerous to mention. Gladstone speaks of the humanism of Auguste Comte, Professor Herford of the humanism of Rousseau, and the Germans in general of the humanism of Herder; whereas Comte, Rousseau, and Herder were all three not humanists, but humanitarian enthusiasts. A prominent periodical, on the other hand, laments the decay of the "humanitarian spirit" at Harvard, meaning no doubt humanistic. We evidently need a working definition not only of humanism, but of the words with which it is related or confused, —humane, humanistic, humanitarian, humanitarianism. And these words, if successfully defined, will help us to a further necessary definition,—that of the college. For any discussion of the place of literature in the college is conditioned by a previous question: whether there will be any college for literature to have a place in. The college has been brought to this predicament not so much perhaps by its avowed enemies as by those who profess to be its friends. Under these circumstances our prayer, like that of Ajax, should be to fight in the light.

I

THE FIRST STEP IN OUR QUEST would seem to be to go back to the Latin words (*humanus, humanitas*) from which all the words of our group are derived. Most of the material we need will be found in a recent and excellent study by M. Gaston Boissier of the ancient meanings of *humanitas*. From M. Boissier's paper it would appear that *humanitas* was from the start a fairly elastic virtue with the Romans, and that the word came to be used rather loosely, so that in a late Latin writer, Aulus Gellius, we find a complaint that it had been turned aside from its true meaning. *Humanitas*, says Gellius, is incorrectly used to denote a "promiscuous benevolence, what the Greeks call philanthropy," whereas the word really implies doctrine and discipline, and is applicable not to men in general but only to a select few,—it is, in short, aristocratic and not democratic in its implication.[1]

The confusion that Gellius complains of is not only interesting in itself, but closely akin to one that we need to be on guard against to-day. If we are to believe Gellius, the Roman decadence was like our own age in that it tended to make love for one's fellow men, or altruism, as we call it, do duty for most of the other virtues. It confused humanism with philanthropy. Only our philanthropy has been profoundly modified, as we shall see more fully later, by becoming associated with an idea of which only the barest beginnings can be found in antiquity—the idea of progress.

It was some inkling of the difference between a universal philanthropy and the indoctrinating and disciplining of the individual that led Aulus Gellius to make his protest. Two words were probably needed in his time; they are certainly needed today. A person who has sympathy for mankind in the lump, faith in its future progress, and desire to serve the great cause of this progress, should be called not a humanist, but a humanitarian, and his creed may be designated as humanitarianism. From the present tendency to regard humanism as an abbreviated and convenient form for humanitarianism there must arise every manner of confusion. The humanitarian lays stress almost solely upon breadth of knowledge and sympathy. The poet Schiller, for instance, speaks as a humanitarian and not as a humanist when he would "clasp the millions to his bosom," and bestow "a kiss upon the whole world." The humanist is more selective in his caresses. Aulus Gellius, who was a man of somewhat crabbed and pedantic temper, would apparently exclude sympathy almost entirely from his conception of *humanitas* and confine the meaning to what he calls *cura et disciplina*; and he cites the authority of Cicero. Cicero, however, seems to have avoided any such one-sided view. Like the admirable humanist that he was, he no doubt knew that what is wanted is not sympathy alone, nor again discipline and selection alone,

1. See *Noctes Atticae*, xiii, 17.

but a disciplined and selective sympathy. Sympathy without selection becomes flabby, and a selection which is unsympathetic tends to grow disdainful.

The humanist, then, as opposed to the humanitarian, is interested in the perfecting of the individual rather than in schemes for the elevation of mankind as a whole; and although he allows largely for sympathy, he insists that it be disciplined and tempered by judgment. One of the most recent attempts to define humanism, that of Brunetière,[2] who was supposed to be out of touch with his own time, suffers, nevertheless, from our present failure to see in the term anything more than the fullness of knowlege and sympathy. Brunetière thinks he has discovered a complete definition of humanism in the celebrated line of Terence: "Humani nihil a me alienum puto." This line expresses very well a universal concern for one's fellow creatures, but fails to define the humanist because of the entire absence of the idea of selection. It is spoken in the play as an excuse for meddling; and might serve appropriately enough as a motto for the humanitarian busybody with whom we are all so familiar nowadays, who goes around with schemes for reforming almost everything—except himself. As applied to literature, the line might be cited as a justification for reading anything, from Plato to the Sunday supplement. Cosmopolitan breadth of knowledge and sympathy do not by themselves suffice; to be humanized these qualities need to be tempered by discipline and selection. From this point of view the Latin *litteræ humaniores* is a happier phrase than our English "humane letters," because of the greater emphasis the Latin comparative puts on the need of selection.

The true humanist maintains a just balance between sympathy and selection. We moderns, even a champion of the past like Brunetière, tend to lay an undue stress on the element of sympathy. On the other hand, the ancients in general, both Greek and Roman, inclined to sacrifice sympathy to selection. Gellius's protest against confusing *humanitas* with a promiscuous

---

2. *Histoire de la Littérature française classique*, t. i, p. 28.

philanthropy instead of reserving it for doctrine and discipline would by itself be entirely misleading. Ancient humanism is as a whole intensely aristocratic in temper; its sympathies run in what would seem to us narrow channels; it is naturally disdainful of the humble and lowly who have not been indoctrinated and disciplined. Indeed, an unselective and universal sympathy, the sense of the brotherhood of man, as we term it, is usually supposed to have come into the world only with Christianity. We may go farther and say that the exaltation of love and sympathy as supreme and all-sufficing principles that do not need to be supplemented by doctrine and discipline is largely peculiar to our modern and humanitarian era. Historically, Christians have always inclined to reserve their sympathies for those who had the same doctrine and discipline as themselves, and only too often have joined to a sympathy for their own kind a fanatical hatred for everybody else. One whole side of Christianity has put a tremendous emphasis on selection—even to the point of conceiving of God Himself as selective rather than sympathetic ("Many are called, few are chosen," etc.). We may be sure that stalwart believers like St. Paul or St. Augustine or Pascal would look upon our modern humanitarians with their talk of social problems and their tendency to reduce religion to a phase of the tenement-house question as weaklings and degenerates. Humanitarianism, however, and the place it accords to sympathy is so important for our subject that we shall have to revert to it later. For the present, it is enough to oppose the democratic inclusiveness of our modern sympathies to the aristocratic aloofness of the ancient humanist and his disdain of the profane vulgar (*Odi profanum vulgus et arceo*). This aloofness and disdain are reflected and in some ways intensified in the humanism of the Renaissance. The man of the Renaissance felt himself doubly set above the "raskall many," first by his doctrine and discipline and then by the learned medium through which the doctrine and discipline were conveyed. The echo of this haughty humanism is heard in the lines of Milton:—

"Nor do I name of men the common rout,
  That wandering loose about,
  Grow up and perish as the summer fly,
  Heads without name, no more rememberèd."

Later on this humanistic ideal became more and more conventionalized and associated with a hierarchy of rank and privilege. The sense of intellectual superiority was reinforced by the sense of social superiority. The consequent narrowing of sympathy is what Amiel objects to in the English gentleman: "Between gentlemen, courtesy, equality, social proprieties; below that level, haughtiness, disdain, coldness, indifference.... The politeness of a gentleman is not human and general, but quite individual and personal." It is a pity, no doubt, that the Englishman is thus narrow in his sympathies; but it will be a greater pity, if, in enlarging his sympathies, he allows his traditional disciplines, humanistic and religious, to be relaxed and enervated. The English humanist is not entirely untrue to his ancient prototype even in the faults of which Amiel complains. There is a real relation, as Professor Butcher points out, between the English idea of the gentleman and scholar and the view of the cultivated man that was once held in the intensely aristocratic democracy of Athens.

II

WE SHOULD OF COURSE REMEMBER that though we have been talking of ancient humanism and humanists, the word humanist was not used until the Renaissance and the word humanism not until a still later period. In studying the humanism of the Renaissance the significant contrast that we need to note is the one commonly made at this time between humanity and divinity. In its essence the Renaissance is a protest against the time when there was too much divinity and not enough human-

ity, against the starving and stunting of certain sides of man by
mediaeval theology, against a vision of the supernatural that imposed a mortal constraint upon his more purely human and
natural faculties. The models of a full and free play of these
faculties were sought in the ancient classics, but the cult of the
ancients soon became itself a superstition, so that a man was
called a humanist from the mere fact of having received an
initiation into the ancient languages, even though he had little
or nothing of the doctrine and discipline that the term should
imply. Very few of the early Italian humanists were really
humane. For many of them humanism, so far from being a
doctrine and discipline, was a revolt from all discipline, a wild
rebound from the mediaeval extreme into an opposite excess.
What predominates in the first part of the Renaissance is a
movement of emancipation—emancipation of the senses, of the
intellect, and in the northern countries of the conscience. It was
the first great modern era of expansion, the first forward push of
individualism. As in all such periods, the chief stress is on the
broadening of knowledge, and, so far as was compatible with
the humanistic exclusiveness, of sympathy. The men of that
time had what Emerson calls a canine appetite for knowledge.
The ardor with which they broke away from the bonds and
leading-strings of mediaeval tradition, the exuberance with
which they celebrated the healing of the long feud between
nature and human nature, obscured for a time the need of
decorum and selection. A writer like Rabelais, for instance, is
neither decorous nor select; and so in spite of his great genius
would probably have seemed to a cultivated ancient barbaric
rather than humane. Such a disorderly and undisciplined
unfolding of the faculties of the individual, such an overemphasis on the benefits of liberty as compared with the benefits
of restraint, brought in its train the evils that are peculiar to
periods of expansion. There was an increase in anarchical self-
assertion and self-indulgence that seemed a menace to the very
existence of society; and so society reacted against the individual
and an era of expansion was followed by an era of concentration. This change took place at different times, and under different circumstances, in different countries. In Italy the change

coincides roughly with the sack of Rome (1527) and the Council of Trent; in France it follows the frightful anarchy of the wars of religion and finds political expression in Henry IV, and literary expression in Malherbe. Of course in so complex a period as the Renaissance we must allow for innumerable eddies and cross-currents and for almost any number of individual exceptions. In an age as well as in an individual there are generally elements, often important elements, that run counter to the main tendency. But if one is not a German doctor who has to prove his "originality," or a lover of paradox for its own sake, it is usually possible to discern the main drift in spite of the eddies and counter-currents.

We may affirm, then, that the main drift of the later Renaissance was away from a humanism that favored a free expansion toward a humanism that was in the highest degree disciplinary and selective. The whole movement was complicated by what is at bottom a different problem, the need that was felt in France and Italy, at least, of protecting society against the individual. One can insist on selection and discipline without at the same time being so distrustful of individualism. Many of the humanists of this period fell into hardness and narrowness (in other words, ceased to be humane) from overemphasis on a discipline that was to be imposed from without and from above, and on a doctrine that was to be codified in a multitude of minute prescriptions. The essence of art, according to that highly astringent genius, Scaliger, who had a European influence on the literary criticism of this age, is *electio et fastidium sui* — selection and fastidiousness toward one's self (in practice Scaliger reserved his fastidiousness for other people). This spirit of fastidious selection gained ground until instead of the expansive Rabelais we have the exclusive Malherbe, until a purism grew up that threatened to impoverish men's ideas and emotions as well as their vocabulary. Castiglione had said in his treatise on the Courtier that there should enter into the make-up of the gentleman an element of aloofness and disdain (*sprezzatura*), a saying that, properly interpreted, contains a profound truth. Unfortunately, aristocratic aloofness, coupled with fastidious selection and unleavened by broad and sympathetic knowledge, leads straight to the attitude that Voltaire has hit off in his sketch of the noble Venetian lord Pococurante,—to the type of scholar who would be esteemed, not like the man of to-day by the inclusiveness of his sympathies, but by the number of things he had rejected. Pococurante had cultivated *sprezzatura* with a vengeance, and rejected almost everything except a few verses of Virgil and Horace. "What a great man is this Pococurante!" says the awe-stricken Candide; "nothing can please him."

The contrast between the disciplinary and selective humanism of the later Renaissance and the earlier period of expansion should not blind us to the underlying unity of aim. Like the ancient humanists whom they took as their guides, the men of both periods aimed at forming the complete man (*totus, teres atque rotundus*). But the men of the later period and the neo-classicists in general hoped to attain this completeness not so much by the virtues of expansion as by the virtues of concentration. It seemed to them that the men of the earlier period had left too much opening for the whims and vagaries of the individual; and so they were chiefly concerned with making a selection of subjects and establishing a doctrine and discipline that should be universal and human. To this end the classical doctrine and discipline were to be put into the service of the doctrine and discipline of Christianity. This attempt at a compromise between the pagan and Christian traditions is visible both in Catholic countries in the Jesuit schools, and in Protestant countries in the selection of studies that took shape in the old college curriculum. No doubt the selection of both divinity and humanity that was intended to be representative was inadequate; and no doubt the whole compromise between doctrines and disciplines, that were in many respects divergent and in some respects hostile, laid itself open to the charge of being superficial. The men of the early Renaissance had felt more acutely the antagonism between divinity as then understood and humanity, and had often taken sides uncompromisingly for one or the other. Machiavelli accused Christianity of having made the world effeminate, whereas Luther looked on the study of the pagan classics, except within the narrowest bounds, as pernicious.

Calvin execrated Rabelais, and Rabelais denounced Calvin as an impostor. Yet, after all, the effort to make the ancient humanities and arts of expression tributary to Christianity was in many respects admirable, and the motto that summed it up, *sapiens atque eloquens pietas*, might still, if properly interpreted, be used to define the purpose of the college.

A desideratum of scholarship at present is a study of the way certain subjects came to be selected as representative and united into one discipline with elements that were drawn from religion; we need, in short, a more careful history than has yet been written of the old college curriculum. Closely connected with this and equally needful is a history of the development of the gentleman, going back to the work of Castiglione and other Italian treatises on manners in the sixteenth century, and making clear especially how the conception of the gentleman came to unite with that of the scholar so as to form an ideal of which something still survives in England. A Castiglione in Italy and a Sir Philip Sidney in England already realize the ideal of the gentleman and scholar, and that with the splendid vitality of the Renaissance. But a Scaliger, for all his fastidious selection, remains a colossal pedant. In general, it is only under French influence that scholarship gets itself disengaged from pedantry and acquires urbanity and polish, that the standards of the humanist coalesce with those of the man of the world. But it is likewise under French influence that the ideal of the gentleman and scholar is externalized and conventionalized, until in some of the later neo-classic Pococurantes it has degenerated into a mixture of snobbishness and superficiality, until what had once been a profound insight becomes a mere polite prejudice. We must not, however, be like the leaders of the great romantic revolt who, in their eagerness to get rid of the husk of convention, disregarded also the humane aspiration. Even in his worst artificiality, the neo-classicist is still related to the ancient humanist by his horror of one-sidedness, of all that tends to the atrophy of certain faculties and the hypertrophy of others, by his avoidance of everything that is excessive and over-emphatic; and, inasmuch as it is hard to be an enthusiast and at the same time moderate, by his distrust of enthusiasm. He cultivates detachment and freedom from affectation (*sprezzatura*) and wonders at nothing (*nil admirari*); whereas the romanticist, as all the world knows, is prone to wonder at everything—especially at himself and his own genius. In his appearance and behavior, the neo-classicist would be true to the general traits of human nature, and is even careful to avoid technical and professional terms in his writing and conversation. "Perfected good breeding," says Dr. Johnson, "consists in having no particular mark of any profession, but a general elegance of manners." (A standard that Dr. Johnson himself did not entirely attain.) At the bottom of the whole point of view is the fear of specialization. "The true gentleman and scholar" (*honnête homme*), says La Rochefoucauld, "is he who does not pride himself on any-thing." We may contrast this with a maxim that is sometimes heard in the American business world: A man who knows two things is damned. In other words, the man of that time would rather have been thought superficial than one-sided, the man of today would rather be thought one-sided than superficial.

III

WE MAY PERHAPS VENTURE to sum up the results of our search for a definition of humanism. We have seen that the humanist, as we know him historically, moved between an extreme of sympathy and an extreme of discipline and selection, and became humane in proportion as he mediated between these extremes. To state this truth more generally, the true mark of excellence in a man, as Pascal puts it, is his power to harmonize in himself opposite virtues and to occupy all the space between them (*tout l'entredeux*). By his ability thus to unite in himself opposite qualities man shows his humanity, his superiority of essence over other animals. Thus Saint François de Sales, we are told, united in himself the qualities of the eagle and the dove—he was an eagle of gentleness. The historian of Greek philosophy we have already quoted remarks on the perfect harmony that Socrates had attained between thought and feeling. If we compare Socrates in this respect with Rousseau, who said that "his heart and his head did not seem to belong to the same individual," we shall perceive the difference between a sage and a sophist. Man is a creature who is foredoomed to one-sidedness, yet who becomes humane only in proportion as he triumphs over this fatality of his nature, only as he arrives at that measure which comes from tempering his virtues, each by its opposite. The aim, as Matthew Arnold has said in the most admirable of his critical phrases, is to see life steadily and see it whole; but this is an aim, alas, that no one has ever attained completely—not even Sophocles, to whom Arnold applies it. After man has made the simpler adjustments, there are other and more difficult adjustments awaiting him beyond, and the goal is, in a sense, infinitely remote.

For most practical purposes, the law of measure is the supreme law of life, because it bounds and includes all other laws. It was doubtless the perception of this fact that led the most eminent personality of the Far East, Gotama Buddha, to proclaim in the opening sentence of his first sermon that extremes are barbarous. But India as a whole failed to learn the lesson. Greece is perhaps the most humane of countries, because it not only formulated clearly the law of measure ("nothing too much"), but also perceived the avenging nemesis that overtakes every form of insolent excess ($\H{\upsilon}\beta\rho\iota\varsigma$) or violation of this law.

Of course, even in Greece any effective insight into the law of measure was confined to a minority, though at times a large minority. The majority at any particular instant in Greece or elsewhere is almost sure to be unsound, and unsound because it is one-sided. We may borrow a homely illustration from the theory of commercial crises. A minority of men may be prudent and temper their enterprise with discretion, but the majority is sure to over-trade, and so unless restrained by the prudent few will finally bring on themselves the nemesis of a panic. The excess from which Greek civilization suffered should be of special interest, because it is plain that so humane a people could not have failed to make any of the ordinary adjustments. Without attempting to treat fully so difficult a topic, we may say that Greece, having lost its traditional standards through the growth of intellectual skepticism, fell into a dangerous and excessive mobility of mind because of its failure to develop new standards that would unify its life and impose a discipline upon the individual. It failed, in short, to mediate between unity and diversity, or, as the philosophers express it, between the absolute and the relative. The wisest Greek thinkers, notably Socrates and Plato, saw the problem and sought a solution; but by putting Socrates to death Athens made plain that it was unable to distinguish between its sages and its sophists.

There is the One, says Plato, and there is the Many. "Show me the man who can combine the One with the Many and I will follow in his footsteps, even as in those of a God." [3] To harmonize the One with the Many, this is indeed a difficult adjustment, perhaps the most difficult of all, and so important, withal, that nations have perished from their failure to achieve it. Ancient India was devoured by a too overpowering sense of the One. The failure of Greece, on the other hand, to attain to this restraining sense of unity led at last to the pernicious pliancy of the "hungry Greekling," whose picture Juvenal has drawn.

The present time in its loss of traditional standards is not without analogy to the Athens of the Periclean age; and so it is not surprising, perhaps, that we should see a refurbishing of the old sophistries. The so-called humanism of a writer like Mr. F. C. S. Schiller has in it something of the intellectual impressionism of a Protagoras.[4] Like the ancient sophist, the pragmatist would forego the discipline of a central standard, and make of individual man and his thoughts and feelings the measure of all things. "Why may not the advancing front of experience," says Professor James, "carrying its imminent

3. *Phaedrus*, 266 B. The Greeks in general did not associate the law of measure with the problem of the One and the Many. Aristotle, who was in this respect a more representative Greek than Plato, can scarcely be said to have connected his theory of the contemplative life or attainment to a sense of the divine unity, with his theory of virtue as a mediating between extremes.

4. Mr. Schiller himself points out this connection (see *Humanism*, p. xvii). As will appear clearly from a later passage (pp. 136 ff.) I do not quarrel with the pragmatists for their appeal to experience and practical results, but for their failure, because of an insufficient feeling for the One, to arrive at real criteria for testing experience and discriminating between judgments and mere passing impressions.

satisfaction and dissatisfaction, cut against the black inane, as the luminous orb of the moon cuts against the black abyss?'' [5] But the sun and moon and stars have their preordained courses, and do not dare, as the old Pythagoreans said, to transgress their numbers. To make Professor James's metaphor just, the moon would need to deny its allegiance to the central unity, and wander off by itself on an impressionistic journey of exploration through space. It is doubtless better to be a pragmatist than to devote one's self to embracing the cloud Junos of Hegelian metaphysics. But that persons who have developed such an extreme sense of the otherwiseness of things as Professor James and his school should be called humanists — this we may seriously doubt. There would seem to be nothing less humane—or humanistic—than pluralism pushed to this excess, unless it be monism pushed to a similar extremity.

The human mind, if it is to keep its sanity, must maintain the nicest balance between unity and plurality. There are moments when it should have the sense of communion with absolute being, and of the obligation to higher standards that this insight brings; other moments when it should see itself as but a passing phase of the everlasting flux and relativity of nature; moments when, with Emerson, it should feel itself "alone with the gods alone"; and moments when, with Sainte-Beuve, it should look upon itself as only the "most fugitive of illusions in the bosom of the infinite illusion." If man's nobility lies in his kinship to the One, he is at the same time a phenomenon among other phenomena, and only at his risk and peril neglects his phenomenal self. The humane poise of his faculties suffers equally from an excess of naturalism and an excess of supernaturalism. We have seen how the Renaissance protested against the supernaturalist excess of the Middle Ages, against a one-sidedness that widened unduly the gap between nature and human nature. Since that time the world has been tending to the opposite extreme; not content with establishing a better harmony between nature and human nature, it would close up the gap entirely. Man, according to the celebrated dictum of Spinoza, is not in nature as one

5. *Humanism and Truth*, p. 16.

empire in another empire, but as a part in a whole. Important faculties that the supernaturalist allowed to decay the naturalist has cultivated, but other faculties, especially those relating to the contemplative life, are becoming atrophied through long disuse. Man has gained immensely in his grasp on facts, but in the meanwhile has become so immersed in their multiplicity as to lose that vision of the One by which his lower self was once overawed and restrained. "There are two laws discrete," as Emerson says in his memorable lines; and since we cannot reconcile the "Law for man" and the "Law for thing," he would have us preserve our sense for each separately, and maintain a sort of "double consciousness," a "public" and a "private" nature; and he adds in a curious image that a man must ride alternately on the horses of these two natures, "as the equestrians in the circus throw themselves nimbly from horse to horse, or plant one foot on the back of one and the other foot on the back of the other."

There is, perhaps, too much of this spiritual circus-riding in Emerson. Unity and plurality appear too often in his work, not as reconciled opposites, but as clashing antinomies. He is too satisfied with saying about half the time that everything is like everything else, and the rest of the time that everything is different from everything else. And so his genius has elevation and serenity, indeed, but at the same time a disquieting vagueness and lack of grip in dealing with particulars. Yet Emerson remains an important witness to certain truths of the spirit in an age of scientific materialism. His judgment of his own time is likely to be definitive: —

> "Things are in the saddle
> And ride mankind."

Man himself and the products of his spirit, language, and literature, are treated not as having a law of their own, but as things; as entirely subject to the same methods that have won for science such triumphs over phenomenal nature. The president of a congress of anthropologists recently chose as a motto for his annual address the humanistic maxim: "The proper study of mankind is man"; and no one, probably, was conscious of any incongruity. At this rate, we may soon see set up as a type of the true humanist the Chicago professor who recently spent a year in collecting cats'-cradles on the Congo.

The humanities need to be defended to-day against the encroachments of physical science, as they once needed to be against the encroachment of theology. But first we must keep a promise already made, and in the following essay try to trace from its origins that great naturalistic and humanitarian movement which is not only taking the place of the humanistic point of view, but actually rendering it unintelligible for the men of the present generation.

II

Two Types of Humanitarians
Bacon and Rousseau

ACCORDING TO RENAN, the capital event of modern thought is the substitution in the sixteenth century of the Copernican astronomy for the old anthropocentric view. With the advent of the new astronomy, man, we are told, first had the sensation of the infinite; it would be less misleading to say that he then had forced upon him as never before the sense of physical immensity. It is this shuddering sense of physical immensity that one finds in Pascal, for example, and which one would seek in vain in a mediaeval writer like Dante. Instead of looking on the world as the center of the universe and himself as the center of the world, man was turned adrift, as it were, in the infinitude of space. Thus swallowed up in vastness, he found it increasingly difficult to assert his own superiority of essence; he regarded himself more and more, not as an empire in another empire, but as a part in a whole. This new feeling of the oneness of nature and human nature brought its own consolations to man for his loss of supernatural privilege. On the sentimental side man was consoled by the boons that, according to Wordsworth, spring from a "wise passiveness"; on the scientific side by the prospect of the dominion that, according to Bacon, he is to win over nature by the very act of obeying her.

Naturalists then have evidently been divided into two great classes, according as the predominant temper has been sentimental or scientific, and corresponding closely to the two classes of naturalists have been the scientific and sentimental humanitarians. The positive and utilitarian movements, we should add, have been inspired mainly by scientific humanitarianism, and sentimental naturalism again has been an important element, if not the most important element, in the so-called romantic movement. We have not space to discuss fully why the various forms of naturalism and humanitarianism have been so closely associated in modern thought. It is evident, however, that the vitally important element in this association has been the idea of progress. The Greeks and Romans studied nature scientifically, and to some extent communed sentimentally with nature. Humanism and naturalism coexisted in the men of classical antiquity, as well as in the men of the Renaissance, and often passed over into one another by almost insensible gradations. But only in comparatively recent times have the conquests of science become so pronounced as to raise the hope of a general and systematic advance of the human race. The old philanthropy, as we have said, has been profoundly modified and converted into humanitarianism by being more closely connected with this idea of progress; and the idea of progress in turn rests mainly on a belief in the benefits that are to come to mankind in the mass as the result of a closer cooperation with nature. The role of science in the new conception has evidently been greater than the role of sentiment. Men have always dreamed of the Golden Age, but it is only with the triumphs of modern science that they have begun to put the Golden Age in the future instead of in the past. The great line that separates the new era from the old is, as Renan remarks, the idea of humanity and the cult of its collective achievements. With the decay of the traditional faith this cult of humanity is coming more and more to be our real religion. We would all like to be Abou ben Adhems (whose tribe *has* increased), and are, indeed, almost incapable of conceiving of the love of God as something apart from the love of man. The new religion threatens even to impair that historical sense which is the special boast of the nineteenth century. Our modern believers in progress view the past as complacently from their own special angle as did the man of the Middle Ages when he imagined nunneries and cathedrals in ancient Troy.

Possibly our definitions of sentimental and scientific humanitarianism may be made still clearer if we remove them from the cloud-land of abstraction and make them concrete and historical; and perhaps this may best be done by picking out for each point of view some individual who not only held it but actually illustrated its working in his life and character. We already have in the sixteenth century a perfect example of the scientific naturalist and humanitarian, in Bacon. For sentimental naturalism, on the other hand, we have to wait until the eighteenth century, when it is embodied with extraordinary completeness in the personality and writings of Rousseau. Bacon and Rousseau represent between them the main tendencies that are at present disintegrating the traditional disciplines, whether humanistic or religious. When in the following pages we speak of any one as a Baconian or a Rousseauist, we do not mean to assert in all cases a direct or even an indirect influence, but merely that these men are prefigured if not actually anticipated in their outlook on life by either Bacon or Rousseau. Thus the direct or indirect obligations of Wordsworth to Rousseau are not always easy to determine, but no careful student can fail to see that the sentimental naturalism of Wordsworth, all that element in his work by which he is an innovator in English poetry, is either latent or more often fully expressed in the earlier naturalism of Rousseau.

The direct and demonstrable influence of Rousseau, is however, enormous; his influence so far transcends that of the mere man of letters as to put him almost on a level with the founders of religions. In his recent lectures on Rousseau, M. Jules Lemaître declared that he was filled with a "sacred horror" (*horreur sacrée*) at the magnitude of this influence; and the fashionable and reactionary elements of Parisian society applauded. Thereupon the friends of Rousseau organized a counter-demonstration in the main hall of the Sorbonne, with thousands present and thousands more turned away, with a white heat of excitement and the kind of speeches that in this country we should associate with a great political convention. We may smile at these characteristically French proceedings, but at bottom the French are right in perceiving how much in modern life is involved in one's attitude toward Rousseau; they are right in centering their attack and defense on the great father of radicalism, instead of fixing their attention on some contemporary radical, who is usually only his remote and degenerate posterity.

Both friends and enemies are agreed as to the commanding position of Rousseau. But in the case of Bacon, some recent writers have inclined to disparage him and his actual contributions to either scientific method or discovery as compared with the contributions of other pioneers like Kepler or Galileo or Descartes.[1] But no disparagement will take away from Bacon the glory of having been more than any one else of his time the prophet of the kingdom of man. Whole generations have been needed to work out in detail the points of view that already existed in a sort of confused unity in Bacon's mind. He was, in short, one of those rare beings over whom brooded almost visibly the "prophetic soul of the wide world dreaming on things to come." Besides Bacon and Rousseau, Petrarch, whose influence radiates along innumerable lines into the Renaissance, is the only other person of the modern centuries who has this supreme significance. Strange circumstance, all three of these great fore-runners of the future were men of weak and in some respects contemptible character. Usually this moral weakness is taken to be more or less a matter of chance. We seem loath to admit that Petrarch and Bacon and Rousseau were prophetic of the modern spirit, not only in their strength, but also in their shortcomings.

For instance, Macaulay's essay on Bacon is, as everybody knows, divided into two parts: the first part is devoted to showing how mean Bacon was as a man; the second part to set-

1. See, for example, the account of Bacon in Höffding's *History of Modern Philosophy* (Bk. II, ch. v).

ting forth the glories of the Baconian idea of progress. And
Macaulay, of course, is not slow to improve this opportunity for
glittering antitheses. But for one who is seeking the truth and
not rhetorical effect, the significance of Bacon's moral breakdown lies in the very fact that it had the same origins as his idea
of progress. He was led to neglect the human law through a too
subservient pursuit of the natural law; in seeking to gain
dominion over things he lost dominion over himself; he is a
notable example of how a man may be "unkinged," as Emerson phrases it, when overmastered by the naturalistic temper
and unduly fascinated by power and success. As we read of the
investigation of Bacon by the parliamentary committee and the
mixture of eminent ability and petty grafting that this investigation revealed, it all seems strangely familiar. We are reminded
irresistibly of the scandalous disclosures about our own leaders
of industry and finance. Like Bacon these men have fallen away
from the "law for man" and been "unkinged," not so much
through a sordid love of gain as through the fascination of power
and success. The one-sided anxiety to "get results" has led to
the excesses that we see, and these excesses are now bringing
down on their perpetrators, as they did on Bacon, the inevitable
nemesis.

In the main drift of his life Bacon tends toward a scientific
positivism, with its setting up of purely quantitative and
dynamic standards. But in so rich and complex a nature we
should not neglect the eddies and counter-currents. In many
respects Bacon remains a humanist of the Renaissance (he has,
for instance, the humanistic disdain for the multitude); in other
respects he is a traditional Christian. He cannot fairly be
accused of any such shallow infatuation with material progress
as appears in Macaulay's essay. He was aware of what Emerson
calls the "double consciousness," and that material progress, so
far from assuring moral progress, may actually imperil man's
higher nature. In the preface of the "Novum Organum" Bacon
prays solemnly that "from the opening up of the pathways of the
senses and a fuller kindling of the natural light, there may not
result in men's souls a weakening of faith and a blindness to the
divine mysteries." It is as though he foresaw the man of the

present time, who has paid as the price of his triumphs over nature and his splendid efficiency a loss of vision; who is too often spiritually "unkinged" at the very moment that he is crowned with the fullness of material power.

Bacon's humanitarianism, the conception of the progress of the race as a whole through scientific investigation and discovery, was slow in exercising an influence on education. It becomes practically effective only when it unites with the movement for the broadening of knowledge and sympathy that makes itself felt throughout Europe in the eighteenth century, especially in the France of Rousseau and Diderot. This movement may be regarded as the second great era of expansion in modern times, the second forward push of individualism. We have seen in Rabelais elements of an unselective naturalism that would close entirely the gap between nature and human nature. There are currents of this sixteenth-century naturalism that disappear under ground, as Sainte-Beuve remarks, during the period of concentration in the seventeenth century, and then, reappearing on the surface, connect our modern naturalism with that of the Renaissance. The naturalism of Diderot, however, has a frankness, not to say a crudity and cynicism, that one would scarcely find even in Rabelais. The principle of selection is obscured on the one hand, by an unbounded exaltation of enthusiasm and sympathy, and, on the other, by the prevalence of quantitative and dynamic over human standards. Diderot had a truly Gargantuan hunger for knowledge, a hunger that in the eyes of the humanist degenerates into a mere lust (*libido sciendi*), because of its lack of measure and restraint. It is at this moment that the craving for the fullness of knowledge and sympathy becomes definitely associated, as it had never been before, with the Baconian humanitarianism. Instead of a fastidious selection, men were to cultivate a universal and encyclopaedic curiosity, and at the same time make this curiosity serve the cause of human progress. The full ambition of a scholar of this type is first to absorb an encyclopaedia and then to make a contribution to knowledge that will deserve a place in some future encyclopaedia. But in practice, the two parts of this ideal—breadth and thoroughness—have been found to be incompatible. Or, is it not rather an example of how any point of view works out into an ironical contradiction of its own principle, unless it is humanized through being tempered by its opposite? The attempt to set up the fullness of knowledge and sympathy as a substitute for selection and judgment leads straight to the narrowness of the modern specialist. For example, the one-sidedness of our latest mediaevalists is already in germ in the magnificent enthusiasms of Herder and the Grimm brothers. One of the characters in Gissing's "Whirlpool" makes a confession that is not only true of many individuals but symbolizes nineteenth century scholarship as a whole. "I am narrowing down," pursued Harvey; "once I had tremendous visions—dreamt of holding half a dozen civilizations in my hand. I came back from the East in a fury to learn the Oriental languages—made a start, you know, with Arabic—dropped one nation after another.... The end will be a country or a town, nay, possibly, a building. Why not devote one's self to the history of a market cross?... Thoroughness is all."

When a man finds that it is impossible to know everything and know it well, it might be supposed that he would seek to apply to the enormous and ever-increasing mass of things to be known some humane principle of selection, and in the search for this principle to fortify his individual insight by the wisdom and experience of the race. But such is not the reasoning of the Baconian. The fullness of knowledge he abandons as something impossible for the individual, and by a sort of fiction transfers it to humanity in the mass. He does not have the humanist's passion for wholeness, for the harmonious rounding out of all the faculties. He is willing to sacrifice this ideal symmetry if only he is allowed to cultivate some special faculty or subject to the utmost. Having thus turned over the fullness of knowledge to mankind and rid himself of the humanistic horror of one-sidedness, he feels free to burrow ever more and more deeply into his own specialty, like the traditional rat in the Holland cheese. What does it matter, he would seem to argue, if a man in himself is but a poor lop-sided fragment, if only this fragment is serviceable, if only it can be built into the very walls of the Temple of Progress? He is satisfied if he can attain to the highest efficiency, and then contribute by this efficiency to human advancement. His entire aim, as he is wont to tell us with so much unction, is training for service and training for power.

But the Baconian, after all, would have been comparatively ineffective in undermining humane standards if he had not been reinforced by the Rousseauist. The scientific and sentimental naturalists are sharply at variance on many points, but in their views on education they often coincide curiously. This coincidence will be plain if one compares, for example, the book on Education, by Herbert Spencer, a scientific humanitarian of the purest water, with Rousseau's "Émile." Indeed, it had always been supposed that Spencer had borrowed directly from Rousseau,[2] but Spencer's private secretary,[3] who recently published a book on Rousseau, asserts that Spencer had never even read the "Émile."

So far as the views of the two types of naturalist are distinguishable, we may say that in the overthrow of humanism the idea of scientific progress that one finds in Bacon has been powerfully aided by the idea of liberty found in Rousseau. Bacon, indeed, in his own utterances on what we should call nowadays the elective principle, speaks less as a scientific humanitarian than as a shrewd observer. "Let parents," he says, "choose betimes the vocations and courses they mean their children should take; for then they are more flexible; and let them not too much apply themselves to the disposition of their children, as thinking they will take best to that which they have most mind to. It is true, that if the affection or aptness of the children be extraordinary, then it is good not to cross it. But generally the precept is good: Select the best, habit will make it easy and agreeable. (*Optimum elige, suave et facile illud faciet consuetudo.*)" This does not sound altogether like President Eliot; yet President Eliot in his general temper and conception of progress is a good Baconian. Only the Baconian idea of progress has been supplemented in his case by an idea of liberty that

2. See, for example, O. Gréard, *Éducation et Instruction*, vol. ii, p. 175 ff.

3. See W. H. Hudson, *Rousseau and Naturalism in Life and Thought*, p. 206 (note).

justifies a well-known French writer on education, M. Compayré, in claiming him as a disciple of Rousseau.[4] President Eliot's character and personal distinction, we need scarcely add, do not connect him with either Bacon or Rousseau, but are derived—so far as they are derived at all—from the best Puritan tradition. But President Eliot speaks as a pure Rousseauist in a passage like the following: "A well-instructed youth of eighteen can select for himself a better course of study than any college faculty, or any wise man who does not know his ancestors and his previous life, can possibly select for him. . . . Every youth of eighteen is an infinitely complex organization, the duplicate of which neither does nor ever will exist." [5] There is then no general norm, no law for man, as the humanist believed, with reference to which the individual should select; he should make his selection entirely with reference to his own temperament and its (supposedly) unique requirements. The wisdom of all the ages is to be as naught compared with the inclination of a sophomore. Any check that is put on this inclination is an unjustifiable constraint, not to say an intolerable tyranny. Now inasmuch as the opinions of even a "well-instructed youth of eighteen" about himself and his own aptitudes are likely to shift and veer this way and that according to the impressions of the moment, we may, perhaps, designate the system that would make these opinions all-important "educational impressionism." This inordinate exaltation of the individual sense as compared with the general or common sense of mankind scarcely antedates Rousseau. But before going any farther let us listen to President Eliot himself on Rousseau and his place in education. The following is from an address before the National Educational Association:—

"Dr. Butler very justly named Rousseau as a great contributor to educational progress. The main work of that man's life tended and still tends toward human liberty, and that one fact has almost sanctified an execrable wretch. Do you know what Rousseau did with five of his wife's babies, one after the other,

4. G. Compayré, *Rousseau et l'Éducation de la Nature*, pp. 98, 99.
5. *Educational Reform*, pp. 132, 133.

in spite of her prayers and tears? He put every one of them in succession into the public *crèche*, knowing that in the then condition of foundling hospitals that destination meant all but certain death. Yet we sit here and listen to the praise of that mean and cruel creature. How shall we account for these two judgments of one man, both just? We can only say that he tied the main work of his intellectual life to the great doctrine of human liberty. Verily, to have served liberty will cover a multitude of sins. May you serve freedom and humanity in all your labors, and then have no sins to cover." [6]

In reading this passage one has something the same sense of a strange psychological anomaly that one has in reading Macaulay's essay on Bacon. Rousseau was an "execrable wretch," who was at the same time a glorious apostle of liberty. Yet nothing is easier to prove than that if Rousseau was an execrable wretch, it was directly because of his idea of liberty; just as Bacon failed morally, not in spite of his idea of progress, but as a result of it.

It has been said that a system of philosophy is often only a gigantic scaffolding that a man erects to hide from himself his own favorite sin. Rousseau's whole system sometimes strikes one as intended to justify his own horror of every form of discipline and constraint. There are certain "self-pleasing minds," says Bacon, in a sentence that seems specially meant for Rousseau, "which are so sensible to every restraint as they will go near to think their girdles and garters to be bonds and shackles." In his eagerness to be rid of every *gêne*, as he would say, Rousseau is ready to tamper with virtue itself. Virtue is no longer to be the veto power of the personality, a bit and a bridle to be applied to one's impulses, and so imposing a difficult struggle. These impulses, Rousseau asserts, are good, and so a man has only to let himself go. Instead of the still small voice that is heard in solitude and urges to self-discipline, virtue is to become a form of enthusiasm; it is to be raised to the dignity of a passion much as the elder Dumas claimed to have raised history to the dignity of the novel. "If not virtuous," says Rousseau

6. *Proceedings National Educational Association*, 1900, p. 199.

sublimely, "I was at least intoxicated with virtue." He was a moral impressionist not so much like the ancient sophist through an excessive intellectual pliancy, as because he would thus rest virtue on the shifting quicksands of sensibility. For him as for Coleridge everything became impossible when it presented itself as a duty or obligation. He will hear of no norm of conduct that is set above individual feeling.

In a passage which is only one of a score of similar purport, Rousseau speaks of "my indomitable spirit of liberty which nothing has been able to overcome. . . . It is certain that this spirit of liberty comes to me less from pride than from indolence —an indolence that is beyond belief. Everything alarms it. The slightest duties of civilized life are unendurable to it. A word to utter, a visit to make, a letter to write, as soon as they are obligatory are torments for me. That is why ordinary intercourse with men is odious to me, and intimate friendship so dear, because it no longer involves any duty. All one has to do is follow one's heart; and that again is why I have been so fearful of benefits, for every benefit calls for gratitude, and I feel that I have an ungrateful heart, for the very reason that gratitude is a duty." [7] The rest of the passage is equally instructive, but enough has been quoted to make clear the relation between Rousseau's idea of liberty and his refusal to accept his duties as a father. It is also clear from this passage that President Eliot has adopted and applied to education only one half of this idea of liberty. Like Rousseau, he would release the student from all outward constraint; like Rousseau, he denies that there is a general norm, a "law for man," the discipline of which the individual should receive. But having bestowed upon the student the full liberty of Rousseau, it is evident that President Eliot would have him use this liberty in a Baconian spirit; he is not to profit by his emancipation, as Rousseau himself would do, to enjoy a "delicious indolence," but he is to work with great energy with reference to his personal interests and aptitudes. Unfortunately many of our undergraduates are more thoroughgoing Rousseauists in this respect than President Eliot. Himself

7. *Lettre à M. de Malesherbes* (4 January, 1762).

one of the most strenuous of men, President Eliot has perhaps not taken enough into account the prodigious *vis inertiae* in average human nature, just as Socrates, the most reasonable of men, was led to underestimate the forces of unreason. Having provided such a rich and costly banquet of electives to satisfy the "infinite variety" of youths of eighteen, President Eliot must be somewhat disappointed to see how nearly all these youths insist on flocking into a few large courses [8]; and especially disappointed that many of them should take advantage of the elective system not to work strenuously along the line of their special interests, but rather to lounge through their college course along the line of least resistance. A popular philosopher has said that every man is as lazy as he dares to be. If he had said that nine men in ten are as lazy as they dare to be, he would have come near hitting a great truth. The elective system has often been regarded as a protest against the doctrine of original depravity. This doctrine at best rests on rather metaphysical foundations, and is hard to verify practically. The Buddhists are perhaps nearer the facts as we know them in putting at the very basis of their belief the doctrine, not of the original depravity, but of the original laziness,[9] of human nature. "It is unimaginable," says Rousseau, who had arrived at the same insight, "to what a point man is naturally lazy. . . . His first and strongest passion, next to that of self-preservation, is to do nothing at all." [10] And Wordsworth, echoing Rousseau, as he so often does, speaks of that "majestic indolence so dear to native man." (Especially dear, every one who has taught in a college would be tempted to

8. I do not mean to assert that the line of least resistance always runs through the large courses. These courses are taken on various other grounds, utilitarian, impressionistic, or simply gregarious—the desire to do what "the other fellows" are doing; sometimes, too, on humanistic grounds, because they are ably conducted courses in standard subjects.

9. The greatest of vices according to Buddha is the lazy yielding to the impulses of temperament (*pamada*); the greatest virtue (*appamada*) is the opposite of this, the awakening from the sloth and lethargy of the senses, the constant exercise of the active will. The last words of the dying Buddha to his disciples were an exhortation to practice this virtue unremittingly (*appamadena sampadetha*).

10. *Essai sur l'origine des langues*, ch. ix (note).

add, to the native undergraduate!) But this indolence, which for the Buddhist is the original curse from which he is to flee, is for Rousseau the very Arcadia of his dreams.

At this point, however, we need to make some important distinctions. We have all heard the unfavorable comparisons the public is fond of making between the idling undergraduate and the strenuous student in the technical school, or between the idleness of the same student in college and the strenuousness he suddenly develops when he gets to the school of law or of medicine. The indolence of which the Buddhist complains is, however, too subtle to be remedied by mere strenuousness. The hustling Baconians, of whom there is no lack in our college faculties, are naturally inclined to give short shrift to the student who has yielded to the charms of a "majestic indolence." If they have their way, they will get rid of laziness in the college, but are likely to get rid at the same time of the whole idea of liberal culture. What the Baconian understands is training for power, training with a view to certain practical or scientific results. In getting his technical or professional education the student is often, of course, immensely stimulated by the plain relation it has to his future livelihood. (Even Rousseau admits that the instinct of self-preservation may triumph over indolence.) At all times it has been difficult to inspire in any considerable body of men the love of a disinterested discipline of the mind, to make them feel the difference between loafing and leisure, and this difficulty has been immensely increased through the weakening of all standards and the encouragement of impressionism by the elective system.

Little seems likely to survive of the idea of liberal culture if it is left on the one hand to the Baconian, who neglects the "law for man" entirely, and on the other to the Rousseauist, who confounds this law with his own temperament. What is important in man in the eyes of the humanist is not his power to act on the world, but his power to act upon himself. This is at once the highest and most difficult task he can set himself if carried out with reference to a humane principle of selection, or what amounts to the same thing, to a true principle of restraint. By right selection even more than by the fullness of knowledge and sympathy, man proves his superiority of essence, and shows that he is something more than a mere force of nature. He is tested not only by what he does, but equally perhaps by what he refrains from doing; just as a writer is great, not only by what he says, but also by what he omits saying. The humanist will insist on the distinction between energy and will, however much the present age seems to have forgotten it. A man may be a prodigy of energy and yet spiritually indolent. Napoleon showed his energy by conquering Europe; he would have shown his will if at the critical moment he had been capable of curbing his own lust for power (*libido dominandi*). "If one man conquer in battle ten thousand times ten thousand men," says the Buddhist proverb, "and another man conquer his own self, he is the greatest of conquerors." That man is most human who can check his faculty, even if it be his master-faculty, and his passion, even his ruling passion, in its mid-career and temper it by its opposite.

Our meaning will become clearer if we digress a moment into the literary field and study the attitude of naturalistic critics toward a writer whom Matthew Arnold calls the most humane of men,—Shakespeare. According to our definition the humanist must maintain a just balance between sympathy and selection. No one, of course, would deny the gift of sympathy to the poet who has coined the happiest of all phrases that express sympathy,—"the milk of human kindness." But both scientific and sentimental naturalists have attempted to dehumanize Shakespeare by refusing him a principle of selection and restraint. For example, Victor Hugo in his book on Shakespeare, which is a thinly disguised apology for Hugo himself and his own art, is interested as a Rousseauist in proving that Shakespeare's genius is purely Titanic and elemental, merely the volcanic upheaval of a temperament. "Shakespeare," says Hugo, "is one of those geniuses badly bridled on purpose by God, so that they may go soaring with free sweep of the wing through the infinite." Taine, again, as a scientific naturalist, would see in Shakespeare a pure product of the Renaissance, which he considers in turn as a vast explosion of uninhibited energy. He insists almost as much as Hugo on the violence, the immoderateness of Shakespeare himself and the characters in his plays.

One thinks of Hamlet's advice to the players: "In the very torrent, tempest, and as I may say, whirlwind of your passion, you must acquire and beget a temperance that may give it smoothness."

In general Shakespeare observes his own precept, though we must admit that at times his art would gain by more severe selection and restraint. If we wish, however, to find the full frenzy of unbridled passion, we should turn, not to Shakespeare, but to certain characters of Victor Hugo. As a French critic remarks, passions that are thus exhibited without any restraining sense of decorum have no place in humane literature at all, but should rather be relegated to the menagerie in the Jardin des Plantes.

Various critics, in the number men so absolutely different as Emerson and Professor Santayana, have complained of the lack of religion in Shakespeare, and it is true that Shakespeare's world compared with that of other great poets, Homer or Sophocles or Dante, impresses one less as a cosmos and more as a romantic chaos. The force of the Renaissance reaction from the Middle Ages may perhaps be measured by the extent to which humanity prevails over divinity in Shakespeare's works. Yet so far as Shakespeare fails to allow sufficiently for religion and the sense of a central unity that it imparts to life, he falls short of being completely humane. However, the strangely violent attack of Tolstoy on Shakespeare, and his repeating of the old charge of lack of religion, is something different and bears directly on our present topic. At bottom the quarrel between Shakespeare and Tolstoy is a quarrel between a humanist and a humanitarian fanatic. Tolstoy, as an avowed disciple of Rousseau,[11] would suppress entirely the principle of selection, and exalt in its place the principle of sympathy, the religion of human brotherhood. What he cannot pardon in Shakespeare is that his wisdom is only for the few, that his view of life is on the whole selective and aristocratic.

The humanist is equally on his guard against the excess of

11. See letter dated 20 March, 1905, in *Annales de la Société Jean-Jacques Rousseau*, vol. i, p. 7: "Rousseau a été mon maître depuis l'âge de quinze ans, etc."

sympathy and the excess of selection, against the excess of liberty and the excess of restraint; he would have a restrained liberty and a sympathetic selection. He believes that the man of to-day, if he does not, like the man of the past, take on the yoke of a definite doctrine and discipline, must at least do inner obeisance to something higher than his ordinary self, whether he calls this something God, or, like the man of the Far East, calls it his higher Self, or simply the Law. Without this inner principle of restraint man can only oscillate violently between opposite extremes, like Rousseau, who said that for him there was "no intermediary term between everything and nothing." With this true restraint, on the other hand, he can harmonize these extremes and occupy the space between them. Rousseau, who would admit of no check upon the unruly desires of the heart (*libido sentiendi*), was therefore led to set up sympathy for one's fellow man as a substitute for religious obligation [12]; and he combined this with a fierce assertion of man's rights and liberties. In encouraging men thus to put a sense of their rights above their obligations, he assumes that the unbounded self-assertion that results will have a sufficient offset in unbounded brotherhood. But is it true that the principle of sympathy will prevail, unaided, against the elemental forces of self-interest that Rousseau would unchain? Yes, replies the political economist, it will prevail if it has to deal with a self-interest that is properly enlightened. Unfortunately, this whole search of our humanitarians for some ingenious mixture of altruistic sympathy and "enlightened self-interest" that will take the place of religious restraint, is too much of an order with the search on the

12. I am, of course, aware that the philosophical theory of sympathy has an important history in modern times quite apart from Rousseau. Bacon already tends to exalt philanthropy above all other virtues. English thinkers like Hutcheson and Shaftesbury anticipate in important respects not only Rousseau's ideas about sympathy, but his whole moral aestheticism. We should connect with these thinkers rather than with Rousseau the rôle ascribed to sympathy by Hume and the political economists (Adam Smith, etc.). The exaltation of pity to the first place in morals is often associated with Schopenhauer, but Schopenhauer himself declares this innovation in ethics to be the great glory of Rousseau. See *Preisschrift über die Grundlage der Moral*, Werke 4, 2, 246 (der 2. Aufl.).

physical plane for the secret of perpetual motion. In the absence of religious restraint, not only individuals but society as a whole will oscillate violently between opposite extremes, moving, as we see it doing at present, from an anarchical individualism to a utopian collectivism. In spite of the copious flow of fine sentiments about human brotherhood, what is already apparent is the inevitable drift toward imperialistic centralization. For, as the French moralist says, men must be either the slaves of duty or the slaves of force. Prometheus, in the ancient fable, is arrested by Violence and Power, the envoys of Zeus, and forced to "desist from his philanthropic ways." [13] The same thing is likely to happen to our modern Promethean individualists.

The issue is somewhat obscured at present because the moral habits of an age that had a definite doctrine and discipline survive for some time after the doctrine itself has become obsolete. As Renan said cynically, in explaining why he remained virtuous even after his loss of the traditional faith, "A chicken will continue to go through the motions of scratching for a time, even after its brain has been removed." But the traditional checks and inhibitions will gradually grow fainter, and society will then feel, and indeed is already beginning to feel, the full impact of a brutal naturalism.

Our lapse into moral impressionism is also hidden from us by the rapid advance of physical science. We assume that because we are advancing rapidly in one direction we are advancing in all directions; yet from what we know of man in history we should rather be justified in assuming the exact opposite. Whatever may be true of the doctrine of progress in the abstract, it is likely, as held by the average American, to prove a dangerous infatuation. We reason that science must have created a new heaven because it has so plainly created a new earth. And so we are led to think lightly of the knowledge of human nature possessed by a past that was so palpably ignorant of the laws of electricity; and in the meanwhile we are blinded to the fact that we have men who are learned in the laws of electricity and ignorant of the laws of human nature. True, the most optimistic

13. Aeschylus, *Prometheus Bound*, Sc. I.

of us cannot help seeing some signs of moral degeneracy. But are we not spending seventy-five million dollars a year on automobiles, with a fair prospect of soon having successful airships? In view of these glorious achievements, why be disquieted by the increase in murders, in suicides, in insanity, in divorce, by all the multiplying symptoms of some serious and perhaps fatal one-sidedness in our civilization that is bringing down on us its appropriate nemesis? The doubts that beset our minds can all be conjured away by the very sound of the magic word Progress. A few years ago I was walking one Sunday evening along a country road in a remote part of New England, and on passing a farmhouse saw through the window the members of the family around the lighted lamp, each one bending over a section of a "yellow" journal. I reflected that not many years before the Sunday reading of a family of this kind would have been the Bible. To progress from the Bible to the comic supplement would seem a progress from religious restraint to a mixture of anarchy and idiocy.

What has just been said is not to be taken as a general arraignment of the modern spirit by a reactionary. No sane person would set out to belittle the immense achievements of science since the Renaissance, and still less that great quickening and broadening out of sympathy during the last two centuries so as to include not only the disinherited among men, but even the animals. The more scientific progress and the more social pity the better. Exception can be taken to these things only when they are set up as absolute and all-sufficient in themselves; when the Baconian would substitute quantitative and dynamic for human standards, or the Rousseauist would exalt social pity into the place of religious restraint as the very keystone of the arch of human nature. The "law for man" suffers in both cases, and in the case of the Rousseauist there is besides a nameless mixture of what used to be called the secular and the theological virtues. Justice Brewer is reported to have said in a recent address that if the law of love only prevailed in the business world there would be no need of jails, no defaulting bank-cashiers, no over-reaching by individuals and trusts, etc. This is not thinking, but humanitarian reverie. If the world of business is ever governed by any laws besides that of the wolf pack, it will not be by the law of love, but by the Ten Commandments, notably the commandment, Thou shalt not steal.

An unrestricted application of the law of love to secular affairs will lead, not to love, but to its opposite, hatred.[14] The same is true of an unrestricted freedom. In praising the liberty of Rousseau, President Eliot is in reality praising the liberty of the anarchist, not because he is himself an anarchist, but because he belongs to a generation which saw so keenly the benefits of liberty that it was unable to see the benefits of restraint. Yet the present would seem no propitious time for indulging in what Burke calls "grand and swelling sentiments of liberty." President Eliot, indeed, reminds one of Bossuet's remark about Marcus Brutus. Brutus, says Bossuet, kept on talking liberty when he should have been talking restraint, and that in the interests of liberty itself. Liberty had already reached that excess in Rome where it was on the point of running into its opposite,—military despotism. Only a doctrinaire could deny that liberty in this country is similarly being strained to the breaking point, that the danger with us, too, is that liberty may "grow to a pleurisy and die in its own too-much." In the case of our railroads, for instance, the difficulty with everybody, from the humblest employee who would rather take chances than obey the rules, to the president and financiers at the top, who have also been running past the red lights in their own way, is a lack of discipline and self-control.

At this crisis, when our crying need is a humane principle of restraint, the best that our sentimental and scientific humanitarians can evolve between them is a scheme of training for service and training for power. Unfortunately a man may be trained for service and trained for power and yet be only a philanthropic anarchist. In Schiller's "Robbers" (1781), which was written when Germany was filled with the influence of Rousseau, one of the robbers praises his chief not only as an

---

14. The International Congress of Socialists, which recently met at Stuttgart in the name of human brotherhood, was described in the newspapers as a "pandemonium of vituperation."

apostle of liberty but as a man of overflowing sympathies. "Honorable men are not ashamed to serve under such a leader. He does not commit murder as we do for the sake of plunder— and as to money, as soon as he has plenty of it at command, he does not seem to care a straw for it; and his third of the booty, which belongs to him of right, he gives away to orphans, or supports *promising young men with it at college*," etc. It seems hardly necessary to draw the analogy between this philanthropic brigand and some captain (Kidd) of industry of our own day. One could recently read in the paper of the philanthropies of the richest man in America, and in another column of the same issue of the prosecution of this man for violation of the law. No one need doubt the genuineness of Mr. Rockefeller's desire for service, and there can, of course, be no question of the success of his training for power: Mr. Harriman, again, has shown amazing efficiency in managing the Southern Pacific and Union Pacific Railroads, and is also in some respects a sincere helper of his fellow men. Yet a few more Harrimans and we are undone.

The mention of these men is not meant to imply any sympathy with most of the attacks that are now being made upon them. A speaker in Boston recently said that Messrs. Rogers and Rockefeller were not human beings, but "ghouls and vampires in human form." This is to go to work in true Rousseau fashion and set up an imaginary dualism in society to take the place of the real dualism in the breast of the individual. The evil principle in society is represented nowadays by the wicked capitalist, much as it was in the old revolutionary times by the wicked king and priest, who were also deemed to be of a different species from the rest of humanity. As a matter of fact, Messrs. Rogers and Rockefeller are not only human beings but representative Americans, who have done with superior capacity what a multitude of the business men of their time would have liked to do. To deny this is to convert what should be an anxious searching into our national standards of success into a semi-socialistic crusade on wealth.

The philanthropic anarchist is, of course, much to be preferred to the anarchist who is not even philanthropic. Yet it is already beginning to dawn dimly on at least a part of the public that a rich man who curbed his own lust for power would be more to the purpose than another rich man who remained uncurbed but devoted a part of his money to "supporting promising young men at college." What is wanted is not training for service and training for power, but training for wisdom and training for character. A list of questions was recently sent around to graduates of the women's colleges as to the relative importance of certain virtues. A majority of those who replied decided that love of humanity is a more important virtue than self-control. This is a view of human nature that may be pardonable in a young woman just out of college. What are we to think of our present leaders of public opinion who apparently hold a similar view? Let a man first show that he can act on himself, there will then be time enough for him to act on other men and on the world. If we are told that we should give no thought to ourselves, but live entirely for others, we should reply with Dr. Johnson that our first endeavor should be to rid our minds of cant, of which every age has its own special variety; and that this being a philanthropic age, it behooves us to rid our minds of the cant of philanthropy.

The eager efforts of our philanthropists to do something for the negro and the newsboy are well enough in their way; but a society that hopes to be saved by what it does for its negroes and its newsboys is a society that is trying to lift itself by its own bootstraps. Our real hope of safety lies in our being able to induce our future Harrimans and Rockefellers to liberalize their own souls, in other words to get themselves rightly educated. Men of heroic capacity such as Messrs. Rockefeller and Harriman have in some respects shown themselves to be are, of course, born, not made; but when once born it will depend largely on the humaneness of their education whether they are to become heroes of good or heroes of evil. We are told that the aim of Socrates in his training of the young was not to make them efficient, but to inspire in them reverence and restraint; for to make them efficient, said Socrates, without reverence and restraint, was simply to equip them with ampler means for harm.[15]

15. The passage I have thus summarized will be found in Xenophon, *Memorabilia*, Bk. iv, ch. iii.

III

The College and the Democratic Spirit

HAVING ARRIVED AT OUR WORKING DEFINITION of the humanist, as well as defined the two main types of humanitarians, we have now to consider their relation to the college. The elective system, so far as it is inspired by the desire of the sentimental humanitarian to set up a pure and unrestricted liberty, to make selection wholly individual, evidently denies the principle on which the college rests. In 1790 Burke wrote with reference to the French followers of Rousseau, who at that time were trying to set up a pure and unrestricted political liberty: "To make a government requires no great prudence.... But to form a *free government*; that is, to temper together these opposite elements of liberty and restraint in one consistent work, requires much thought, deep reflection, a sagacious, powerful, and combining mind." This is a truly humane utterance, and no less true of the educational problem than of the problem in politics. To set up pure restraint, as was the tendency of the mediaeval educator, is easy. To set up pure liberty, as our modern radical tends to do, is likewise easy. But to temper liberty with restraint in education requires "a sagacious, powerful and combining mind." The attempt to establish an unrestricted freedom not only strikes at the foundation of the college, but is in some respects a palpable affront to common sense. Now the Anglo-Saxon, though often lamentably lacking in general ideas, is strong in common sense, and a reaction is already setting in against the excesses of the elective principle. Educational *laissez faire* such as prevailed at Harvard in the 1880s and 1890s, for instance, is plainly doomed. The new scheme for degrees with distinction at Harvard is an important departure from pure electivism toward the group system that has found favor in so many American institutions. The group system in itself seems a fair compromise between individual inclination and general standards; but if it is not to lead to premature specialization, it must evidently be administered by men who are in sympathy with the aims of the American College, and not by men whose scholarly ideals are "made in Germany." Liberty, to be humanized, must be tempered by true restraint, and not simply by strenuousness. We must insist once more on our distinction between energy and will.

A true principle of restraint involves constant reference, not merely to one's own temperament and aptitudes, but to a more general human law; it implies not only an anxiety to express one's own mind, but to put this mind into some kind of accord with what Emerson calls "the constant mind of man." The humanitarian triumph in the college has weakened this humane restraint and selection, and as an offset has exalted, on the one hand, the principle of sympathy, and on the other, scientific method or discipline in the "law for thing." The idea of quality, of high and objective standards of human excellence, has been equally compromised by the impressionism of the Rousseauist and by the Baconian's neglect of everything that cannot be expressed in terms of quantity and power. As formerly conceived, the college might have been defined as a careful selection of studies for the creation of a social elite. In its present tendency, it might be defined as something of everything for everybody.

This is precisely what we glorify as the triumph of the democratic spirit—a democracy of studies to meet the needs of a student democracy. The "democratic spirit" is another of those popular catchwords that are the delight of the sophist and the declaimer and the despair of the serious thinker. Evidently the college should be democratic in the sense that it should get rid of all distinctions of family and rank. We want no American equivalents for the types that Thackeray has catalogued in his chapters on university snobs. Now the snob may be defined as a man who, in his estimate of things, is drawn away from their true and intrinsic worth and dazzled by outer advantages of wealth, or power, or station. There is of course the snob who crawls at the feet of the possessor of these advantages, as well as the possessor of them who looks down at those who are less fortunate than himself. In a few of our Eastern colleges the snobbishness of family exists, but not to a dangerous degree. Some of the more luxurious of our college dormitories and clubhouses testify to an extravagant and foolish use of money, but from the snobbishness of wealth our colleges as a whole are likewise comparatively free. This is the more gratifying when we reflect how rampant this snobbishness is in the country at large, so much so that the yellow journals show by the very nature of their attacks on the rich that they are pandering to an intense snobbishness in their readers. There is also a laudable desire in our colleges to give everybody a chance. Indeed the more humanitarian members of our faculties are ready to waste their energies in trying to elevate youths above the level to which they belong, not only by their birth, but by their capacity.

We are not to assume, however, that our colleges are free from snobbishness simply because we read in the papers that forty Yale undergraduates are paying their way as motormen and trolley-conductors and forty more as waiters and bellboys in summer hotels. The real snobbishness that prevails among our collegians arises, not from the worship of family or of wealth, but of power in the special form in which it is familiar to them,—that of athletic prowess. In his estimate of athletic as compared with intellectual achievement, the average American undergraduate is an undoubted snob, and is encouraged in his snobbishness by the newspapers and the public. The principal of a preparatory school who gave a position as teacher to a young man who could not even get his degree but had been prominent athletically, is a snob of a very offensive type—at least, as offensive as the Oxford dons who used to grant degrees to lords without the formality of an examination. Indeed, the American has suffered more seriously in his humane standards by his pampering of the athlete than the Englishman by his truckling to the lord. The Oxford student still retains something of the *sprezzatura* or aloofness of the amateur, who sees in athletic sport only one, and that a somewhat subordinate element, in the total make-up of a man and a gentleman; whereas the American student pursues athletics as an end in themselves, and succumbs in true Baconian fashion to the glitter of success. In his anxiety to win at any cost, he already displays on the football field the spirit he will afterwards carry into business. That a community like the college, which has met together to do homage to the things of the mind, should in practice worship at the feet of the successful athlete — this is an irony that no amount of beautiful effusions about the democratic spirit can disguise. It is urged with much reason that athletic training is needed as an offset to certain enervating influences of modern life; but without the restraining presence of humane standards it will be possible to oscillate between effeminacy and brutality, and at the same time miss the note of real manliness.

The democratic spirit that the college needs is a fair field and no favors, and then the more severe and selective it is in its requirements the better. Most of those, however, who talk about the democratic spirit obviously mean something different. All of us who have had anything to do with college discipline are familiar with the type of sentimental humanitarian in whom the delicate balance between sympathy and judgment has been lost, and who is ready to lower the standard of an institution rather than inflict an apparent hardship on an individual. In general, the humanitarian inclines to see in the college a means not so much for the thorough training of the few as of uplift for the many; his aim, in short, is extensive, not intensive. He is always likely to favor any scheme that will bring the bachelor's degree within reach of a greater number, even at the imminent risk of cheapening the degree itself. The Rousseauist, by his exaltation of social pity, tends along a different path to the same end as the Baconian when he confuses growth in the human sense with mere bigness and expansion. An interesting contrast between the humanitarian and the humanistic temper appears in the three years' degree as it is being worked out in this country, and the three years' degree that actually exists at Oxford. At Oxford the inferior man is allowed to leave at the end of the third year with a pass degree; the more capable student remains another year and works intensively for a degree with honors. In this country the good man is encouraged to leave at the end of three years, and the inferior or idle student who remains is labored over by a humanitarian faculty in accordance with its great design of leavening the lump and raising the social average. The scientific humanitarian usually takes a hand at this point and suggests a scheme of mechanical equivalents, by which a man who does second-rate work, let us say, in fifteen courses for four years, is to be accounted the academic equal of the man who does first-rate work in twelve courses for three years. A more flagrant example of the confusion of quality in the human with quality in the scientific sense, it would be hard to imagine. A scheme of this kind will have value when it is proved that the human mind can be measured and tested in the same way as an electric current.

In one sense the purpose of the college is not to encourage the democratic spirit, but on the contrary to check the drift toward a pure democracy. If our definition of humanism has any value, what is needed is not democracy alone, nor again an unmixed aristocracy, but a blending of the two—an aristocratic and selective democracy. In the lower schools the humanitarian point of view should have a large place. The university, again, by its very name implies an encyclopaedic fullness; one should be able to say of it in Dryden's phrase, "Here is God's plenty." It should offer ample opportunity to the humanist to perfect himself in his own discipline; yet the primary purpose of the university is not to maintain the principle of selection.

The function of the college, on the other hand, should be to insist on the idea of quality; it should hold all the faster to its humane standards now that the world is threatened with a universal impressionism. Athens is the best example of a selective democracy; the standards of quality it set still remain in some lines unsurpassed. But at Athens these qualitative achievements did not rest perhaps on a sufficiently broad base of quantity and numbers. What shall we say of our American democracy? We can often see our faults reflected, as by a magnifying glass, in foreign opinion, and we should take a hint from the fact that the verb to "Americanize" means in European languages to adopt cheap and flashy machine methods. Our Pittsburgh millionaires are giving us a foretaste of what may be expected from a democracy that leads the quantitative life and combines it with moral impressionism. We seem certain to break all known records of bigness, but unless this bigness is tempered by quality we shall sprawl helplessly in the midst of our accumulated wealth and power, or at best arrive at a sort of senseless iteration. Many of our rich men are scarcely on a higher level than the Mexican peon, who, having suddenly come into a great fortune through mining, and remembering that his wife desired a piano, built her a castle with a thousand rooms, and in each room a piano.

There is another aspect of the democratic spirit—the tendency, namely, that the elective system has fostered in the college toward a democracy of studies; and this can be refuted in the name of a higher democracy. Assuming that the selection of studies in the old curriculum was purely arbitrary, that the respect accorded to certain studies over others was superstitious, there would be, even then, a great deal to be said in its favor. No one, says Emerson, knows what moral vigor is needed to supply the girdle of a superstition. But this selection was neither arbitrary nor superstitious. It embodied the seasoned and matured experience of a multitude of men, extending over a considerable time, as to the studies they actually found helpful and formative. In arriving at a humane selection the individual is powerfully abetted by the selection of time. In the matter of literary production, for instance, what a tremendous selection, as Emerson remarks, has taken place, even at the end of ten years. When books like the Greek and Latin classics have survived for centuries after the languages in which they are written are dead, the presumption is that these books themselves are not dead, but rather very much alive — that they are less related than most other books to what is ephemeral and more related to what is permanent in human nature. By innumerable experiments the world slowly winnows out the more essential from the less essential, and so gradually builds up standards of judgment. The Rousseauist would subordinate this permanent element of judgment, whether in an individual man or in a body of men, to the impulse of the moment. The good sense of the whole people tends to triumph in the long run—this is true democracy according to Lincoln.[1] The will of a popular majority at any particular instance should be supreme — this is the pseudo-democracy of Rousseau. We may safely trust the democratic spirit, if by democracy we mean the selective democracy of the sober second thought, and not the democracy of the passing impression.

Both our colleges and preparatory schools need to concentrate on a comparatively small number of standard subjects selected in this democratic way, that is to say, so as to register the verdict and embody the experience of a large number of men extending over a considerable time. Those who are for taking up with every new subject and untried fashion are not educational democrats, but educational impressionists. As a result of this impressionism, our colleges and preparatory schools, instead of doing thorough work in a few studies of approved worth, are falling into that "encyclopaedic smattering and miscellaneous experiment" [2] which according to Plato are especially harmful in the training of the young. The scientist is interested apparently only in natural selection; the impressionist would make selection purely individual; but what is imperative in the college

1. Why then, it may be asked, should not democracy select without restraint? The answer is, that democracy should not be restrained in its judgments, but only in its impressions. Three institutions in this country—the Senate, Constitution, and Supreme Court—were especially intended to embody the more permanent judgments and experience of democracy and at the same time serve as a bulwark against popular impulse. Attacks on these institutions are usually inspired by the rankest Rousseauism.

2. *Laws*, 819 A. If we are to judge by the papers and addresses of Mr. Wilson Farrand of the Newark Academy, preparatory school teachers are already beginning to feel the need of more concentration and less "encyclopaedic smattering" in college entrance requirements.

is humane selection, in other words, a choice of studies that will reflect in some measure the total experience of the race as to the things that have been found to be permanently important to its essential nature.

Common sense will aid in finding out what these humane studies are. There are many persons in this country who would have felt the benefits of a college training in their own case, and who almost instinctively would like to see the college stick to its traditional business of teaching a few standard subjects with a view to a general liberalizing of the mind; who almost instinctively distrust our humanitarian enthusiasts and their readiness to discard the sifted experience of generations in order that they may apply their own educational nostrums. But common sense, although it will do a great deal, will not do everything. Humanism may survive in England simply as a part of the Tory tradition, in virtue of that happy stupidity which, according to Bagehot, is the great superiority of the Englishman, or in virtue of what Burke more politely terms the Englishman's "invincible persistence in the wisdom of prejudice." It is doubtful, however, whether even in England humanism can long survive in this purely traditional way; it certainly cannot do so in America. The radical has used ideas in attacking the humanistic tradition; the humanist must meet him on his own ground and give a clear account of the faith that is in him, and then perhaps he will have a valuable auxiliary in the instinctive good sense of many who are not directly interested in his generalizations.

Friedrich Paulsen, possibly the most distinguished of recent German writers on education, remarks that in the sixteenth century Germany had the beginnings of a college as something quite distinct from either preparatory school or university, and regrets that these beginnings did not develop into something like the college in England or America. We should think twice before sacrificing an institution that on the whole has worked so admirably as to excite the envy even of enlightened Germans; especially before sacrificing it, as we seem in much danger of doing at present, to a mixture of intellectual muddle and humanitarian cant. There is no intention to disparage that great movement of education expansion during the past thirty years of which President Eliot, and in a lesser degree President Gilman, have been the worthy leaders. But such is the one-sidedness of human nature that this movement, which was necessary for the creating of an American university, now menaces the very existence of the college. The heads of our colleges should not let a just admiration for President Eliot blind them to the fact that they need to cultivate not only the virtues of expansion, but even more the virtues of concentration; that the guiding spirit of the college, if it is to continue to live at all and not be lost in the university and the preparatory school, must be the maintenance of humane standards (though, of course, the hollow shell may survive for a time after this spirit has departed); that the purpose of the college, in short, if it is to have any separate purpose, must be in a quantitative age to produce men of quality.

IV

Literature and the College

IT WAS WITH SOMETHING OF THE SPIRIT of true prophecy that Herbert Spencer proclaimed, in his work on Education, the approaching triumph of science over art and literature. Science, he said, was to reign supreme, and was no longer to be the "household drudge" who had "been kept in the background that her haughty sisters might flaunt their fripperies in the eyes of the world." The tables indeed have been turned so completely that art and literature have not only ceased to be "haughty," but have often been content to become the humble handmaids of science. It is to this eagerness of the artistic imagination to don the livery of science that we already owe the "experimental" novel. A Harvard Commencement speaker promised, not long ago, that we are soon to have poetry that shall be less "human" and more "biological." While awaiting these biological bards of the future, we may at least deal scientifically with the poets of the past, if we are to trust the title of a recently published Laboratory Method for the study of poetry. Another writer, after heaping contempt on the traditional views of poetry, produces his own formula and informs us that

$$\text{Poem} = x + \text{HI} + \text{VF}$$

Many of us nowadays would seem to be convinced, with the

118

French naturalist, that if happiness exists anywhere it will be found at the bottom of a crucible. Renan regretted in his old age that he had spent his life on so unprofitable a subject as the history of Christianity instead of the physical sciences. For the proper study of mankind is not man, but chemistry; or, perhaps, our modern attitude might be more correctly defined as an attempt to study man by the methods of physics and chemistry. We have invented laboratory sociology, and live in a nightmare of statistics. Language interests us, not for the absolute human values it expresses, but only in so far as it is a collection of facts and relates itself to nature. With the invasion of this hard literalness, the humanities themselves have ceased to be humane. I was once told as convincing proof of the merit of a certain classical scholar that he had twenty thousand references in his card catalogue.

The humanism of the Renaissance was a protest against the excesses of the ascetic. Now that science aspires to be all in all, somewhat after the fashion of theology in the Middle Ages, the man who would maintain the humane balance of his faculties must utter a similar protest against the excesses of the analyst, in whom a ''literal obedience to facts has extinguished every spark of that light by which man is truly man.'' It is really about as reasonable to use a dialogue of Plato merely as a peg on which to hang philological disquisitions as it was in the Middle Ages to turn Ovid's ''Art of Love'' into an allegory of the Christian life. In its mediaeval extreme, the human spirit strove to isolate itself entirely from outer nature in a dream of the supernatural; it now tends to the other extreme, and strives to identify itself entirely with the world of phenomena. The spread of this scientific positivism, with its assimilation of man to nature, has had especially striking results in education. Some of our higher institutions of learning are in fair way to become what a certain eminent scholar thought universities should be, — ''great scientific workshops.'' The rare survivors of the older generation of humanists must have a curious feeling of loneliness and isolation.

The time has perhaps come, not so much to react against this nineteenth-century naturalism, as to define and complete it, and especially to insist on its keeping within proper bounds. The nature cult is in danger of being pushed too far, not only in its scientific but in its sentimental form. The benefits and blessings that Herbert Spencer promises us from the scientific analysis of nature are only to be matched by those that Wordsworth promises from sentimental communion with nature.

> "One impulse from a vernal wood
>   May teach you more of man,
> Of moral evil and of good,
>   Than all the sages can."

The sentimental and scientific worship of nature, however far apart they may be at some points, have much in common when viewed in relation to our present subject,—their effect on college education. The former, working up into the college from the kindergarten, and the latter, working downward from the graduate school, seem likely between them to leave very little of humanistic standards. The results are sometimes curious when the two tendencies actually meet. I once overheard a group of undergraduates, in search of "soft" courses, discussing whether they should elect a certain course in Old Egyptian. The exaggerations of Wordsworth and Herbert Spencer may have served a purpose in overcoming a counter-excess of tradition and conventionalism. But now the nature cult itself is degenerating into a kind of cant. The lover of clear thinking cannot allow to pass unchallenged many of the phrases that the votaries of the Goddess Natura have come to utter so glibly, — such phrases, for instance, as "obedience to nature" and "natural methods." The word nature — covering as it does both the human world and the world of phenomena—has been a source of intellectual confusion almost from the dawn of Greek philosophy to the present day. To borrow an example from French literature, it is equally in the name of "nature" that La Fontaine humanizes his animals and that Zola bestializes his men. By juggling with the twofold meaning of the word, Renan arrived only a few years ago at his famous dictum that "nature does not care for chastity."

It is a disquieting fact that Rousseau, the man whose influ-

ence is everywhere in the new education, was remarkable for
nothing so much as his inability to distinguish between nature
and human nature. He counts among his disciples all those
who, like him, trust to the goodness of "nature," and so tend to
identify the ideal needs of the individual with his temperamental
leaning; who exalt instinct and idiosyncrasy; who, in their
endeavor to satisfy the variety of temperaments, would push the
principle of election almost down to the nursery, and devise, if
possible, a separate system of education for every individual.
For we are living in a privileged age, when not only every man,
as Dr. Donne sang, but every child

> "thinks he hath got
> To be a Phoenix, and that there can be
> None of that kind, of which he is, but he."

Our educators, in their anxiety not to thwart native aptitudes,
encourage the individual in an in-breeding of his own temperament, which, beginning in the kindergarten, is carried upward
through the college by the elective system, and receives its final
consecration in his specialty. We are all invited to abound in our
own sense, and to fall in the direction in which we lean. Have we
escaped from the pedantry of authority and prescription, which
was the bane of the old education, only to lapse into the
pedantry of individualism? One is sometimes tempted to
acquiesce in Luther's comparison of mankind to a drunken
peasant on horseback, who, if propped up on one side, slips over
on the other. What would seem desirable at present is not so
much a Tory reaction toward the old ideal as a sense of measure
to save us from an opposite excess—from being entirely "disconnected," as Burke has expressed it, "into the dust and
powder of individuality." The need of discipline and community of ideal enters into human nature no less than the craving
for a free play of one's individual faculties. This need the old
curriculum, with all its faults, did something to satisfy. According to Dean Briggs of Harvard, discipline is often left in the new
education to athletics; and athletics also meet in part the need
for fellowship and communion. However much members of the
same college may be split up in their intellectual interests by

different electives, they can at least commune in an intercollegiate football game. Yet there should likewise be a place for some less elemental form of communion; so many of the very forces in the modern world that make for material union would seem at the same time to tend toward spiritual isolation. In this as in other respects we are at the furthest remove from mediaeval Europe, when men were separated by almost insuperable obstacles in time and space, but were knit together by common standards. When it comes to the deeper things of life, the members of a modern college faculty sometimes strike one, in Emersonian phrase, as a collection of "infinitely repellent particles." The mere fact that men once read the same book at college was no slight bond of fellowship. Two men who have taken the same course in Horace have at least a fund of common memories and allusions; whereas if one of them elect a course in Ibsen instead of Horace, they will not only have different memories, but, so far as they are touched by the spirit of their authors, different ideals. Only a pure radical can imagine that it is an unmixed gain for education to be so centrifugal, or that the outward and mechanical devices that are being multiplied to bring men together can take the place of this deeper understanding.

The sentimental naturalist would claim the right to elect Ibsen instead of Horace simply because he finds Ibsen more "interesting"; he thus obscures the idea of liberal culture by denying that some subjects are more humane than others in virtue of their intrinsic quality, and quite apart from individual tastes and preferences. The scientific naturalist arrives at the same result by his tendency to apply only quantitative tests and to translate everything into terms of power. President Eliot remarks significantly that the old distinction between the degrees of Bachelor of Arts and Bachelor of Science "is fading away, and may soon disappear altogether; for the reason that the object in view with candidates for both degrees is fundamentally the same, namely, training for power." Our colleges are very much taken up at present with the three years' scheme; but what a small matter this is, after all, compared with the change in the degree itself from a qualitative basis to a quantitative and dynamic one! If some of our educational radicals have their way, the A. B. degree will mean merely that a man has expended a certain number of units of intellectual energy on a list of elective studies that may range from boiler-making to Bulgarian; the degree will simply serve to measure the amount and intensity of one's intellectual current and the resistance overcome; it will become, in short, a question of intellectual volts and amperes and ohms. Here again what is wanted is not a hard and fast hierarchy of studies, but a sense of measure that will save us from the opposite extreme, from the democratic absurdity of asserting that all studies are, and by right should be, free and equal. The rank of studies will finally be determined, not by the number of intellectual foot pounds they involve, but by the nearness or remoteness of these studies to man, the boundaries of whose being by no means coincide with those of physical nature:—

> "Man hath all which Nature hath, but more,
> And in that *more* lie all his hopes of good."

The future will perhaps arrive at a classification of studies as more or less humane. However desirable this humane revival may be, we should not hope to bring it about mechanically by proposing some brand-new educational reform. For this would be to fall into the great error of the age, and attempt to create the spirit by means of appliances instead of taking as our very point of departure the doctrine that man is greater than machinery. The hope for the humane spirit is not in the munificence of millionaires, but in a deeper and more earnest reflection on the part of the individual. Emerson's address on the American Scholar is a plea for a humanism that shall rest on pure intuition; the only drawback to Emerson's programme is that he assumes genius in his scholar, and genius of a rare kind at that. On the other hand, a humanism so purely traditional as that of Oxford and the English universities has, along with elements of great strength, certain obvious weaknesses. Perhaps the chief of these is that it seems, to the superficial observer at least, to have forgotten real for conventional values—the making of a man for the making of a gentleman. Herbert Spencer writes of this English education: "As the Orinoco Indian puts on his paint before leaving his hut, . . . so, a boy's drilling in Latin and Greek is insisted on, not because of their intrinsic value, but that he may have the 'education of a gentleman.' " All that may be affirmed with certainty is that if the humane ideal appear at all in the future, it must be in the very nature of things more a matter of individual insight and less a matter of tradition than heretofore. The weakening of traditional authority that our age has seen has some analogy with what took place in the Greece of Pericles. One may perhaps say, without pushing the analogy too far, that we are confronted with the same alternative,—either to attain to the true individualism of Socrates, the first of the humanists as he has been called, or else to fall away into the intellectual and moral impressionism of the sophists. Unpleasant signs of this impressionism have already appeared in our national theatre and newspaper press, in our literary criticism, our philosophy, and our popular novel. Our greatest danger, however, is educational impressionism.

Changes may very well be made in the mere form of the A. B. degree, provided we are careful to retain its humane aspiration. But through lack of clear thinking, we seem likely to forget the true function of the college as opposed to the graduate school on the one hand, and the preparatory school on the other. This slighting of the college is also due in part to German influences. Some of our educational theorists would be willing to unite the upper part of the college course with the graduate school and surrender the first year or two of it to the preparatory school, thus arriving at a division similar to the German gymnasium and university. This division is logical if we believe with Professor Münsterberg that there are but two kinds of scholars, "productive" and "receptive" scholars — those who discover knowledge, and those who "distribute" it; and if we also agree with him in thinking that we need give "the boy of nineteen nothing different in principle from what the boy of nine receives." [1] But the youth of nineteen does differ from the boy of nine in one important particular,—he has become more capable

1. *American Traits*, p. 89.

of reflection. This change from the receptive to the reflective and assimilative attitude of mind is everything from the humane point of view, and contains in fact the justification of the college. Professor Münsterberg stigmatizes our college scholarship not only as "receptive," but as "passive" and "feminine" (though, to be sure, this bad state of affairs has been somewhat mended of late by the happy influence of Germany). But this is simply to overlook the humane endeavor which it is the special purpose of the college to foster — that effort of reflection, virile above all others, to coördinate the scattered elements of knowledge and relate them not only to the intellect but to the will and character; that subtle alchemy by which mere learning is transmuted into culture. The task of assimilating what is best in the past and present, and adapting it to one's own use and the use of others, so far from lacking in originality, calls for something akin to creation. Professor Münsterberg regards the relation between the productive scholar and the college teacher as about that between an artist like Sargent and a photographer. He goes on to say that "the purely imitative thinker may make a most excellent teacher. Any one who has a personality, a forcible way of presentation, and an average intellect, will be able to be a fine teacher of any subject at six weeks' notice." [2] This German notion of knowledge as something that is dumped down on one mind and then "distributed" in the same mechanical fashion to other minds, is precisely what we need to guard against. The ambition of the true college teacher is not to "distribute" knowledge to his students, not "to lodge it with them," as Montaigne says, "but to marry it to them and make it a part of their very minds and souls." We shall have paid a heavy price for all the *strengwissenschaftliche Methode* we have acquired from Germany if it makes us incapable of distinguishing between mere erudition and true scholarship.

Granting, then, that the receptive attitude of mind must largely prevail in the lower schools, and that the productive scholar should have full scope in the graduate school, the

2. *Ibid.*, p. 95.

college, if it is to have any reason at all for existing separately, must stand, not for the advancement, but for the assimilation of learning, and for the perpetuation of culture. This distinction is fairly obvious, and one would almost be ashamed to recall it, did it not seem to be overlooked by some of the men who are doing the most to mould American education. The late President Harper, for example, in his address on the future of the small college, proposed that some of these colleges be reduced to the rank of high schools, that others be made into "junior colleges" (in due subordination to the larger institutions, and taking the student only to the end of the sophomore year), and that others justify their existence by cultivating specialties. The great universities, for their part, are to be brought into closer relations with one another so as to form a sort of educational trust. Now President Harper was evidently right in thinking that the small colleges are too numerous, and that no one would be the loser if some of them were reduced to the rank of high schools. Yet he scarcely makes mention in all his scheme of what should be the real aim of the small college that survives, namely, to teach a limited number of standard subjects vivified and informed by the spirit of liberal culture. From whatever side we approach them, these new theories are a menace to the small college. Thus the assumption that a student is ready for unlimited election immediately on completing his preparatory course puts at a manifest disadvantage all save a very few institutions; for only a few institutions have the material resources that will permit them to convert themselves into educational Abbeys of Thélème and write over their portals the inviting legend: STUDY WHAT YOU LIKE. The best of the small colleges will render a service to American education if they decide to make a sturdy defense of the humane tradition instead of trying to rival the great universities in displaying a full line of educational novelties. In the latter case, they may become third-rate and badly equipped scientific schools, and so reënact the fable of the frog that tried to swell itself to the size of the ox.

The small colleges will be fortunate if they appreciate their own advantages; if they do not fall into the naturalistic fallacy of confusing growth in the human sense with mere expansion; if they do not allow themselves to be overawed by size and quantity, or hypnotized by numbers: Even though the whole world seem bent on living the quantitative life, the college should remember that its business is to make of its graduates men of quality in the real and not the conventional meaning of the term. In this way it will do its share toward creating that aristocracy of character and intelligence that is needed in a community like ours to take the place of an aristocracy of birth, and to counteract the tendency toward an aristocracy of money. A great deal is said nowadays about the democratic spirit that should pervade our colleges. This is true if it means that the college should be in profound sympathy with what is best in democracy. It is false if it means, as it often does, that the college should level down and suit itself to the point of view of the average individual. Some of the arguments advanced in favor of a three years' course imply that we can afford to lower the standard of the degree, provided we thereby put it within reach of a larger number of students. But from the standpoint of the college one thoroughly cultivated person should be more to the purpose than a hundred persons who are only partially cultivated. The final test of democracy, as Tocqueville has said, will be its power to produce and encourage the superior individual. Because the claims of the average man have been slighted in times past, does it therefore follow that we must now slight the claims of the superior man? We cannot help thinking once more of Luther's comparison. The college can only gain by close and sympathetic contact with the graduate school on the one hand, and the lower schools on the other, provided it does not forget that its function is different from either. The lower schools should make abundant provision for the education of the average citizen, and the graduate school should offer ample opportunity for specialization and advanced study; the prevailing spirit of the college, however, should be neither humanitarian nor scientific, — though these elements may be largely represented,—but humane, and, in the right sense of the word, aristocratic.

In thus sketching out an ideal it costs nothing, as a French writer remarks, to make it complete and pretentious. One reason why we are likely to fall so far short of our ideal in practice is the difficulty, as things now are, of finding the right kind of college teacher. Professor Münsterberg praises his German teachers because they never aspired to be more than enthusiastic specialists, and he adds that "no one ought to teach in a college who has not taken his doctor's degree." This opinion is also held by many Americans, and hence the fetish worship of the doctor's degree on the part of certain college presidents. But one may shine as a productive scholar, and yet have little or nothing of that humane insight and reflection that can alone give meaning to all subjects, and is especially appropriate in a college teacher. The work that leads to a doctor's degree is a constant temptation to sacrifice one's growth as a man to one's growth as a specialist. We must be men before being entomologists. The old humanism was keenly alive to the loss of mental balance that may come from knowing any one subject too well. It was perhaps with some sense of the dangers of specialization that the ancient flute-player replied to King Philip, who wished to argue a point of music with him: "God forbid that your majesty should know as much about these things as I do." England is perhaps the only country in which something of this ideal of the elegant amateur — "l'honnête homme qui ne se pique de rien" — has survived to our own day. Compared with the Germans the English still are, as some one recently called them, a nation of amateurs. However, a revulsion of feeling is taking place, and one might imagine from the tone of some recent English articles that the writers would like to see Oxford converted into a polytechnic school. The whole problem is a most difficult one: the very conditions of modern life require us nearly all to be experts and specialists, and this makes it the more necessary that we should be on our guard against that maiming and mutilation of the mind that come from over-absorption in one subject. Every one remembers the passage in which Darwin confesses with much frankness that his human appreciation of art and poetry had been impaired by a one-sided devotion to science.

We should at least insist that the college teacher of ancient or modern literature be something more than a mere specialist. To regard a man as qualified for a college position in these subjects simply because he has investigated some minute point of linguistics or literary history—this, to speak plainly, is preposterous. If we are told that this is a necessary test of his originality and mastery of method, we should reply that as much originality is needed for assimilation as for production,—far more, indeed, than enters into the mechanical compilations so often accepted for doctors' theses in this country and Germany. This outcry about originality is simply the scientific form of that pedantry of individualism, so rampant at the present hour, which, in its sentimental form, leads, as we have seen, to an exaggerated respect for temperament and idiosyncrasy. One of the surest ways of being original nowadays, since that is what we are all straining so anxiously after, would be simply to become a well-read man (in the old-fashioned sense of the term), to have a thorough knowledge and imaginative appreciation of what is really worthwhile in the literature of the past. The candidate for the doctor's degree thinks he can afford to neglect this general reading and reflection in the interests of his own private bit of research. This pedantic effort to be original is especially flagrant in subjects like the classics, where, more than elsewhere, research should be subordinated to humane assimilation. What are we to think of the classical student who sets out to write his thesis before he has read widely, much less assimilated, the masterpieces of Greece and Rome? Unfortunately, this depreciation of assimilative and reflective scholarship falls in with what is most superficial in our national temperament — our disregard for age and experience in the race or the individual, our small esteem for the ''ancient and permanent sense of mankind'' as embodied in tradition, our prejudice in favor of young men and new ideas. In our attitude toward age and tradition, some of us seem bent on going as far in one direction as the Chinese have gone in the other. Youth has already come to be one of the virtues chiefly appreciated in a minister of the gospel! Tocqueville remarks that the contempt for antiquity is one of the chief dangers of a democracy, and adds with true insight that the study of the classics, therefore, has special value for a democratic community. In point of fact, the classical teacher could attempt no higher task than this imaginative interpretation of the past to the present. It is to be accounted one of the chief disasters to our higher culture that our classical teachers as a body have fallen so far short of this task, that they have come instead so entirely under the influence of the narrowest school of German philology, the school of Lachmann and Gottfried Hermann. The throng of scholiasts and commentators whom Voltaire saw pressing about the outer gates of the Temple of Taste now occupy the sanctuary. The only hope for the future of classical studies is in a quite radical change of direction. For instance, a better test than a doctor's degree of a man's fitness to teach classics in the average college would be an examination designed to show the extent and thoroughness of his reading in the classical languages and his power to relate this knowledge to modern life and literature. This foundation once laid, the research instinct might develop naturally in those who had a turn for research, instead of being developed, as it is now, in all alike under artificial pressure. But it is hardly probable that our classical teachers will welcome any such suggestion. For, unlike the old humanists as they may be in most other respects, they still retain something of their pride and exclusiveness; they are still careful to remind us by their attitude that Latin and Greek are *litterae humaniores*, however little they do to make good the claim to this proud distinction. They may be compared to a man who inherits a great name and estate, the possession of which he does not sufficiently justify by his personal achievement.

The teaching of the classics will gain fresh interest and vitality by being brought into close contact with mediaeval and modern literature; we should hasten to add that the teaching of modern languages will gain immensely in depth and seriousness by being brought into close contact with the classics. Neither condition is fulfilled at present. The lack of classical teachers with an adequate foreground and of modern language teachers with an adequate background is one of the chief obstacles to a revival of humane methods. Yet nothing could be more unprofitable under existing conditions than the continuance in any form of the old quarrel of the Ancients and Moderns. "I prefer the philosophy of Montaigne," says Charles Francis Adams in his address on the College Fetish, "to what seem to me the platitudes of Cicero." As though it were possible to have a full understanding of Montaigne without knowledge of the "platitudes" of Cicero, and the whole of Latin literature into the bargain! The teacher of French especially, if he would avoid superficiality, needs to be steadied and ballasted by a thorough classical training. It is so much easier to interest a class in Rostand than in Racine that he is in constant danger of falling into cheap contemporaneousness. A French instructor in an Eastern college told me that as a result of long teaching of his subject he had come to know the "Trois Mousquetaires" better than any other work in all literature; and the "Trois Mousquetaires" is a masterpiece compared to other texts that have appeared, texts whose literary insignificance is often equaled only by the badness of the editing.[3] The commercialism of the large publishers works hand in hand here with the impressionism of modern language teachers, so that the undergraduate of to-day sometimes has the privilege of reading a novel of Georges Ohnet where a generation ago he would have read Plato.

Those who have faith in either ancient or modern languages as instruments of culture should lose no time in healing their minor differences if they hope to make head against their common enemies,—the pure utilitarians and scientific radicals. Herbert Spencer, who may be taken as the type of these latter, holds that scientific analysis is a prime necessity of life, whereas art and literature are only forms of "play," the mere entertainment at most of our idle moments. And he concludes in regard to these subjects: "As they occupy the leisure part of life, so should they occupy the leisure part of education." That this doctrine which reduces art and literature to a sort of dilettanteism should find favor with pure naturalists is not surprising. The case is more serious when it is also accepted, often unconsciously perhaps, by those who are working in what should be the field of literature. Many of the students of linguistics who

---

3. There has been improvement in this respect during the past few years.

have intrenched themselves in our college faculties are ready to grant a place to literature as an occasional relaxation from the more serious and strenuous labors of philological analysis. Only a man must not be too interested in literature under penalty of being thought a dilettante. A young philologist once said to me of one of his colleagues: "He is almost a dilettante—he reads Dante and Shakespeare." It is perhaps the Spencerian view of art that accounts also for a curious predilection I have often noticed in philologists for vaudeville performances and light summer fiction. Certain teachers of literature, it must be confessed,—especially teachers of English,—seem to have a similar conception of their role, and aspire to be nothing more than graceful purveyors of aesthetic solace, and arbiters of the rhetorical niceties of speech. The philologist and the dilettante are equally far from feeling and making others feel that true art and literature stand in vital relation to human nature as a whole, that they are not, as Spencer's theory implies, mere refined modes of enjoyment, mere titillations of the aesthetic sensibility. Some tradition of this deep import of humane letters for the higher uses of man was maintained, along with other knowledge of value, in the old college curriculum. Now that this humane tradition is weakening, the individual, left to his own resources, must seek a substitute for it in humane reflection.

In other words,—and this brings us once more to the central point of our discussion,—even if we sacrifice the letter of the old Bachelor of Arts degree, we should strive to preserve its spirit. This spirit is threatened at present in manifold ways,—by the upward push of utilitarianism and kindergarten methods, by the downward push of professionalism and specialization, by the almost irresistible pressure of commercial and industrial influences. If we sacrifice both the letter and the spirit of the degree, we should at least do so deliberately, and not be betrayed through mere carelessness into some educational scheme that does not distinguish sufficiently between man and an electric dynamo. The time is above all one for careful thinking and accurate definition. Money and enthusiasm, excellent as these things are, will not take the place of vigorous personal reflection. This, it is to be feared, will prove unwelcome doctrine to the ears of an age that hopes to accomplish its main ends by the appointment of committees, and has developed, in lieu of real communion among men, nearly every form of gregariousness. Professor Münsterberg thinks that our highest ambition should be to rival Germany in productive scholarship. To this end he would have us establish a number of twenty-five-thousand-dollar professorships, and appoint to them our most meritorious investigators and masters of scientific method; in addition he would have us heap on these chosen heroes of research every manner of honor and distinction. But he will seriously mislead us if he persuades us that productive scholarship is our chief educational problem. We must insist that a far more important problem just now is to determine the real meaning and value of the A. B. degree. However, we should be grateful to Professor Münsterberg for one thing: in dealing with these fundamentals of education, he is comparatively free from that indolent and impressionistic habit of mind that so often marks our own manner of treating them. He does us a service in forcing us to search more carefully into our own ideas if only in order to oppose him. Almost any opinion that has been thoroughly thought out is better than a mush of impressionism. For, as Bacon has said, truth is more likely to be helped forward by error than by confusion.

V

Literature and the
Doctor's Degree

IT IS RELATED OF DARWIN THAT after a morning of hard work in
his study he was wont to come out into the drawing-room and
rest on the sofa while listening to a novel read aloud. This anec-
dote may serve as a symbol not only of the scientific attitude
toward literature, but of the place that literature is coming to
occupy in life. The modern man reserves his serious energy for
science or sociology or finance. What he looks for when he turns
to pure literature is a soothing and mildly narcotic effect. Many
people, of course, do not seek in books even the solace of their
idle moments, but leave art and literature to women. "Poetry,"
as Lofty says, speaking for men of business, "is a pretty thing
enough for our wives and daughters, but not for us." In the
educational institutions, especially the large universities of the
Middle West, the men flock into the courses on science, the
women affect the courses in literature. The literary courses,
indeed, are known in some of these institutions as "sissy"
courses. The man who took literature too seriously would be
suspected of effeminancy. The really virile thing is to be an elec-

trical engineer. One already sees the time when the typical teacher of literature will be some young dilettante who will interpret Keats and Shelley to a class of girls. As it is, the more vigorous and pushing teachers of language feel that they must assert their manhood by philological research. At bottom they agree with the scientist — and the dilettante — in seeing in literature the source not of a law of life, but of more or less agreeable personal impressions.

The distinction between the dilettante and the philologist is closely related to the more general distinction we have already made between the sentimental and the scientific naturalist, or, as we have agreed to call them, between the Rousseauist and the Baconian. Many of the grammarians in ancient Alexandria did work very similar to that of our contemporary philologists. Evidently, however, they took a much more modest view of their profession, and this was because the Alexandrian was not like the modern philologist, exalted in his own eyes by the feeling that he was contributing by his research to the advancement of learning and pushing at the great car of progress. It is by their definite contribution to knowledge that our modern linguistic Baconians would wish to be esteemed; provided they can get at the precise facts in their study of language, and then disengage from these facts the laws that are supposed to govern them, they are content to turn the human values over to the Rousseauist and to the vagabondage of intellect and sensibility in which the Rousseauist delights.

Once more, however, we are arrested by the need of right definition. The word philology is used nowadays to cover everything from Vedic noun inflections to literary criticism and the Epistles of St. Paul.[1] By the very classifications they insert in university catalogues, our philologists make clear that they look upon literature itself as only a department of philology. We can scarcely hope to define this strangely elastic term in a way that will be generally acceptable, but we can at least define it for our present use.

1. See *Harvard University Catalogue*, 1906-07, pp. 439, 440.

In coming at our definition we need to return for a moment to Emerson's distinction between the two laws "not reconciled." So far as language falls under the "law for thing," it is philology; so far as it expresses the "law for man," it is literature. In following out the phenomenal relationships of language and literature, philology has a vast and important field. It becomes an abuse and a usurpation only when it would set up these phenomenal relationships as a substitute for the still more important relationships of language and literature to the human spirit. Again, the appeal of literature to the individual intellect and sensibility has a large and legitimate place. Impressionism and dilettanteism arise only when the individual would emancipate himself entirely from the discipline of more general standards.

The philologist as we know him nowadays is not always a grammarian who differs from his Alexandrian prototype merely in being puffed up by the Baconian sense of contributing to human progress. That variety of philologist, to be sure, is still extremely common, especially among our classical teachers. But there is another school of philology which has found full expression only in comparatively recent times and is more closely akin to history than to linguistics; or it would be more correct to say that the keener sense of historical relativity, of growth and development, that marked the nineteenth century has profoundly modified all forms of history, including the history of literature. Unfortunately it has proved extremely difficult in practice to combine the historical method with a due regard for intrinsic values. To do this properly is to mediate between the absolute and the relative, and this, as we have seen, is the most difficult of all the adjustments the humanist has to make. The great danger of the whole class of philologists we are discussing is to substitute literary history for literature itself—a danger that has been especially manifest in a field where literary phenomena are numerous and genuine literature comparatively scarce, that of the Middle Ages.[2] The interest of a certain type of

2. The Middle Ages had plenty of intellectual power, but this was largely diverted from the vernaculars into Latin and the scholastic philosophy. With the exception of Dante's poem, the Middle Ages hardly succeeded in expressing themselves completely in literature as they did, for example, in the Gothic cathedral.

mediaevalist in the object of his study would often seem to be in inverse ratio to its real importance. The vital question, after all, is not whether one *chanson de geste* is derived from another *chanson de geste*, but whether either work has in itself any claim to the attention of a serious person. I have heard of Ph.D. examinations of candidates who were planning to teach modern literature, where the questions were almost entirely on the mediaeval field; and on minute points of linguistics and literary history, at that, with only incidental mention of the mediaeval authors who are important for the humanist,—Dante, Chaucer, Petrarch, Boccaccio.

Our modern philologists often accuse their classical brethren of being narrow and illiberal because they do not make a fuller use of the historical method. But the trouble lies deeper, and is not to be remedied by substituting one school of philology for another. The historical method is invaluable, but only when it is reinforced by a sense of absolute values.[3] In itself a great deal of the *Quellenforschung* that goes on at present is really on a lower level than good old-fashioned grammar or text criticism. The man who has that dry book-keeping habit of mind, which is perennial, wins repute as a scholar to-day by some study of origins and influences, much as he might have got on as a critic in neo-classic days by talking about the "rules" and cataloguing "beauties" and "faults." Comparative literature owes its sudden prosperity to the talismanic virtues that are supposed to belong to the historical and comparative methods. But comparative literature will prove one of the most trifling of subjects unless studied in strict subordination to humane standards. For instance, the relationship of Petrarch to the sonneteers of the Renaissance is interesting, but the weightier problem is how both Petrarch and his disciples are related, not to one another, but to the "constant mind of man." Comparative literature may become positively pernicious if it is allowed to divert under-

---

3. What I say here on the historical and comparative methods needs to be completed by what I say on the same subject in the essays on the "Rational Study of the Classics" and on "Ancients and Moderns."

graduates from gaining a first-hand acquaintance with the great classics, to a study of interrelationships and interdependencies either of individual authors or of national literatures. Besides, there is no necessary connection between an author's historical influence and significance and his true worth. Petrarch deserves on the whole a larger place in literary history than Dante, and yet is far inferior to Dante both as a writer and as a man.

The corruption of literature by historical philology resembles what has taken place in history itself. The historians, likewise, have been too exclusively occupied with the phenomena of their subject, and have failed to adjust the rival claims of the absolute and the relative. In one of his essays, Bacon tries to get at some of the underlying laws of the human spirit as they are manifested in the phenomena of history, and at the same time warns us against fixing our gaze too intently on these phenomena themselves. "It is not good," he says, "to look too long on these turning wheels of vicissitude. As for the philology of them, that is but a circle of tales, and therefore not fit for this writing." Here is a correct use of the word philology by a great master of thought and language—so correct, indeed, as almost to seem a prophecy of our most recent scholarship and the excess to which it has fallen. The danger of a former type of scholar was to gloss over the infinite complexity of the facts with a few facile generalizations. The danger of the scholar of to-day is rather to philologize everything, to turn literature and history and religion itself into a mere "circle of tales,"—in other words, to make endless accumulations of facts, and then fail to disengage from these accumulated stores their permanent human values.

What has just been said may seem to some to echo the attacks of Carlyle on Dryasdust, and in general the attacks of the whole romantic school on the abuse of scientific analysis. But at bottom nothing could be more different from each other than the protests of the humanist and the romanticist against the excess of dry analysis and fact-collecting. The romanticist protests because this excess interferes with enthusiasm, with the free play of emotion; the humanist protests because it interferes with judgment and selection. In spite of the opprobrious epithets Carlyle heaped upon him, Dryasdust has prospered, and is now teaching history — and literature—in our American colleges. Indeed, one may go farther and say that Dryasdust has been helped rather than hindered by the romanticist. The excess of dry fact-collecting is the natural rebound from an excess of undisciplined emotion. How often Carlyle himself fails to distinguish between the ''law for man'' and what is simply law for Carlyle! But Carlyle, after all, is something more than a mere romantic impressionist. Our meaning will perhaps be better illustrated by a historian like Michelet, who was a thoroughgoing Rousseauist. A person who reads continuously Michelet's account of the French Revolution is tempted to exclaim at last: In Heaven's name, let us have the cold facts, unembroidered by these arabesques of a disordered fancy, and undistorted by the hallucinations of a revolutionary temperament! Since a man cannot put the human element into his work without thus being wantonly subjective, let him eliminate the human element entirely, and attain at least to the objectivity of the scientist. This is the reasoning that the whole of French literature went through after the riot of subjectivity indulged in by the romantic school of 1830. The great writers have known how to be at once objective and human; but the French writers who tried to escape from the romantic excess of emotion by scientific detachment, by subjecting man entirely to the ''law for thing,'' fell, as a French critic expresses it, into a ''stark inhumanity.'' And this is usually what happens to the fact-collecting, scientific historian. By selecting his facts and affirming a judgment he would, of course, run the risk of expressing nothing higher than his own temperament; but even this is better than to run the risk of expressing nothing human at all.

We have been talking all along as though the scientist and the impressionist, the philologist and the dilettante were necessarily separate and antagonistic persons; but this is very far from being the case. Philology and dilettanteism are in reality only the analytical and the aesthetic, or, as one would be tempted to say, the masculine and the feminine aspects of the same naturalistic movement. They are often combined in the same person, or rather exist alongside one another in him, as a special form of that unreconciled conflict between intellect and feeling that one finds in Rousseau and his descendants. As Renan says somewhat inelegantly of himself, one half of his nature made monkey faces at the other half. Renan, indeed, was so completely the philologist in all the senses we have defined — in language, in history, and in religion—that he may come to be looked upon in the future as the best representative of the type in the nineteenth century. At the same time he was an impressionist and dilettante and — such is the practical complexity of human nature — in some respects a humanist, especially in his conception of style. From the start he was an eminent but also an incurably subjective thinker — a thinker who betrayed the inability of the Rousseauist to get away from his own temperament. And so he gradually lost faith in the seriousness of his own thinking, until at last he allowed it to degenerate into a sort of superior intellectual vaudeville. The only thing that he took seriously at the end was his contribution to philological fact. There is pathos in the slip of paper found on his desk after his death, on which he had written that the achievement that gave him the most satisfaction was his collection of Semitic Inscriptions, the most aridly erudite of all his works, the one into which, humanely speaking, he had put the least of himself.

Most of our philologists, of course, are not Renans. The philological discipline is not in itself conducive either to ideas or to the art of expressing ideas, and Renan, after all, had both. There often exists, however, even in the average philologist, along with the scientific method, which is his masculine side, a feminine or dilettante side. He often combines his strict philologizing with that impressionism which is only the excess of the sympathetic and appreciative temper. The judicial and selective temper he neither possesses himself nor understands in others. What he admires next to philology is the cleverness of the dilettante, and he sometimes succeeds in attaining to it himself.

This curious interplay of philology and impressionism, sometimes united in the same person, but more often existing separately, runs through the whole of our language-teaching, but is most visible perhaps in the teaching of English. At one extreme of the average English department is the philological mediaevalist, who is grounded in Gothic and Old Norse and

Anglo-Saxon; at the other extreme is the dilettante, who gives courses in "daily themes," and, like the sophists of old, instructs ingenuous youth in the art of expressing itself before it has anything to express.

The philologists are better organized than the dilettantes, and command the approaches to the higher positions through their control of the machinery of the doctor's degree. The dilettante is generally relegated to a subordinate place, and is often fitted for it by a pliant and subservient temper. Indeed, it might not be an exaggeration to say that a majority of the more important chairs of ancient and modern literature in this country are already held by men whose whole preparation and achievement have been scientific rather than literary. This situation is on the face of it absurd, and in some respects even scandalous. Yet the philological syndicate can scarcely be blamed for pushing forward men of its own kind; and the problem is in itself so difficult that one should sympathize with the perplexities of college presidents. The young doctor of philosophy has at least submitted to the discipline of facts and given evidence of some capacity for hard work. The dilettante has usually given evidence of nothing, except perhaps a gentle epicureanism. Temperamental indolence and an aversion to accuracy have been known to disguise themselves as a love of literature; so that the college president is often justified in his preference.

Yet it is this acceptance of the doctor's degree as proof of fitness for a chair of literature that is doing more than any one thing to dehumanize literary study and fix on our colleges a philological despotism. The degree as now administered puts a premium, not on the man who has read widely and thought maturely, but on the man who has shown proficiency in research. It thus encourages the student to devote the time he still needs for general reading and reflection to straining after a premature "originality." Any plan for rehabilitating the humanities would therefore seem to turn on the finding of a substitute for the existing doctorate. What is wanted is a training that shall be literary, and at the same time free from suspicion of softness or relaxation; a degree that shall stand for discipline in ideas, and not merely for a discipline in facts. Our language instruction needs to emphasize more than it is now doing the relationship between literature and thought, if it is to be saved from Alexandrianism. Alexandria had scholars who were marvels of aesthetic refinement, and others who were wonders of philological industry. Yet Alexandrian scholarship deserves its doubtful repute because of its inability to vitalize either its aestheticism or is philology,—because of its failure, on the whole, to make any vigorous and virile application of ideas to life. The final test of the scholar must be his power to penetrate his facts and dominate his impressions, and fuse them with the fire of a central purpose (*ergo vivida vis animi pervicit*). What is disquieting about our teachers of language is not any want of scientific method or aesthetic appreciativeness, but a certain incapacity for ideas. Some of our classical scholars have done distinguished work of a purely linguistic kind. A number of our scholars in the modern field have achieved eminence not only in linguistic work, but also in that investigation of literary history which passes with many for literature itself. But we do not get from our teachers of the classics any equivalent of such writing as that of Professor Butcher in England, or of M. Boissier in France—writing that should be almost the normal product of a humanistic scholarship; nor do our teachers of modern languages often attain to that union of finished form and mature generalization which is a common occurrence in the French doctor's thesis.

One of our scholars of German training, evidently alarmed at the growing dissatisfaction with the present Ph.D., admits that the American thesis should try to combine the solidity of German scholarship with the French finish of form. Satisfactory doctor's theses, however, are not to be compounded by any such easy recipe. Most German theses, on literary subjects, at least, are as flimsy in substance as they are crude in form; and finish of form in the French thesis has value only in so far as it is the outer sign of maturity of substance. One can scarcely contemplate the German theses, as they pour by hundreds into a large library, without a sort of intellectual nausea. American scholarship should propose to itself some higher end than simply to add a tributary to the stream.

Hope for literary study in this country would seem to lie in questioning the very things that to our philologists of German training seem self-evident. Thus they assume not only that the chief aim of our graduate schools should be to train investigators, but that our graduate students have as a rule a preparation sufficiently broad to justify them in embarking at once on their investigations. They assume — and this is perhaps the underlying assumption of the whole German school—that there are two kinds of scholars: the receptive scholar, who takes things on authority and is still in his intellectual nonage; and the originative scholar, who by independent research proves that he is intellectually of age. But this is to overlook the all-important intermediary stage when the mind is neither passively receptive nor again originative, but is assimilative in the active and masculine sense. It it this oversight which leads to the exaggerated estimate of the man who brings forward new material as compared with the man who has really assimilated the old. Nothing was more remarkable about Greek literature than the balance it maintained between the forces of tradition and the claims of originality,[4] so that Greek literature at its best is a kind of creative imitation. It is precisely the lack of this creative imitation that is the special weakness of our contemporary literature, just as the lack of creative assimilation is the special weakness of our contemporary scholarship. A pseudo-originality is equally the bane of both.

The trouble with most of our imitation of German scholarship is that it has not been creative, as all fruitful imitation must be, but servile. We should be grateful to the Germans for all we have learned from them, but at the same time we should not be their dupes. The uncritical adoption of German methods is one of the chief obstacles to a humanistic revival. The Germanizing of our classical study in particular has been a disaster not only to the classics themselves, but to the whole of our higher culture. It was not so very long ago that a man could win reputation as a classical scholar merely by editing some Greek or Latin text with

4. This point is clearly made in a recent paper by Professor H. W. Smyth of Harvard on "Aspects of Greek Conservatism."

notes mainly translated from the German. A feeling for form and proportion, good taste, measure and restraint, judgment and discriminating selection — these are the humanistic virtues that should be associated with a study of the classics. It can scarcely be claimed that these humanistic virtues are the ones in which the Germans chiefly excel. Dante notes as a special German failing the lack of sobriety. The Germans occasionally display this intemperance on the planes of thought and feeling. Their prodigality of sentiment we probably all recognize; but the German philosophy, the profundity of which we admire, is often only a form of the *libido sciendi*, the failure to observe the law of measure in the matters of the mind; it is often, again, only the views of a French writer, Rousseau,[5] done into obscure and pedantic phraseology. Coleridge probably did more than any other person, except possibly Carlyle, to instill into English and Americans that exaggerated and superstitious regard for things German as compared with things French which in one form or another has persisted from that day to this. Yet even Coleridge admits that there is a certain "nimiety" about the Germans. By this imperfect observance of the law of measure the Germans betray the fact that they are a people still young in civilization. Scientific method and immense erudition they have acquired, and they have always had abundant enthusiasm. But it is easier to be scientific or erudite or enthusiastic than civilized. Of course we ourselves, in some respects, do not differ from the Germans, but for that very reason we should gain more, perhaps, from models whose virtues and failings are not so

---

5. For the relation of Kant to Rousseau, see Kuno Fischer, *Geschichte der neueren Philosophie*, vol. III, b. I. cap. xiv; C. Dieterich, *Kant und Rousseau*, etc. R. Fester has treated the whole subject from a somewhat special angle in his *Rousseau und die deutsche Geschichtsphilosophie*. It is only fair to remember that the immense influence of Rousseau in Germany was largely due to the fact that the Germans found in Rousseau a brilliant literary expression of what was already latent in themselves. The deeper affiliations of Rousseau's temperament are with Germany rather than with England. The book of M. Joseph Texte (*J.-J. Rousseau et le cosmopolitisme littéraire*) has been misleading in this respect. The best general account of Rousseau's German influence remains that of H. Hettner in his *Literaturgeschichte des XVIII Jahrhunderts*, vol. v.

much like our own. The French are very far from faultless, yet French life is more complementary to our life than that of the Germans, and contact with it is therefore more likely to lead to the completing and rounding out of ourselves that the humanist desires.

In the matter of the doctor's degree especially our practice might at least have been tempered by hints from England and France, both of them countries with older literary traditions than Germany. For instance, a First Class at Oxford has little in common with our undergraduate honors, but offers a training comparable in difficulty to that of the doctorate. This training, however, is of an entirely different kind; it is at once a test of humane assimilation, and a discipline in thoroughness and accuracy. The Frenchman, again, who has gained in the lycée the educational equivalent of the gymnasium, cannot, like the German, proceed at once to specialize; he must in all cases receive the *licence* and in nearly all cases actually does receive the *agrégation* — involving years of assimilative work — before he arrives at his special investigation. Even with these restrictions, Sainte-Beuve, himself one of the greatest and most accurate of investigators, complained of the harm done to humane letters in France by an undue emphasis on "originality" and research. In our own time, the same complaint has been repeated with less amenity by Brunetière. As Sainte-Beuve says, "L'ère des scholiastes et commentateurs se rouvre et recommence." Sainte-Beuve's prophecies of a new Alexandrianism are justified by the poverty of real intellectual achievement on the part of our modern language teachers as compared with their eager interest in such subjects as the making of concordances, dialect-study, and spelling reform.

Our inferiority in literary scholarship might be remedied in some measure if it were led up to and encouraged with us, as it is in France and England, by an appropriate degree. Such distinctions as a First Class in an Oxford honor school or the French *agrégation* would not in themselves be suited to our needs; but they at least illustrate how a degree that stands primarily for reading and assimilation may be made as severe and searching as a degree that stands primarily for research. If the general principle of such a degree were once accepted, its details could easily be adapted to our special requirements. Perhaps the desired end could best be accomplished by a comprehensive plan for graduate and undergraduate honors in literature. Graduate honors could be used to give the degree of A.M. the meaning it has hitherto lacked, and undergraduate honors to help restore to the degree of A.B. the meaning it is so rapidly losing. Graduate honors should not take more than two years, and should hardly attempt to cover more than a single literature; but in that case they ought ordinarily to presuppose undergraduate honors, which, like the new honors in literature at Harvard, correlate the ancient and modern fields.

Who can doubt that a teacher of French who had thus widely read in the ancient and modern classics would be of more use to the average college than the man who had demonstrated his "originality" by collecting examples of the preposition in Old French from Godefroy's Dictionary? Or that the classical scholar who knew his Plato and Aristotle both in themselves and in their relation to the humane tradition of the world would do more to advance his subject than the man who had devoted painful vigils to writing a thesis on the Uses of *dum, donec,* and *quoad*? The successful honor candidate would, like the French *agrégé* and unlike the American doctor, have been prepared directly for the work he would normally be expected to do; and then, if he had a gift for research, he could, like the *agrégé*, cultivate this gift at leisure and at last publish something that might compare in maturity with the French doctoral dissertation. Students at the age at which they ordinarily attend the graduate school may attain to scientific method; they may become distinguished fact-collectors either in the line of linguistic work pure and simple or in the line of historical research; but the maturity of judgment that can alone give value to literary scholarship comes, as Longinus has said, if it comes at all, only as the crowning fruit of long experience. Students with literary tastes should not be encouraged to sacrifice to the fetish of productive scholarship the time they still need for assimilation.

The new degree that we propose, though putting a diminished emphasis on research, should rest its discipline in ideas on a solid discipline in facts. Language should be thoroughly mastered both linguistically and as a medium for the adequate and artistic expression of thought. To attempt to train in ideas students who have received no previous discipline, not even the discipline of common accuracy, is to expect them to fly before they have learned to walk. It will probably be easy enough to start a reaction against the present methods of our philologists, but this movement of protest will prove worse than useless if it is simply to turn to the profit of the dilettante. The natural tendency of the philologists themselves when goaded beyond a certain point by their critics is to promote a few dilettantes to college positions as a sort of sop to the literary element. If the philologist has to choose between a humanist and a dilettante, he is likely to prefer the latter, moved perhaps by an obscure instinct of self-preservation, but even more by that secret alliance which we have already noted between his own nature and that of the dilettante. In fact, the danger just now is greater from the dilettante than from the philologist, provided we include the dilettanteism of the philologist himself. There has been a decrease of late in scientific dogmatism, that dogmatism of the nineteenth century which was often as profound and unconscious as that of mediaeval theology. The arrogance of the philologist is bound to diminish, and indeed is already diminishing, with that of the scientist. One can even now observe in the philologist who has "arrived" an increasing anxiety to assume a literary pose. His friends talk with bated breath of his literary sense. He not only convinces himself and his friends, but college presidents, that he is "literary." Indeed, if the abuse of the word literary continues at the present rate, one will soon have to abandon the word entirely to the dilettante and the philologist in his dilettante moods. It is only just to the philologist to admit that his way of giving courses in literature is often a rather convincing substitute for a genuinely humanistic treatment. As Sainte-Beuve phrases it, when seen from a distance, and from behind, and by moonlight, the literary philologist and the humanist might almost be mistaken for one another. The philologist profits by the common failure to distinguish between literature and literary history. And then, too, he often has that enthusiastic and appreciative temper which is not only easier to attain than the judicial attitude, but also more popular. He usually betrays himself, however, when he tries to handle general ideas and especially to relate these ideas to something higher than his own temperament.

The humanist who at present enters college teaching should not underestimate the difficulties he is likely to encounter. He will find a literature ancient and modern controlled by a philological syndicate, a history dehumanized by the abuse of scientific method, and a political economy that has never been humane.[6] Under these circumstances the humanist will have to undertake the task that Wordsworth so modestly proposed to himself, that of creating the taste by which he is to be enjoyed. He will be more or less out of touch with his colleagues; and, though he will attract some students of the more serious sort, will not necessarily win wide and sudden popularity among undergraduates. As a result of long practice, from the kindergarten up the American undergraduate has often acquired a remarkable dexterity in dodging every kind of discipline. If he takes a course given in a humanistic spirit, he is likely to have exacted from him a good part of the philological discipline in facts, and an additional discipline in ideas with which the philologist is generally not over-much concerned. It is not surprising that many students should prefer the kind of course given by the dilettante who is less preoccupied with the whole question of discipline, and so freer to devote himself to being clever and entertaining. A man of ideas once said in my presence that intellect will tell in the long run — even in a college faculty. In the meanwhile he himself resigned a college position and took up

6. From the outset the orthodox political economy has been humanitarian rather than humane. The end of man, as it views him, is not the attainment of wisdom but the production of wealth. It therefore tends to reduce everything to terms of quantity and power and, as an offset, resorts to various mixtures of altruistic sympathy and "enlightened self-interest." Everything of course depends on the individual teacher. Political economy taught by a Walter Bagehot would be more humane than Plato as taught by many of our American classicists.

another occupation in the evident fear that otherwise he might
suffer the fate of Dryden's Achitophel:—

> "Yet still he saw his fortune at a stay—
> Whole droves of blockheads choking up his way."

Academic recognition is likely to come at present not to the man
of ideas, but to the man who can present the most plausible
mixture of philology and impressionism. It requires courage to
prefer to what is so plainly the "way to promotion and pay" the
difficult and unpopular task of thinking.

We should, however, be charitable to the philologists, and
grant that the difficulty with them is not so much a deliberate
hostility to ideas as a sheer inability to recognize ideas when they
see them. This inability explains as much as any one thing the
condition into which our classical departments have fallen. A
committee which recently investigated one of our Eastern colleges reported that the courses in the classics were mainly taken
by "grinds" as part of their professional training for teaching,
whereas the courses in political economy were taken by large
numbers of undergraduates for the purposes of general culture.
Our classical professors are prone to look upon themselves as the
victims of manifest destiny and inevitable tendencies; and it is
true that classical studies have a formidable foe in the very spirit
of the age. But that this foe is not insuperable is shown by the
prompt response of our public to classical lecturers like Professors Butcher and Murray, who are at the same time men of
ideas. The English humanism, as I have tried to show elsewhere, does not exactly meet our present needs. Yet rather than
suffer indefinitely from the German incubus, we had better try
to induce some of the best of the Oxford honor men to come to
this country as teachers of the classics. An occasional returning
Rhodes scholar may also be of some use. A man with Oxford
training is at least likely to know something of his Plato and
Aristotle, and that is already a great deal.

With more liberal methods, we may hope in time to get more
American students, and of a stronger type, to go into the classics. I have known first-class men in both the ancient and the
modern field who have been literally driven away in disgust by

the present requirements for the Ph.D. I have known others who have accepted these requirements, but in bitterness of spirit. The wail of the dilettante who lacks backbone to acquire the philological discipline we can afford to neglect. The case is more serious, however, when the student humanistically inclined is likewise repelled from a career of literary teaching by the barbed-wire entanglements with which our philologists have obstructed its entrance.

Herein lies the justification of the new degree, or at least of a radical revision of the requirements for the existing degree. The problem, of course, is not so much to devise some new form of academic machinery as to change the spirit which is responsible for the present superstition of the doctor's degree. This will be a necessary preliminary to the liberalizing of our study of either the ancient or modern languages. But though we must have the spirit first of all, we must not be neglectful of our methods. It already savors of the dilettante to have too fine a scorn for questions of method. Right methods without strong men and strong men without right methods are equally unavailing. Taken individually and apart from their methods our classical scholars are probably as able a body of men as will be found in any other department.

For these and other reasons, then, a new degree would seem to be required as an alternative, if not a substitute, for the present Ph.D.; a degree that would lay due stress on aesthetic appreciativeness and linguistic accuracy, but would insist above all on wide reading and the power to relate this reading so as to form the foundation for a disciplined judgment. There would then be some hope of our having humanists as well as philologists and dilettantes, and our literary instruction would be safeguarded from the dry rot of Alexandrianism.

VI

The Rational Study
of the Classics[1]

DEAN SWIFT, IN HIS DESCRIPTION of the battle between the
ancient and modern books in the king's library, has very wisely
refrained from telling the outcome of the encounter. The conflict
is not even yet fought to a finish, but the advantage is more and
more on the side of the moderns. By its unconscious drift not less
than by its conscious choice of direction, the world seems to be
moving away from the classics. The modern mind, as the
number of subjects that solicit attention increases, tends, by an
instinct of self-preservation, to reject everything that has even
the appearance of being non-essential.

If, then, the teacher of the classics is thus put on the defensive,
the question arises how far his position is inevitable, and how far
it springs from a failure to conform his methods to existing
needs. Present methods of classical teaching reflect the change
that has taken place during the past thirty years in our whole

1. It might be well to point out that this essay was written in 1896, from six
to eleven years before the other essays in the volume, and refers in places to
conditions that have since undergone some change.

151

higher education. This period has seen the rise of graduate schools organized with a view to the training of specialists on the German plan, and superimposed on undergraduate systems belonging to an entirely different tradition. The establishment of the first of these graduate schools, that of the Johns Hopkins University, and the impulse there given to work of the type leading to the German doctor's degree, is an event of capital importance in American educational history. President Gilman contemplated with something akin to enthusiasm the introduction of the German scientific spirit, of *strengwissenschaftliche Methode*, the instinct for research and original work, into the intellectual life of the American student. The results have more than justified his expectations. In all that relates to accurate grasp of the subject in hand, to strenuous application and mastery of detail, the standard of American scholarship has risen immensely during the last few years, and will continue to rise. Our universities are turning out a race of patient and laborious investigators, who may claim to have rivaled the Germans on their own ground, as Horace said the Romans had come to rival the Greeks:—

> "Venimus ad summum fortunae; pingimus atque
> Psallimus et luctamur Achivis doctius unctis."

There are, however, even among those who recognize the benefits of the German scientific spirit, many who feel at the same time its dangers and drawbacks. A reaction is beginning against a too crude application of German methods to American educational needs. There are persons at present who do not believe that a man is fitted to fill a chair of French literature in an American college simply because he has made a critical study of the text of a dozen mediaeval beast fables and written a thesis on the Picard dialect, and who deny that a man is necessarily qualified to interpret the humanities to American undergraduates because he has composed a dissertation on the use of the present participle in Ammianus Marcellinus. It is held by others, who put the matter on broader grounds, that German science is beginning to show signs of a decadence similar to the decadence that overtook Greek science in the schools of Alexandria. Matthew Arnold declares the great Anglo-Saxon failing during the present century to have been an excessive faith in machinery and material appliances. May we not with equal truth say that the great German failing during the same period has been an excessive faith in intellectual machinery and intellectual appliances? What else but intellectual machinery is that immense mass of partial results which has grown out of the tendency of modern science to an ever minuter subdivision and analysis? The heaping up of volumes of special research and of investigations of infinitesimal detail has kept pace in Germany with the multiplication of mechanical contrivances in the Anglo-Saxon world. One sometimes asks in moments of despondency whether the main achievement of the nineteenth century will not have been to accumulate a mass of machinery that will break the twentieth century's back. The Cornell University library already contains, for the special study of Dante alone, over seven thousand volumes; about three fourths of which, it may be remarked in passing, are nearly or quite worthless, and only tend to the confusion of good counsel. Merely to master the special apparatus for the study of Dante and his times, the student, if he conforms to the standard set for the modern specialist, will run the risk of losing his intellectual symmetry and sense of proportion, precisely the qualities of which he will stand most in need for the higher interpretation of Dante.

Nowhere, perhaps, is this disposition to forget the end of knowledge in the pursuit of its means and appliances more apparent than in the study of the classics. There is no intention, in saying this, to underrate the services that nineteenth-century scholars, especially those of Germany, have rendered the cause of classical learning. In their philological research and minute criticism of texts they are only following a method which, though first formulated and systematically applied by Bentley, goes back in its main features to the great scholars of the Renaissance. Is there not, however, a fallacy in assuming that material so strictly limited in amount as that remaining to us from classical antiquity is forever to be primarily the subject of scientific investigation? The feudal institutions which saved France from anarchy during the Middle Ages had come, in the eighteenth century, to be the worst of anachronisms; and in like manner the type of scholarship which was needed at the beginning of the Renaissance to rescue and restore the texts of the classical writers will come to be a no less flagrant anachronism if persisted in after that work has been thoroughly done. The method which in the sixteenth century produced a Stephanus or a Casaubon will only give us to-day the spectacle of the "German doctor desperate with the task of saying something where everything has been said, and eager to apply his new theory of fog as an illuminating medium." As the field of ancient literature is more and more completely covered, the vision of the special investigator must become more and more microscopic. The present generation of classical philologists, indeed, reminds one of a certain sect of Japanese Buddhists which believes that salvation is to be attained by arriving at a knowledge of the infinitely small. Men have recently shown their fitness for teaching the humanities by writing theses on the ancient horse-bridle and the Roman doorknob.

Doubtless the time has not yet come for what may be called the age of research in the ancient languages to be finally brought to a close. Of Greek literature especially, we may say, in the words of La Fontaine, "That is a field which cannot be so harvested that there will not be something left for the latest comer to glean." But while there may still be subjects of research in the classics that will reward the advanced student, it is doubtful whether there are many such whose study the beginner may profitably undertake as a part of his preparation in his specialty. In doing the work necessary under existing conditions to obtain the doctor's degree in the classics, it may be questioned whether a man has chosen the best means of getting at the spirit, or even the letter, of ancient literature or of qualifying himself to become an exponent of that literature to others. It is claimed by the advocates of research that the training the student gets in his investigation, even though he fail to arrive at any important result, is in itself valuable and formative to a high degree. He is at least initiated into that *strengwissenschaftliche Methode* on which President Gilman lays such particular stress. We must recognize a large measure of truth in the claims thus put forward by the advocates of research. It is by his power to gather himself together, to work within limits, as Goethe has told us in a well-known phrase, that the master is first revealed. In so far, then, as the German scientific method forces us to gather ourselves together and to work within limits, thereby increasing our power of concentration, our ability to lay firm hold upon the specific fact, we cannot esteem it too highly. There can be no more salutary discipline for a person who is afflicted with what may be termed a loose literary habit of mind than to be put through a course of exact research. The lack of the power to work within limits, to lay firm hold upon the specific fact, is a fault of the gravest character, even when it appears in a mind like that of Emerson.

The question arises, however, whether an unduly high price has not been paid for accuracy and scientific method when these qualities have been obtained at the sacrifice of breadth. Would it not be possible to devise a series of examinations, somewhat similar in character, perhaps, to those now held for honors at Oxford and Cambridge,—examinations which would touch upon ancient life and literature at the largest possible number of points, and which might serve to reveal, as the writings of a doctor's thesis does not, the range as well as the exactness of a student's knowledge? Some test is certainly needed which shall go to show the general culture of a candidate as well as his special proficiency, his familiarity with ideas as well as with words, and his mastery of the spirit, as well as of the mechanism, of the ancient languages.

It is precisely in the failure to distinguish between the spirit and the mechanism of languages, in the unwillingness to recognize literature as having claims apart from philology, that the danger of the present tendency chiefly consists. The opinion seems to be gaining ground that the study of literature by itself is unprofitable, hard to disassociate from dilettanteism, and not likely to lead to much except a lavish outlay of elegant epithets of admiration. A professor of Greek in one of the Eastern colleges is reported to have said that the literary teaching of the classics would reduce itself in practice to ringing the changes on the adjective "beautiful!" It is rigorous scientific method, we are told, that needs to be painfully acquired. If a man has a certain right native instinct, his appreciation of the literature will take care of itself; and if this native instinct is lacking, it is something that no pressure from without will avail to produce. It is, then, *strengwissenschaftliche Methode* with its talismanic virtues that our every effort should be directed to impart, whereas the taste for literature is to be reckoned in with Dogberry's list of things that come by nature. It is in virtue of some such sentiments as this that the study of philology seems at present to be driving the study of literature more and more from our Eastern universities. Do not the holders of this view, we may ask, emphasize unduly the influence their method will have upon individuals, and at the same time fail to consider the effect it may have in the formation of a tendency? In the long run the gradual working of any given ideal upon the large body of average men, who simply take on the color of their environment, will produce a well-nigh irresistible movement in the direction of that ideal. If the minutiae rather than the larger aspects of the classics are insisted upon, the taste for small things will spread like a contagion among the rank and file of classical scholars, and we shall soon be threatened with an epidemic of pedantry. A particular type of school is as much in need of a congenial atmosphere in which to flourish as a plant is in need of a congenial soil and climate in which to flower and bring forth fruit. We cannot readily imagine a Professor Jowett appearing under existing conditions at the University of Berlin. Besides, the danger is to be taken into account that if present methods are pushed much further, the young men with the right native instinct for literature are likely to be driven out of the classics entirely. Young men of this type may not all care to be educated as though they were to be "editors, and not lovers of polite literature;" they may not feel the fascination of spending months in a classical seminary, learning how to torment the text and the meaning of a few odes of Horace,—

> "And torture one poor word ten thousand ways."

There is, to be sure, a very real danger in some subjects, especially in English literature, that the instruction may take too belletristic a turn. The term "culture course" has come to mean, among the undergraduates of one of our Eastern colleges, a course in which the students are not required to do any work. It is one of the main advantages of Latin and Greek over modern languages that the mere mastering of an ancient author's meaning will give to a course enough bone and sinew of solid intellectual effort to justify the teacher in adding thereto the flesh and blood of a literary interpretation. In a civilization so hard and positive in temper as our own, it is not the instinct for philology, but rather the instinct for literature and the things of the imagination, which is likely to remain latent if left to itself. A certain dry, lexicographical habit of mind is said by Europeans to be the distinctive mark of American scholarship. Instead of fostering this habit of mind in the study of the classics by an undue insistence on philology, it should be our endeavor to counteract it by giving abundant stimulus and encouragement to the study of them as literature. In the classics more than in other subjects, the fact should never be forgotten that the aim proposed is the assimilation, and not the accumulation, of knowledge. In the classics, if nowhere else, mere erudition should be held in comparatively little account except in so far as it has been converted into culture; and culture itself should not be regarded as complete until it has so penetrated its possessor as to become a part of his character. Montaigne has said somewhere in his essays that he loved to forge his mind rather than to furnish it. The metaphor of Montaigne's phrase is somewhat mixed, but the idea it embodies is one that men born into a late age of scholarship cannot ponder too carefully. As the body of learning transmitted from the past increases in volume, it becomes constantly more difficult to maintain the exact relation between the receipt and the assimilation of knowledge which has been declared by the greatest of the Hindu sages to be the root of all wisdom. "Without knowledge," says Buddha, "there is no reflection, without reflection there is no knowledge; he who has both knowledge and reflection is close upon Nirvâna."

The risk we run nowadays is that of having our minds buried beneath a dead-weight of information which we have no inner energy, no power of reflection, to appropriate to our own uses and convert into vital nutriment. We need to be on our guard against allowing the mere collector of information to gain an undue advantage over the man who would maintain some balance between his knowledge and reflection. We are, for instance, putting a premium on pedantry, if we set up as the sole test of proficiency in the classics the degree of familiarity shown with that immense machinery of minute learning that has grown up about them. This is to exalt that mere passive intellectual feeding which is the bane of modern scholarship. It is to encourage the man who is willing to abandon all attempt at native and spontaneous thought and become a mere register and repertory of other men's ideas in some small department of knowledge. The man who is willing to reduce his mind to a purely mechanical function may often thereby gain a mastery of facts that will enable him to intimidate the man who would make a larger use of his knowledge; for there are among scholars, as Holmes says there are in society, "fellows," who have a number of "ill-conditioned facts which they lead after them into decent company, ready to let them slip, like so many bulldogs, at every ingenious suggestion or convenient generalization or pleasant fancy." There has always existed between the man of the literal fact and the man of the general law, between the man of cold understanding and the man of thought and imagination, an instinctive aversion. We can trace the feud that has divided the two classes of minds throughout history. They were arrayed against each other in fierce debate for centuries during the Middle Ages under the name of Realists and Nominalists. The author of one of the oldest of the Hindu sacred books pronounces an anathema on two classes of people, the grammarian and the man who is over-fond of a good dinner, and debars them both from the hope of final salvation.

The remark has frequently been made that quarrels would not last long if the fault were on one side only. We may apply this truth to the debate in question, which considered in its essence, springs from the opposition between the lovers of synthesis and the lovers of analysis. Now, Emerson has profoundly said, in his essay on Plato, that the main merit of the Greeks was to have found and occupied the right middle ground between synthesis and analysis; and this will continue to be the aim of the true scholar.

The old humanism, such as it still survives at Oxford, has in it much that is admirable; but it has become, in some respects at least, antiquated and inadequate. It would sometimes seem to lead, as it did in the case of Walter Pater, to an ultra-aesthetic and epicurean attitude toward life—to a disposition to retire into one's ivory tower, and seek in ancient literature merely a source of exquisite solace. The main fault of this English humanism, however, is that it treats the classical writers too much as isolated phenomena; it fails to relate them in a broad and vital way to modern life. It would seem, then, that new life and interest are to be infused into the classics not so much by a restoration of the old humanism as by a larger application to them of the comparative and historical methods. These methods, we hasten to add, should be informed with ideas and reinforced by a sense of absolute values. Especially in the case of a language like Latin, whose literature is so purely derivative, and which has in turn radiated its influence along so many different lines to the modern world, any mere disconnected treatment of individual authors is entirely insufficient. The works of each author, indeed, should first be considered by themselves and on their own merits, but they should also be studied as links in that unbroken chain of literary and intellectual tradition which extends from the ancient to the modern world.

It is by bringing home to the mind of the American student the continuity of this tradition that one is likely to implant in him, more effectually, perhaps, than in any other way, that right feeling and respect for the past which he so signally lacks. For if the fault of other countries and other times has been an excess of reverence for the past, the danger of this country to-day would seem rather to be an undue absorption in the present. No great monument of a former age, no Pantheon or Notre Dame, rises in the midst of our American cities to make a silent plea for the past against the cheap and noisy tendencies of the passing hour. From various elements working together obscurely in his consciousness — from the theory of human perfectibility inherited from the eighteenth century, from the more recent doctrine of evolution, above all from the object lesson of his own national life—the average American has come to have an instinctive belief that each decade is a gain over the last decade, and that each century is an improvement on its predecessor; the first step he has to take in the path of culture is to realize that movement is not necessarily progress, and that the advance in civilization cannot be measured by the increase in the number of eighteen-story buildings. The emancipation from this servitude to the present may be reckoned as one of the chief benefits to be derived from classical study. Unfortunately this superficial modernism turns many away from the study of the classics alto-gether, and tends to diminish, even in those who do study them, that faith and enthusiasm so necessary to overcome the initial difficulties.

The American, it is true, is often haunted, in the midst of all his surface activity, with a vague sense that, after all, his life may be deficient in depth and dignity; it is not so often, however, that he succeeds in tracing this defect in his life to its lack of back-ground and perspective, to the absence in himself of a right feeling for the past,—that feeling which, as has been truly said, distinguishes more than any other the civilized man from the barbarian. As has already been remarked, this feeling is to be gained, in the case of the classics, not so much by treating them as isolated phenomena as by making clear the manifold ways in which they are related to the present, by leaving no chasm between ancient and modern life over which the mind is unable to pass. One of the important functions, then, of the classical teacher should be to bridge over the gap between the Greek and Roman world and the world of to-day. No preparation can be too broad, no culture too comprehensive, for the man who would fit himself for the adequate performance of such a task. His knowledge of modern life and literature needs to be almost as wide as his knowledge of the life and literature of antiquity. The ideal student of the classics should not rest satisfied until he is able to follow out in all its ramifications that Greek and Latin thought which, as Max Müller says, runs like fire in the veins of modern literature. In the case of an author like Virgil, for instance, he should be familiar not only with the classical Virgil, but also with the Virgil of after-centuries, — with Virgil the magician and enchanter who haunted the imagination of the Middle Ages, with Virgil the guide of Dante, and so on, down to the splendid ode of Tennyson. If he is dealing with Aristotle, he should be able to show the immense influence exercised by Aristotle over the mediaeval and modern European mind, both directly through the Latin tradition and indirectly through Averrhoës and the Arabs. If his author is Euripides, he should know in what way Euripides has affected modern dramatic art; he should be capable of making a comparison between the "Hippolytus" and the "Phèdre" of Racine. If he is studying Stoicism, he should be able to contrast the stoical ideal of perfection with the Christian ideal of the perfect life as elaborated by writers like St. Bonaventura and St. Thomas Aquinas. He should neglect far less than has been done heretofore the great patristic literature in Greek and Latin, as giving evidence of the process by which ancient thought passed over into thought of the mediaeval and modern types. These are only a few examples, chosen almost at random, of the wide and fruitful application that may be made of the comparative method.

How much, again, might be done to enhance the value of classical study by a freer use than has hitherto been made of the historical method! The word "historical" is intended to be taken in a large sense; what is meant is not so much a mere cataloguing of the events of ancient civilization as an investigation of the various causes that led to the greatness or decline of ancient societies. The last word on the reasons for the rise and fall of the Romans has not been spoken by Montesquieu. An investigation of the kind referred to would allow the application of many of the theories of modern science, but its results would have far more than an abstract scientific interest; they would provide us with instruction and examples to meet the problems of our own times. From the merest inattention to the teachings of the past, we are likely, in our national life, to proceed cheerfully to

"Commit the oldest sins the newest kind of ways."

A sober reflection on the history of the ancient republics might put us on our guard against many of the dangers to which we ourselves are exposed. It might cure us in part of our cheap optimism. It might, in any case, make us conscious of that tendency of which Macchiavelli had so clear a vision,—the tendency of a state to slip down an easy slope of prosperity into vice:—

"Et in vitium fortuna labier aequa."

How much light must be shed—to give but a single illustration of what is meant—on contemporary as well as on Roman politics by a course, properly conducted, on the correspondence of Cicero!

The method just suggested of studying the classics might possibly render them less liable to the complaint now made that they are entirely remote from the interests and needs of the present. It is this feeling of the obsoleteness of the classics, joined to the utilitarian instinct so deeply imbedded in the American character, that is creating such a wide-spread sentiment in favor of giving the place they now hold to modern languages. The American student of the future is evidently going to have a chance to follow in the footsteps of that remarkable young woman, Miss Blanche Amory of "Pendennis," who, it will be remembered, "improved her mind by a sedulous study of the novels of the great modern authors of the French language." It would appear, from a comparison of the catalogues of one of our Eastern universities, that its undergraduates now have an opportunity to read "La Débâcle" of Émile Zola, where twenty years ago they would have been required to read the "Antigone" of Sophocles.

We will not attempt for the present a full discussion of this important question as to the relative educational value of ancient and modern languages, but a few reasons may be given briefly in support of the view that modern languages, however valuable as a study supplementary to the classics, are quite inadequate to take their place.

M. Paul Bourget, in a recent autobiographical sketch, tells us that, as a young man, he steeped his mind in the works of Stendhal and Baudelaire and other modern literature of the same type. He fails to explain, either to himself or others, the fact that these modern books, though written, as he says, in all truth and sincerity, should yet have given him a view of life which later led only to bitter disappointment and disillusion. M. Bourget's difficulty might have been less if he had taken into account that the authors of whom he speaks, so far from serving as a stimulus to his will and reason, merely invited him to retire into a corner and try strange experiments on his own emotional nature, and draw new and novel effects from his own capacity for sensation; that they held out to him, in short, the promise of a purely personal and sensuous satisfaction from life,—a promise which life itself may be counted upon not to keep. Now modern authors are not all, like Baudelaire, of the violently subjective type, but the intrusion of the author and his foibles into his work, the distortion of the objective reality of life by its passage through the personal medium, is much more frequent in modern than in ancient literature. Much of modern literature merely encourages to sentimental and romantic revery rather than to a resolute and manly grappling with the plain facts of existence. Romanticism may not mean the Commune, as Thiers said it did, but we may at least say that literature of the romantic type, compared with that in the classical tradition, is so deficient in certain qualities of sobriety and discipline as to make us doubt its value as a formative influence upon the minds of the young. Classical literature, at its best, does not so much tend to induce in us a certain state of feelings, much less a certain state of the nerves; it appeals rather to our higher reason and imagination—to those faculties which afford us an avenue of escape from ourselves, and enable us to become participants in the universal life. It is thus truly educative in that it leads him who studies it out and away from himself. The classical spirit, in its purest form, feels itself consecrated to the service of a high, impersonal reason. Hence its sentiment of restraint and discipline, its sense of proportion and pervading law. By bringing our acts into an ever closer conformity with this high, impersonal reason, it would lead us, although along a different path, to the same goal as religion, to a union ever more intimate with

> "our only true, deep-buried selves,
> Being one with which we are one with the whole world."

By a complete and harmonious development of all our faculties under the guidance and control of this right reason, it would raise us above the possibility of ever again falling away

> "Into some bondage of the flesh or mind,
> Some slough of sense, or some fantastic maze
> Forged by the imperious, lonely thinking power."

This high message contained in classical literature calls for the active exercise of our own best faculties, of our intellect and imagination, in order to be understood. It may be because of this purely intellectual appeal of the classics that there is so much initial inertia to overcome in awakening an interest in them. Indeed, to transform into a Greek scholar the average young man of to-day, whose power of attention has been dissipated in the pages of the American newspaper, whose mind has been relaxed by reading the modern erotic novel, — this, to borrow one of Phillips Brooks's phrases, would sometimes seem about as promising an enterprise as to make a lancehead out of putty. The number of those who can receive the higher lessons of Greek culture is always likely to be small. The classical spirit, however, is salutary and formative wherever it occurs, and if a man is not able to appreciate it in Pindar, he may in Horace; and if not in Horace, then in Molière. French literature of the seventeenth century is, as a whole, the most brilliant manifestation of the classical spirit in modern times, and one might teach French with considerable conviction, were it not for the propensity of the American student to confine his reading in French to inferior modern authors, and often, indeed, to novels of the decadence.

Decadent novels and other fungous growths of a similar nature are not peculiar to French, but are multiplying with alarming rapidity in all the great European literatures. Modern literature has been more or less sentimental since Petrarch, and a morbidly subjective strain has existed in it since Rousseau, while of late a quality is beginning to appear which we cannot better describe than as neurotic. We may say, to paraphrase an utterance of Chamfort's, that the success of some contemporary books is due to the correspondence that exists between the state of the author's nerves and the state of the nerves of his public. Spiritual despondency, which under the name of *acedia* was accounted one of the seven deadly sins during the Middle Ages, has come in these later days to be one of the main resources of literature. Life itself has recently been defined by one of the lights of the French deliquescent school as "an epileptic fit between two nothings." It is no small resource to be able to escape from these miasmatic exhalations of contemporary literature into the bracing atmosphere of the classics; to be able to rise into that purer ether

> "where those immortal shapes
> Of bright aerial spirits live insphered
> In regions mild of calm and serene air."

We can, then, by no means allow the claims of those who find in modern languages an adequate substitute for the classics. However, we agree with those who assert that if the classics are to maintain their traditional place, they should be related more largely to the needs and aspirations of modern life. With this end in view, classical study must take a new direction; we need to emulate the spirit of the great scholars of the Renaissance, but to modify their methods. As to the present excess of German tendency in American classical scholarship, it may be left to remedy itself. The German research method appeals, indeed, to certain hard, positive qualities in the American mind, but other sides of the German ideal the American will find distasteful, on closer acquaintance; above all, he will prove incapable, in the long run, of the sublime disinterestedness of the German specialist, who, so far from asking himself whether his work will ever serve any practical purpose, never stops to inquire whether it will serve any purpose at all. A reaction, then, against the exaggerations of German method and of the scientific spirit will do no harm, though the classics need to benefit by a full application of the historical and comparative methods. There is needed in the classics to-day a man who can understand the past with the result, not of loosening, but of strengthening his grasp upon the present. There is needed a type of scholar intermediary between the high school pedagogue and the university specialist, who can interpret the classics in a large and liberal spirit to American undergraduates, carrying with him into his task the consciousness that he is forming the minds and characters of future citizens of a republic. The teaching of the classics thus understood could be made one of the best preparations for practical life, and less might be heard of the stock complaint about wasting time in the study of the dead languages. As to this last charge, we may quote from the most eloquent appeal that has been made of late years for a more liberal study of the classics,—that of Lowell in his Harvard Anniversary address. If the language of the Greeks is dead, he there says, "yet the literature it enshrines is rammed with life as perhaps no other writing, except Shakespeare's, ever was or will be. It is as contemporary with to-day as with the ears it first enraptured, for it appeals not to the man of then or now, but to the entire round of human nature itself. Men are ephemeral or evanescent, but whatever page the authentic soul of man has touched with her immortalizing finger, no matter how long ago, is still young and fair as it was to the world's gray fathers. Oblivion looks in the face of the Grecian Muse only to forget her errand. . . . We know not whither other studies will lead us, especially if dissociated from this; we do know to what summits, far above our lower region of turmoil, this has led, and what the many-sided outlook thence."

There was never greater need of the Hellenic spirit than there is to-day, and especially in this country, if that charge of lack of measure and sense of proportion which foreigners bring against Americans is founded in fact. As Matthew Arnold has admirably said, it is the Greek writers who best show the modern mind the path that it needs to take; for the modern man cannot, like the man of the Middle Ages, live by the imagination and religious faculty alone; on the other hand, he cannot live solely by the exercise of his reason and understanding. It is only by the union of these two elements of his nature that he can hope to attain a balanced growth, and this fusion of the reason and the imagination is found realized more perfectly than elsewhere in the Greek classics of the great age. Those who can receive the higher initiation into the Hellenic spirit will doubtless remain few in number, but these few will wield a potent influence for good, each in his own circle, if only from the ability they will thereby have acquired to escape from contemporary illusions. For of him who has caught the profounder teachings of Greek literature we may say, in the words of the "Imitation," that he is released from a multitude of opinions.

VII

Ancients and Moderns

THE MODERN LANGUAGES have had so much practical success in supplanting Greek and Latin that they have hardly felt the need as yet of justifying themselves theoretically. The ancient humanities have been in general retreat in spite of the sturdy defense of Oxford and a few other strongholds of tradition. Sainte-Beuve's last secretary tells us that he once overheard the great critic, himself one of the last of the humanists, muttering: "Les anciens ont perdu la partie." The Quarrel of Ancients and Moderns, remarks M. Faguet, will soon cease, because there will soon be nobody left who knows enough about the ancients even to argue the question. The new programmes for secondary education recently adopted in France, which did more than any other country to impose the imitation of antiquity as a dogma upon Europe, now tends in its attitude toward classical study to fall from superstition into irreverence.

Modern languages, then, have had little to do but succeed. They have benefited by their utilitarian appeal, and in the case of one's mother tongue by their appeal to sentiment. They have benefited by the constantly increasing influence of women in literature and education. As a substitute for Greek and Latin, they have attracted the vast multitude which in its choice of studies follows more or less consciously the line of least resistance. In the meanwhile certain fundamental questions have remained unsettled regarding the real value of modern languages, especially one's own language, as instruments of discipline and culture. Indeed, one may say that modern languages owe their popularity not so much to their being instruments of discipline as to their having afforded a means of escape from a definite discipline. They were greatly aided in their triumph over Latin and Greek by that movement to substitute sympathy for restraint which we have associated with Rousseau. But to make this point clear we shall need to review rapidly the Quarrel of Ancients and Moderns.

I

IN ITS PURELY LITERARY ASPECTS, the first phase of the Quarrel has become obsolete. If this first phase is still important, it is because of its being so closely related to the beginnings of the idea of progress.[1] Only one of all the writers and wits who were engaged on either side of the Quarrel may be said to have perceived clearly the grounds on which the moderns were finally to break away from the imitation of the ancients and affirm the legitimacy of their own modes of thought and expression. This writer was St. Évremond. He was already an adept in what was to be known later as the historical method. He looks upon the Latin and Greek masterpieces not as absolute models raised above time and space, but as the product of special conditions of climate, religion, environment, etc. Now that all these conditions have changed, modern literatures have a right to change with them. To impose Greek and Latin authors dogmatically is to forget that they, no less than the moderns, were subject to the law of universal relativity.

St. Évremond, however, was somewhat isolated in his own time, and as an inspirer of historical method can hardly be said

1. The best treatment of this first phase of the quarrel is still that of H. Rigault: *La querelle des anciens et des modernes* (1856).

to have been influential.[2] For the modern phase of the Quarrel of Ancients and Moderns we do not need to go farther back than Rousseau, who had far less historical sense than St. Évremond. Yet Rousseau is the most important initiator in the movement that was finally to dislodge the ancient languages from their exclusive position as standards of form and good taste. In the name of feeling, Rousseau headed the most powerful insurrection the world has ever seen against every kind of authority; and it was inevitable that he should attack the authority that classicism arrogated to itself over the individual sensibility, its pretension to regulate emotion in the name of fixed standards. Rousseau was especially bitter against the classical, or rather the pseudo-classical, notion of decorum, which proscribed spontaneity, or, as he would have said, silenced the voice of the heart in the name of a wearisome dignity.

It was reserved for a German disciple of Rousseau, Herder,[3] to take the decisive step in carrying Rousseauism into the field of literature and history. Herder resembles Rousseau in that the significance of his work is often greater than its intrinsic value. He has immense importance as an initiator. He probably did more than any other man of his time to promote a sympathetic and imaginative interpretation of the past, and prepare the way for the triumph of that historical method which has proved so powerful a solvent of both Christian and classical dogma. In applying the historical method Herder did not, like St. Évremond, show the cold and cautious temper of the man of the world, but rather the temper of the romantic and humanitarian enthusiast. Herder transfers to the nation the idea of organic growth and development that Rousseau had employed in his "Émile" to revolutionize the education of the individual child. He dwells with particular interest on the origins of nationalities, —especially of his own nationality,—and idealizes this first age of spontaneity and instinct much as Rousseau had exalted child-

2. St. Évremond (1610–1703) spent the last forty years of his life in exile at London. His influence on Dryden possibly appears in Dryden's occasional anticipations of the historic method.

3. English influences such as Ossian and Percy's Reliques coöperated in Herder with the influence of Rousseau.

hood as the Golden Age of the individual. Folk songs and all forms of poetry that arise spontaneously are to be preferred to the conscious creations of academic art. The Iliad and the Odyssey had been looked on by the previous age as the works of a single poet who wrote with direct reference to the rules of the epics laid down in LeBossu. Under the new influence Homer ceases to be a person, and becomes a mere name for a collection of popular ballads.

The philosophical theory behind Herder's method is an interesting extension of Rousseau's idea of sympathy. According to Rouseau every man is to cultivate his own originality to the utmost, and then sympathize with other men who do likewise. According to Herder every nation is to cultivate to the utmost its own national genius, and then, as an offset to this self-assertion, have a comprehensive sympathy for other national originalities. Nationalism is to be tempered by internationalism. Nationalism and internationalism, as we have thus defined them, first became effective as world forces with the French Revolution; but the theory is already complete in Herder and Rousseau.[4] Our modern cosmopolitanism is simply one form of Rousseau's attempt to substitute sympathy for restraint as the foundation of ethics. Any one who believes that the instincts for brotherhood are strong enough to prevail unaided over the egoistic instincts in the relations between man and man may readily believe in a similar altruistic triumph in international relations. But in the eyes of the old-fashioned moralist there is something chimerical in the underlying assumption of the Rousseauist. The whole notion that the diverse and clashing egoisms either of individuals or nationalities will have a sufficient counterpoise in sympathy alone, or in sympathy reinforced by an "enlightened

4. The cosmopolitanism of sympathy is clearly formulated by Rousseau in a passage like the following: "La commisération naturelle...ne réside plus que dans quelques grandes âmes cosmopolites qui franchissent les barrières imaginaires qui séparent les peuples et qui à l'exemple de l'être souverain qui les a créés embrassent tout le genre humain dans leur bienveillance" (*Discours sur l'origine*, etc.). For the extent to which Rousseau encouraged the inbreeding of national temperament, see the scheme of education outlined in his *Considérations sur le gouvernement de la Pologne*.

self-interest," may very well turn out to be—as some one said of the ten commandments — an "iridescent dream." The Rousseauist would have men commune in their differences, or, to be more precise, would rest communion among men on a mixture of sympathy and self-assertion. Almost on the face of it, the older doctrine is less utopian which insisted, as a necessary preliminary to the free play of sympathy among men, that they should unite in a common discipline. This was the cosmopolitanism of mediaeval Europe, when men were knit together in a single faith; and we should not forget that the Europe of the Middle Ages was in some respects more genuinely cosmopolitan than the Europe of to-day.

There was also a literary cosmopolitanism before Rousseau, which likewise rested, so far as it went, on discipline rather than on sympathy. The neo-classical doctrine that held sway for over two centuries tended to impose on all cultivated Europeans, irrespective of country, common literary standards. It insisted that one should be a man before being a German or Englishman or Frenchman. Local or personal peculiarities that interfered with conformity to the general norm were to be either disciplined or suppressed. This general norm that the neo-classicists set up suffered from artificiality and convention. Neo-classicism undoubtedly went too far in its tendency to proscribe all localism, all sharp emphasis on either individual or national traits. This extreme of self-effacement is one, at all events, of which we have been thoroughly cured. The Irish member of Parliament who recently arose and insisted on addressing the house in Gaelic had evidently attained to a high degree of both individual and racial self-assertion. He was a long way, in any case, from the old-fashioned notion of the gentleman, who, it will be remembered, did not pride himself on anything—not even on being an Irishman.

The movement, then, begun by Rousseau and Herder involved an intense individualism and nationalism, and at the same time a cult of the primitive, the spontaneous, the instinctive. This cult assumed not only a poetical and imaginative, but also a strictly erudite form. We already have in the Grimm brothers a mingling of exact scholarship and romantic enthusiasm. As one application of Rousseau's exaltation of the felicities of instinct over conventional life, the new school turned away from the age of national maturity when a few great writers gave the full measure of their perfection, and devoted the powers of comprehension and sympathy, on which it prided itself, to the study of origins. Now the study of origins as the term was so often understood by the romanticists—*i.e.*, national and collective origins — means in practice for all the European peoples a return to the Middle Ages. Mediaevalism benefited immensely by the weakening of the classical tradition. Heine says that the Schlegels were interested in India only because they saw in India a sort of elephantine Middle Ages. But there was more than this in the study of the Far East; it became in the hands of the romanticists a means of undermining the classical orthodoxy. The revelation of remote times and countries that were plainly cultivated, and yet in a way so strangely different from our own, had in it a potent suggestion of the new doctrine of relativity; it taught men to see,—

> "Beyond their passion's widest range
> Far regions of eternal change."

It helped them to feel that there was no one standard of taste, as the classicists maintained, but a multiplicity of standards, each one justified by the special circumstances of its age and environment.

The person who did more than any one else to popularize the new nationalism and cosmopolitanism was Madame de Staël. She was a direct disciple of Rousseau and at the same time a disciple of the Germans, chiefly through A. W. Schlegel, the tutor of her children. Her book on Germany marks an epoch in the Quarrel of Ancients and Moderns, and is probably more packed with thought than any other book ever written by a woman. A reading of Madame de Staël suggests that the ancients have suffered about as much from the influence of women who want a literature of sentiment and romance as they have from the influence of the scientific radicals, who can scarcely be said to want any literature at all. Her work also suggests how much one is aided in becoming a modern by a defec-

tive sense of form. "Les Grecs," says Madame de Staël, "tout
etonnants qui'ils sont, laissent peu de regrets." [5] No one could
have written that who really knew the Greeks at first hand, and
at the same time had even a remote perception of that "antique
symmetry" which Leonardo da Vinci lamented his failure to
attain (*defuit una mihi symmetria prisca*). Conversely a man may be
an arch-iconoclast, — he may, like M. Anatole France, display
an anarchical irreverence for every traditional belief, — and yet,
if he has only a glimpse of the antique symmetry, he will be a
doubtful recruit for the moderns. "It is difficult," says M.
France, "to join in the illusions of those who think that Latin
studies will be saved as soon as they share the noble name of
classics with modern rivals, which, try as they may, will never
equal them in dignity, strength, grace, and beauty."

An illuminating comparison might be made from the point of
view of our present topic between Madame de Staël and a contemporary who had likewise come under the influence of
Rousseau and Herder. Goethe's position in the Quarrel of
Ancients and Moderns is of peculiar interest because he was at
once a great scientist and a great man of letters, and also one of
the earliest adepts in the new cosmopolitanism. At the same
time he had a keen perception of the antique symmetry, and so,
as he grows older, tends to return to the classical tradition. He
refuses to treat Latin and Greek in a purely historical way, and
affirms for them not only a relative but an absolute worth. In his
later work one can even detect curious lapses into certain
classical, or rather pseudo-classical, errors. Yet Goethe can still
be of help in showing how humanism may be conciliated with
the new cosmopolitanism. We shall have paid a heavy price for
our historical method if as a result of attaining it we lose our
sense of values and are set afloat on a boundless sea of relativity.
The adjustment involved in escaping this danger is, as we
already have said, the most difficult that the humanist has to
make. We should add that Goethe's way of dealing with this
difficulty is substantially the same as that of Sainte-Beuve.

---

5. It is only fair to Madame de Staël to say that this sentence is taken from
her earlier and less mature work *De la Littérature* (1° Partie, ch. iv).

"The time of universal literature has come," says Goethe, and he urges us to cultivate in our attitude toward foreign literatures a world-wide sympathy. But he adds that if "we are looking for masterpieces we must think neither of the Chinese nor of the Servians, nor of Calderon nor of the Niebelungenlied, but must turn to the ancient Greeks, for in their work is found the model of man in his true beauty. The rest we should consider only historically and in order to appropriate to ourselves whatever good we may find in it." And again: "Nowadays we are expected to be Greeks and Latins, English and French; and now they are mad enough to send us to the Far East. A young man must really lose his wits. To console Meyer, I showed him my colossal head of Juno as a symbol, telling him that he could remain with the Greeks and find tranquillity."

In strict philosophy, Goethe's position is, of course, untenable. Greece was subject, like other countries, to the law of relativity. Things classical as well as things modern are a part of the universal flux. Yet Goethe's solution has, if not a theoretical, at least a practical value. The fixed stars are not really fixed, but for ordinary purposes may be considered so. In like manner some of the ancients and a few of the greatest of the moderns may be regarded as the fixed stars of literature. We may safely take our bearings with reference to them and be guided by them in deciding what is essence and what is accident in human nature. They are a sort of concrete *idea hominis*. There is something definitive in their rendering of life, — something that is purged of all localism, and deserves to be received as typical, even if not in quite the sense that the neo-classic dogmatist supposed. For example, how many centuries may pass before we have another picture of womanhood at once so large, so simple, and so representative as the Nausicaa episode in the Odyssey! "If we earnestly study classical antiquity," says Goethe, "a feeling comes over us as though it were only then that we really become men." And he naturally concludes: "May the study of Greek and Roman literature ever remain the basis of the higher culture."

II

GOETHE OCCASIONALLY REVERTS to the neo-classic narrowness in his later opinions; yet in the main he illustrates admirably how it is possible to attain the widest knowledge and sympathy and at the same time insist on judgment and selection. Like a true humanist, he combines opposite extremes and occupies all the space between them. One who has been sufficiently fortified in his sense of values may benefit greatly by what we have defined as Rousseauism. If a man has thoroughly assimilated the great masterpieces and attained a firm grasp on the humane tradition, he may profitably round out his humanism by the new cosmopolitan virtues and the historical method. But Rousseauism left to itself tends to inbreed individual and national temperament, and to substitute miscellaneous sympathies (or antipathies) for firm principles of judgment. Obviously the danger of impressionism is greater for the modern than for the ancient languages: first because of the very nature of the new cosmopolitanism to which the modern languages owe their success; second, because the problem of selection has not been simplified for the moderns, as for the ancients, by time. Only those books come down which deserve to last, says Emerson; and it may be said of most of the books which a teacher of the classics is likely to use that they are intrinsically important as well as important for their influence on the thought and literature of the world. The choice of books in the modern field, on the other hand, is likely to represent nothing higher than purely individual or national preferences, and often mere caprice. There is the constant peril in the modern languages of a cheap contemporaneousness. From the lists of books read in schools and colleges and from the publishers' catalogues one might infer that what is now taking the place of the masterpieces of Greece and Rome is a hodge-podge of second-rate French and German novels. Even the best judges are likely to be impressionists in dealing with contemporaries; so that from the point of view of the college one would be tempted to lay down the rule that the only good authors are dead authors.

In selecting reading, the modern-language teacher often does not consult even his own impressions, but the impressions of his students, and in his endeavor to secure their interest condescends deliberately to their crudity and immaturity. I once knew a French teacher who submitted the choice of books to be read to the vote of his class,—a truly democratic deference to the will of the majority. The danger, as another teacher explained to me, is that, if too high a standard of reading is set, the modern languages will be made as dull as Latin. It is true that something may well be sacrificed in the elementary courses to secure the interest of students, but this principle is being pushed too far. The test of a teacher, after all, is his power so to stimulate his students as to raise their interest to a higher level. From the point of view of the college the vital question is not whether a teacher inspires interest, but what kind of interest he inspires and in what quality of undergraduate. The college teacher should strive to interest his more capable men, even at the risk of boring the dullards.

The danger of a trivial and inferior choice of reading is not confined to contemporaries. Emerson's dictum that only those books come down which deserve to last has truth, if only it is taken to mean a real survival. A remarkable feature of modern scholarship, however, has been its tendency to disinter things to which the past had given decent burial. What are we to think, for instance, of the seventeenth-century English dramatists as a field of study for girl undergraduates? "Set the maiden fancies wallowing in the troughs of"—Wycherley. Of course the difficulty we refer to comes largely from the confusion of college and university standards, and we realize what a delicate adjustment is involved in institutions that set out to be at once college and university. Wycherley has his place in a university course, along with many other things that are contrary to the principle of selection on which the college rests. We should add that this latitude is desirable, even in the university, only when a large proportion of those who frequent it have already had a humane training. The confusion of university and college standards is one from which even the smaller college suffers. The young Ph.D., with his one-sided interest in his own specialty, is turned loose upon it, and often allowed to inflict his naïve enthusiasms on undergraduates.

It is hardly necessary to enlarge further on the danger of impressionism in modern language study. This danger is generally recognized. The real difference of opinion is as to the remedy. The counter-irritant that is at present most in favor is philology. Impressionism tempered by philological research (mainly in the mediaeval field) — that would seem to sum up the present tendency in modern languages. The emphasis on the Middle Ages is due in part, of course, to German influence. Our American scholarship, like the German scholarship from which it is imitated, has a predilection for origins, for "art's spring-birth so dim and dewy." But our mediaevalism is also due to the need that is felt of some counterpoise to the "softness" of the more strictly modern period — especially in English. Discipline in philology, however, will not take the place of the restraint that comes from a recognition of humane standards. Linguistic accuracy we must have in any case. The practical question is whether the average student in the modern field cannot get this accuracy and at the same time more assistance in forming humane standards from a classical rather than from a mediaeval background. Reasons that favor the classics may be drawn from the historical method itself. For the historical method is not concerned only with philological facts and their interrelationship, but also with the transmission of ideas. Now if the modern languages are related philologically [6] to the Middle Ages, they are related imaginatively and intellectually in at least an equal degree to ancient Greece and Rome. It is an historical fact that one may regret, but a fact none the less, that there is a sharp break, or, as the French express it, a solution of continuity, between mediaeval and modern France. A student of modern French who neglects the Latin classics to become familiar with the Chanson de Roland or the mystery plays of Chrétien de Troyes is allowing himself to be diverted from something that

6. No one can be a good mediaevalist who is not also a good Latinist. If the direct linguistic relation of modern language is with the Middle Ages, the remoter relationship is, of course, in the case of the Romance languages almost entirely, and in the case of English largely, with Latin.

the great French writers were steeped in to something of which they had little or no knowledge. The break with the mediaeval past was less abrupt in England than in France; yet even for the student of English literature an acquaintance with the Middle Ages before Chaucer is vastly less important than an acquaintance with the classics. The best avenue of approach to the great English poets, for example, is not through Caedmon and Beowulf, as some misguided moderns would have us believe, but through Homer and Virgil.

In theory, several of our institutions, especially Harvard, admit the importance of the classical background. But practically, when a graduate student is once started on his bit of mediaeval research, he not only has to forego his classics, but in preparing for his doctor's examination often has to cram from manuals a hasty knowledge of the very parts of the modern field that he is afterwards to teach. In pleading for a less rampant mediaevalism, we do not mean to disparage the Middle Ages. The value of mediaeval studies in themselves is not in question, but merely the wisdom of subordinating to these studies other fields of study that are still more valuable. It is a pity that life is so short and human energy so limited, for otherwise one might do full justice to all three periods,—classical, mediaeval, and modern. A man who was not planning to be a mediaeval specialist might without sacrifice of proportion take a course even in Gothic, if only he had what Lowell calls "the centurial adolescence of Methuselah."

The average student of modern languages should have a general grounding in the Middle Ages, and should have above all the knowledge of mediaeval life that comes from a careful study of Dante and Chaucer. But hope for a revival of sound literary standards lies, not in our present insistence on mediaeval philology, but rather in linking together the two ends of the humane tradition that have been disjoined by an unprofitable antagonism between ancients and moderns. As I have said elsewhere, an entirely new chapter in the relations of ancients and moderns will begin when they realize that they must not only cease to quarrel, but actually coöperate, if they are to make head against their common enemies, the pure utilitarians and scientific radicals. Latin and Greek must not attempt to arrogate to themselves alone the title of *litterae humaniores*. It is still more or less true in England, though less true than formerly, that a teacher of the classics enjoys prestige and dignity, whereas a teacher of modern languages is regarded as being about on a level with a teacher of dancing. The ancient humanities cannot maintain permanently this haughty isolation. The moderns are even now battering at the gates of Oxford, and Oxford will be fortunate if in making a necessary adjustment it does not become involved, as we have been, in all kinds of dubious radical experiments. The ancient humanities will gain greatly in interest by closer contact with the moderns; the moderns for their part will deserve to rank as humanities at all only by recognizing fully their indebtedness to the ancients. The classics with the modern foreground will be safeguarded against dryness and stagnation; the moderns with the classical background will be saved from impressionism and superficiality.

III

This whole problem of interrelating ancients and moderns is one, however, that concerns the college much more nearly than it does the graduate school. Graduate students of modern languages should already have a firm classical foundation. As it is, many of these students, as well as a fair proportion of their teachers, resemble Shakespeare [7] in at least one respect,—they have "small Latin and less Greek." This lack is the natural outcome of the predominance of moderns over ancients in undergraduate study. At Harvard, for example, there are over five times as many undergraduate enrollments in modern language electives (including English) as in the classics. Some of the more thoughtful of the moderns are beginning to see that such a difference in their favor is already undesirable; and that if it con-

---

7. Or rather the popular notion of Shakespeare. The atmosphere in which Shakespeare wrote was so saturated with Greek and Latin influence as to make his direct acquaintance with the classics a secondary question.

tinues to grow until college and university study of the classics is relegated to a few specialists the result will be disastrous to the interest of culture. Passing mention has been made of the Honors in Literature established at Harvard in 1903. This new scheme, quite apart from the practical question whether it will prove attractive to undergraduates, deserves some attention as a declaration of principles. To quote from the preliminary announcement, the purpose of Honors in Literature is "to offer in addition to the existing schemes for honors a plan that will encourage undergraduates to combine reading in the classics with reading in the modern languages. It is desired to emphasize in this way the underlying unity of literary study, and especially the interdependence of classical and modern literature." The plan is, in short, an attempt, probably the first attempt on the part of a college faculty, not only at a truce between ancients and moderns, but at a cordial coöperation in the interests of a broader and sounder literary training.

The new Harvard honors have some analogy with the examinations for classical honors at Oxford. They resemble the Oxford honors in encouraging the student to independent reading; in subordinating philology to literature; in testing primarily the student's powers of assimilation; and in not requiring even so much research as is represented by a thesis. There is an evident danger in eliminating so completely the linguistic element. Special vigilance will be needed to save the scheme from the charge of "softness," and to make clear that it is intended to produce humanists and not dilettantes. Our language teachers, trained for the most part almost exclusively in the methods of scientific research, are only too prone to confuse the humanist with the dilettante, to grant the name of scholar only to the man who is concerned with the collecting and classifying of facts. An equivalent, therefore, must be found in most cases for the Plato and Aristotle that give bone and sinew to the honor examinations at Oxford. A more thorough grasp of Greek philosophy is indeed one of the great *desiderata* of American scholarship; yet Greek philosophy can hardly hope to occupy the same position here as in the English universities, even if we should some day have classical scholars less interested in the uses of the optative in Plato and Aristotle and more interested in the supreme position of these writers in the history of human thought.

Theoretically—in coördinating the ancient and modern fields —the Harvard Honors in Literature represent an important advance on anything at Oxford; practically, neither this nor the other honor schemes at Harvard or other American institutions are likely soon to rival Oxford either in the standard of assimilative scholarship they attain or in the number of students they attract. The average educated American usually knows that a pass degree in the English universities is easy to get; he is often ignorant of the far more important fact that a large proportion of the students at Oxford, for example, take not a pass degree, but a degree with honors. Not only are many more honor degrees granted at Oxford [8] than at Harvard, but the Oxford honor examinations are much more difficult than the corresponding Harvard examinations. Of course, for the average Harvard undergraduate a college education does not mean honor work at all, but only too often a mere patchwork of large elementary courses, supplemented by professional or semi-professional study toward the end.

Stated, then, in the simplest terms, Harvard undergraduate work represents a low grade, Oxford a high grade, of assimilative scholarship. An unfriendly critic might add that if our colleges are inferior in assimilative scholarship to England, our graduate schools are inferior in productive scholarship to Germany. The first inferiority, however, is even more certain than the second, and, one is tempted to add, more serious, as affecting even more directly the whole tone of our national life. In spite of the immense stir we have been making of late about higher education, publishers assure us that for years past the demand for good reading has been decreasing rather than increasing. The Harvard Honors in Literature are intended to cultivate not only a taste for good reading, but the habit of doing

8. According to the report of the Curzon committee, 531 men received honors at Oxford in 1907. The Oxford Calendar for 1906 shows 3,663 undergraduates in residence. It would seem to follow from these figures that at least one half the Oxford undergraduates take degrees with honors.

this reading relatedly. The highest ambition of the friends of the college as opposed to the university should be to build up a popular honor system. The building up of such a system may prove, after all, the most practical means of rehabilitating the Bachelor of Arts degree, of giving it the meaning and seriousness it is so rapidly losing. It would hardly be going too far to say that the American college, with most of the things it has traditionally represented, is threatened at present with utter extinction. The Bachelor of Arts degree is menaced not merely by the curtailment of the term of residence,[9] but even more seriously, perhaps, by the widening out of the conditions on which the degree is granted, until it ceases to have any meaning. For instance, at Leland Stanford University a student may enter, not only without Latin and Greek, but without any language or nonscientific subject whatsoever except English composition, and then receive his Bachelor of Arts degree on completing a certain number of hours' work in mechanical engineering.[10] At this rate, the Bachelor of Arts degree may soon come to be granted to a student as a reward for getting his professional training as a plumber! At all events, so far as Leland Stanford is concerned, the Bachelor of Arts degree has already been emptied utterly of its traditional content. The whole question is one in which the alumni of the older institutions should take an active interest, and not leave it, as they have seemed inclined to do heretofore, to the educational experts. They should remember that a majority of these supposed experts are men of German training, whose primary interest is not in the college, but in the graduate school.

The day, then, may soon come, if indeed it has not come already, when the Bachelor of Arts degree, to have any real significance, will not only need to be accompanied by the name of the institution, but will need furthermore to be an honor degree. No doubt much may be done toward improving undergraduate instruction by a more careful tutorial supervision of the large

9. President Butler's proposal to reduce the term of residence to two years has naturally been followed by proposals from aspiring high-school teachers to annex what is left of the college course to the preparatory schools.

10. See *Leland Stanford Register*, 1906–07, pp. 36, 74.

courses, and by raising the standard of course examinations. There should be, in addition to all this, however, some proof of a connected plan of study, such as is furnished by a man who has won even a fourth class in an honor school at Oxford. The problem is to prevent incoherencies of choice on the part of the student, while allowing him every reasonable freedom of election. To meet undergraduate needs, an honor group should be broad and flexible; it should be primarily assimilative in purpose, and make no premature attempt to encourage research; finally, it should not take all of the student's time, but should leave him leisure for the pursuit of minor subjects. An honor system conceived in this spirit might be made the means, not of reacting against the elective system, but of completing it, unless, indeed, like some educational radicals, we conceive of the elective system as a mere orgy of individualism.

No honor scheme, any more than the present system of course examinations, will ever avail to distinguish between the student of humanistic instincts and the mere "grind." However, it might be easier to distinguish between the two kinds of students by a general examination on an honor group than by adding up marks in separate and often unrelated courses. The test of a student from the point of view of the college is not what he can do in any particular course, but how far he is able to organize the work he has done in all his courses into an orderly whole. Emphasis is rightly laid in the preparatory school on work done in separate courses; this emphasis may be lessened in the college, the purpose of which is to test not only the acquisitive, but even more the assimilative powers of the mind. We should not lose sight of the elementary truth that any honor scheme, however ingenious, is not worth much more than the living spirit of the men who are behind it. The success of undergraduate literary instruction will finally depend on the securing of men who are fitted for it both by native endowment and by adequate training in the graduate school or elsewhere. The evident danger of any form of the group system when not administered by the right kind of men is that it will lead to premature specialization.

It is possible to conceive of honor schemes that will have a fair measure of success.[11] The Honors in History and Literature established at Harvard in 1906 promise well in this respect. One should not, however, be too sanguine as to the immediate success of any plan for interrelating the study of the ancient and the modern languages, though the principle involved is, from the humane point of view, the most important of all. One great drawback is the unpopularity of the classics in this country. The case of our American classical departments is about the reverse of that of the lion's den in the fable: all tracks lead *away* from them. A much graver obstacle to the union of ancients and moderns in a common humane endeavor is the evident intention of the moderns to push their present advantage to the utmost. One can only deplore the complacency with which modern-language teachers as a body seem to regard the rapid decline of Greek studies during the past few years as well as the prospect of a demand in the near future for a Bachelor of Arts degree without Latin. The current utilitarianism, which appears to exalt the study of the modern at the expense of the ancient languages, will, if yielded to, deprive this very study of a large part of its seriousness and dignity. President Hadley may, as he said in a recent address, prefer "Wilhelm Meister' to Plato; but no one, it should be remembered, would be more offended by the doctrine implied in this utterance than Goethe himself. The modern languages will escape from the suspicion of being a cheap substitute for the traditional discipline only when taught with due reference to the classical background by men who are themselves good classical scholars.

11. The success in a large way of schemes for honors might necessitate the creation of separate examining boards, or else a great simplification in the present system of course examinations. The conducting of both course and honor examinations would impose an unfair burden on our already overworked faculties.

VIII

On Being Original

THERE HAS BEEN A RADICAL CHANGE during the last hundred
years in the world's attitude toward originality. An age of conformity has given way to an age of self-assertion; so that nowadays a man makes a bid for fame by launching a paradox, much
as he might have done in the time of Pope by polishing a commonplace. Then, even a person of genuine originality was in
danger of being accounted freakish. Now, many a man passes
for original who is in reality only freakish. Boileau, speaking for
the old criticism, says that Perrault was "bizarre;" Sainte-
Beuve, speaking for the new, says that Perrault had genius.
From the outset, the neo-classic critics stifled free initiative in
the name of the "rules," and opposed to every attempt at innovation the authority of Aristotle and the ancients. The relation
of the literary aspirant to the "models" during this period is not
unfairly summed up in the words of the comic opera,—

> "Of course you can never be like us,
> But be as like us as you're able to be."

Later, under French influence, the tyranny of etiquette was
added to the tyranny of classical imitation. Aristotle was reinforced by the dancing master. Social convention so entwined

itself about the whole nature of a Frenchman of the Old Régime that it finally became almost as hard for him as we may suppose it is for a Chinaman to disengage his originality from the coils of custom. The very word original was often used as a term of ridicule and disparagement. Brossette writes of the Oriental traveler Tavernier that he is "brutal and even a bit original." "When it is desired to turn any one to ridicule," writes Boursault about the same time, "he is said to be an *original sans copie*." Anything in literature or art that departed from the conventional type was pronounced "monstrous." La Harpe applies this epithet to the "Divine Comedy," and points out how inferior the occasional felicities of this "absurd and shapeless rhapsody" are to the correct beauties of a true epic like Voltaire's "Henriade."

And so we might go on, as Mr. Saintsbury, for example, does for scores of pages in his "History of Criticism," exposing the neo-classic narrowness, and setting forth in contrast the glories of our modern emancipation. But this is to give one's self the pleasure, as the French would say, of smashing in open doors. Instead of engaging in this exhilarating pastime, we might, perhaps, find more profit in inquiring, first, into the definite historical reasons that led to the triumph of the so-called school of good sense over the school of genius and originality; and second, in seeking for the element of truth that lurked beneath even the most arid and unpromising of the neo-classic conventions. For if, like Mr. Saintsbury and many other romanticists, we reject the truth along with the convention, we shall simply fall from one extreme into another.

The whole subject of originality is closely bound up with what is rather vaguely known as individualism. We must recollect that before the disciplinary classicism of the later Renaissance there was an earlier Renaissance which was in a high degree favorable to originality. At the very beginning of this earlier period, Petrarch made his famous plea for originality, in a letter to Boccaccio, and established his claim, in this as in other respects, to be considered the first modern man. "Every one," says Petrarch, "has not only in his countenance and gestures, but also in his voice and language, something peculiarly his own (*quiddam suum ac proprium*), which it is both easier and wiser to cultivate and correct than it is to alter.'' And so many of the Italians who followed Petrarch set out to cultivate the *quiddam suum ac proprium*, often showing real ardor for self-expression, and still oftener, perhaps, using the new liberty merely as a cloak for license. Society finally took alarm, not only at the license, but at the clash of rival originalities, each man indulging in his own individual sense without much reference to the general or common sense of mankind. We need not, however, repeat what we have already said in our first essay about the reaction of the later Renaissance against an excessive individualism. This reaction, especially in France and Italy, soon ran into excesses of its own. Yet we must not forget that, at the moment when the neo-classic disciplinarian appeared on the scene, the great creative impulse of the early Renaissance was already dying out or degenerating into affection. The various forms of bad taste that spread like an epidemic over Europe at the end of the sixteenth century and beginning of the seventeenth (cultism, Marinism, euphuism, préciosité, etc.), have their common source in a straining to be original in defiance of sound reason. We may say of the writers of these different schools as a class that, in spite of occasional lyrical felicities, they have ''all the nodosities of the oak without its strength and all the contortions of the Sibyl without the inspiration.''

The school of good sense was the natural and legitimate protest against this pseudo-originality. But this school can be justified on higher grounds than simply as a reaction from a previous excess. It tried to apply, however imperfectly, the profound doctrine of Aristotle that the final test of art is not its originality, but its truth to the universal. The question is one of special interest because we are living in an age that comes at the end of a great era of expansion, comparable in some ways to that of the Renaissance. Now, as then, there is a riot of so-called originality. In the name of this originality art is becoming more and more centrifugal and eccentric. As the result of our loss of standards, the classicist would complain, we are inbreeding personal and national peculiarities and getting farther and farther away from what is universally human.

In other words, the chief ambition of our modern art, which resembles in this respect some of the art of the later Renaissance, is to be original. The first aim of both classic and neo-classic art, on the other hand, was to be representative. Aristotle has said that it is not enough to render a thing as it is in this or that particular case, but as it is in general; and he goes on to say that the superiority of poetry over history lies in the fact that it has more of this universality, that it is more concerned with the essentials and less with the accidents of human nature. The weakness of neo-classic art was that it substituted the rule of thumb and servile imitation for direct observation in deciding what were accidents and what were essentials. It was ready to proscribe a thing as "monstrous," — that is, as outside of nature,—when in reality it was simply outside the bounds set by certain commentators on Aristotle. The artist had to conform to the conventional types established in this way, even if he sacrificed to them poignancy and directness of emotion. He was limited by the type not only in dealing with any particular literary form, — tragedy, epic, and so forth, — but even in his creating of individual characters. For example, he must be careful not to paint a particular soldier, but the typical soldier, and of course he was not to depart too far from the classical models in deciding what the traits of the typical soldier are. Thus Rymer condemns Iago because he is not true to the "character constantly worn by soldiers for some thousands of years in the world." According to Rymer, again, the queen in one of Beaumont and Fletcher's plays oversteps the bounds of decorum. Some particular queen, Rymer admits, may have acted in this way; but she must be rid of all her "accidental historical impudence" before she can become an orthodox, typical queen, entitled to "stalk in tragedy on her high shoes."

The attempt of the neo-classicists to tyrannize over originality and restrict the creative impulse in the name of the type was bound in the long run to provoke a reaction. To carry through the difficult and delicate task of breaking with convention some man of more than Socratic wisdom was needed; instead, this task was undertaken by the "self-torturing sophist, wild Rousseau." In almost the opening sentence of his "Confessions"

Rousseau strikes the note that is heard throughout the nineteenth century, from the early romanticists to Ibsen and Sudermann: "If I am not better than other men, at least I am different." By this gloating sense of his own departure from the type Rousseau became the father of eccentric individualists. By his insistence on the rights and legitimacy of unrestrained emotion he inaugurated the age of storm and stress, not only in Germany, but throughout Europe. Our modern impressionists, who would make of their own sensibility the measure of all things, are only his late-born disciples.

Emotion, insists the classicist, must be subdued to what is typical; else it will be eccentric and not true to the human heart. "The human heart of whom?" cries Alfred de Musset, like a true disciple of Jean-Jacques. "The human heart of what? Even though the devil be in it, I have my human heart of my own—*j'ai mon coeur humain, moi.*" The whole of French romanticism is in that *moi.* Away with stale authority, usage, and tradition, that would come between a man and his own spontaneity, and keep him from immediate contact with "nature." Let him once more see the world bathed in the fresh wonder of the dawn. To this end let him discard books ("a dull and endless strife") and live as if "none had lived before him."

Every man, in short, is to be an original genius. It was the assumption of this attitude by Rousseau's followers in Germany that gave its name to a whole literary period (*Geniezeit*). Germany sought its emancipation from convention, not, as Lessing would have wished, through the discipline of reason, but through "genius" and "originality," which meant in practice the opening of the floodgates of sentiment. We can imagine the disgust with which Lessing looked on the Rousseauism of the youthful Goethe. In "Werther," critics are accused of being in a conspiracy against originality. Their rules are compared to a system of dams and trenches with which the critics protect their own little cabbage-patches against genius, whose impetuous waves would otherwise burst forth and overwhelm them, and at the same time astound the world. One thinks of Lessing's admirable defense of criticism, of the passage in which he confesses that he owes all he has, not to genius and originality, but to a patient assimilation of the wisdom of the past. "Without criticism, I should be poor, cold, short-sighted. I am, therefore, always ashamed or annoyed when I hear or read anything in disparagement of criticism. It is said to suppress genius, and I flattered myself that I had gained from it something very nearly approaching genius. I am a lame man who cannot possibly be edified by abuse of his crutch."

We are still inclined to side with original genius against what Lessing calls criticism. Criticism itself has come to mean nowadays mere appreciativeness, instead of meaning, as it did for Lessing, the application of standards of judgment. It may, however, appear some day how much the great romantic leaders, Shelley for example, suffered from the absence of just what Lessing called criticism. Men may then grow weary of a genius and originality that are at bottom only an outpouring of undisciplined emotion. One whole side of our American transcendental school is only a belated echo of German romanticism, which itself continues the age of original genius. There is special danger even in Emerson's conception of originality, and the unbounded deference with which it fills him for the untrained individual. Every man, to become great, merely needs, it would appear, to plant himself indomitably on his instincts; but it is not safe for the average person to trust so blindly to what Rymer would have called his own "maggot." Hawthorne, the best observer of the group, has left an account of some of the nightmare originalities that were developed under the Concord influence.

We read of a certain character in one of Marivaux's plays: "He is a man whose first impulse is to ask, not, 'Do you esteem me?' but, 'Are you surprised at me?' His purpose is not to convince us that he is better than other people, but that he resembles himself alone." The comedy in which this eighteenth-century Bernard Shaw figures was written a number of years before Rousseau assumed the Armenian costume and began to agitate Europe with his paradoxes. Since Rousseau the world has become increasingly familiar with the man who poses and attitudinizes before it and is not satisfied until he can draw its attention to the traits that establish his own uniqueness. The eccentric individualist not only rejoices in his own singularity, but is usually eager to thrust it on other people. His aim is to startle, or, as the French would say, to *épater le bourgeois*, to make the plain citizen "stare and gasp." Dr. Johnson said of Lord Monboddo that if he had had a tail he would have been as proud of it as a squirrel. Perhaps Rousseau was never more deeply hurt than by the lady who said, on breaking with him, "You're just like other men." This, as a French critic remarks, was a home thrust that one of Molière's soubrettes could not have improved upon. The claim of Rousseau and his earlier followers was to be not simply unique, but unique in feeling. This sentiment of uniqueness in feeling speedily became that of uniqueness in suffering—on the familiar principle, no doubt, that life, which is a comedy for those who think, is a tragedy for those who feel. Hence arose in the romantic school a somewhat theatrical affectation of grief. Byron was far from being the first who paraded before the public "the pageant of his bleeding heart." Chateaubriand especially nourished in himself the sense of fated and preëminent sorrow and was ready to exclaim at the most ordinary mischance: "Such things happen only to me!" Sainte-Beuve makes an interesting comparison between Chateaubriand and another native of Brittany, the author of "Gil Blas." "A book like 'René,' " says Sainte-Beuve, "encourages a subtle spiritual pride. A man seeks in his imagination some unique misfortune to which he may abandon himself and which he may fold about him in solitude. He says to himself that a great soul must contain more sorrow than a little one; and adds in a whisper that he himself may be this great soul. 'Gil Blas,' on the other hand, is a book that brings you into full contact with life and the throng of your fellow creatures. When you are very gloomy and believe in fatality and imagine that certain extraordinary things happen to you alone, read 'Gil Blas,' and you will find that he had that very misfortune or one just like it, and that he took it as a simple mishap and got over it."

The same contrast might be brought out by comparing Montaigne and Rousseau, the two writers who, in a broad sense, are the masters respectively of Lesage and Chateaubriand. This contrast is easily missed, because at first glance Montaigne seems an arch-egotist like Rousseau, and is almost equally ready to bestow his own idiosyncrasies on the reader. Yet in the final analysis Montaigne is interested in Montaigne because he is a human being; Rousseau is interested in Rousseau because he is Jean-Jacques. Montaigne observes himself impartially as a normal specimen of the genus homo. Rousseau, as we have seen, positively gloats over his own otherwiseness. Montaigne aims to be the average, or, it would be less misleading to say, the representative man; Rousseau's aim is to be the extraordinary man, or original genius. Rousseau is an eccentric, Montaigne a concentric individualist. The sentence of Montaigne that sums him up is, "Every man bears within him the entire image of the human lot." Rousseau is rather summed up in his phrase, "There are souls that are too privileged to follow the common path," with its corollary that he is himself one of these privileged souls.

The nineteenth century saw the rise of a race of eccentric individualists, especially in art and literature, who, like Rousseau, scorned the common path and strove to distinguish themselves from the bourgeois and philistine in everything, from the details of their dress to the refinements of their sensations. In this quest of the rare and the original they attained to a departure from the norm that was not only eccentric, but pathological. Every man was to have the right to express not only his own particular vision of life, but his own particular nightmare. We finally come to a writer like Baudelaire, who builds himelf a "little strangely scented and strangely colored kiosk on the extreme tip of the romantic Kamchatka" and "cultivates his hysteria with delight and terror;" who, instead of being true to the human heart, as the old-fashioned classicist would say, makes it his ambition to create a "new shudder." All the modern writer cares for, says M. Anatole France, is to be thought original. In his fear of becoming commonplace he prides himself, like Victor Hugo, on reading only those books that other men do not read, or else he does not read at all, and so comes to resemble that eighteenth-century Frenchwoman who was said to have "respected in her ignorance the active principle of her originality." The danger of the man who is too assimilative, who possesses too perfectly the riches of tradition, is to feel that originality is henceforth impossible. It is related of a French critic that he used to turn away wearily from every new volume of poetry that was submitted to him, with the remark: "All the verses are written."

Genuine originality, however, is a hardy growth, and usually gains more than it loses by striking deep root into the literature of the past. La Bruyère begins his "Characters" by observing that "Everything has been said," and then goes on to write one of the most original books in French. Montaigne wrote a still more original book which often impresses the reader as a mere cento of quotations. An excessive respect for the past is less harmful than the excess from which we are now suffering. For example, one of our younger writers is praised in a review for his "stark freedom from tradition...as though he came into the world of letters without ever a predecessor. He is the expression in literary art of certain enormous repudiations." It is precisely this notion of originality that explains the immense insignificance of so much of our contemporary writing. The man who breaks with the past in this way will think that he is original when he is in reality merely ignorant and presumptuous. He is apt to imagine himself about a century ahead of his age when he is at least four or five centuries behind it. "He comes to you," as Bagehot puts it, "with a notion that Noah discarded in the ark, and attracts attention to it as if it were a stupendous novelty of his own."

We may be sure that the more enlightened of the Cave Dwellers had already made deeper discoveries in human nature than many of our modern radicals. Goethe said that if as a young man he had known of the masterpieces that already existed in Greek he would never have written a line. Goethe carries his modesty too far; but how grateful just a touch of it would be in the average author of to-day! With even a small part of Goethe's knowledge and insight, he would no longer go on serving up to us the dregs and last muddy lees of the romantic and naturalistic movements as originality and genius. He would see that his very paradoxes were stale. Instead of being a half-baked author, he would become a modest and at the same time judicious reader; or, if he continued to write, he would be less anxious to create and more anxious to humanize his creations. Sooner or later every author, as well as the characters he conceives, will have to answer the question that was the first addressed to any one who designed to enter the Buddhist church: "Are you a human being?" The world's suffrage will go in the long run to the writer or artist who dwells habitually in the centre and not on the remote periphery of human nature. Gautier paid a doubtful compliment to Victor Hugo when he said that Hugo's works seemed to proceed not from a man, but an element, that they were Cyclopean, "as it were, the works of Polyphemus." Hugo remained the original genius to the end, in contrast with Goethe, who attained humane restraint after having begun as a Rousseauist.

Romanticism from the very beginning tended to become eccentric through over-anxiety to be original; and romanticism is now running to seed. Many of our contemporary writers are as plainly in an extreme as the most extreme of the neo-classicists. They think that to be original they need merely to arrive at self-expression without any effort to be representative. The neo-classicist, on the other hand, strove so hard to be representative that he often lost the personal flavor entirely and fell into colorless abstraction. Both extremes fail equally of being humane. For, to revert to our fundamental principle, the humanist must combine opposite extremes and occupy all the space between them. Genuine originality is so immensely difficult because it imposes the task of achieving work that is of general human truth and at the same time intensely individual. Perhaps the best examples of this union of qualities are found in Greek. The original man for the Greek was the one who could create in the very act of imitating the past. Greek literature at its best is to a remarkable degree a creative imitation of Homer.

The modern does not, like the Greek, hope to become original by assimilating tradition, but rather by ignoring it, or, if he is a scholar, by trying to prove that it is mistaken. We have been discussing thus far almost entirely the originality of the Rousseauist or sentimental naturalist; but we should not fail to note the curious points of contact here as elsewhere between sentimental and scientific naturalism. The Baconian aims less at the assimilation of past wisdom than at the advancement of learning. With him too the prime stress is on the new and the original. Formerly there was a pedantry of authority and prescription. As a result of the working together of Rousseauist and Baconian there has arisen a veritable pedantry of originality. The scientific pedant who is entirely absorbed in his own bit of research is first cousin to the artistic and literary pedant who is entirely absorbed in his own sensation. The hero of modern scholarship is not the humanist, but the investigator. The man who digs up an unpublished document from some musty archive outranks the man who can deal judiciously with the documents already in print. His glory will be all the greater if he can make the new document a pretext for writing a book, for attempting a rehabilitation. The love of truth shades imperceptibly into the love of paradox; and Rousseauist and Baconian often coexist in the same person.

A royal road to a reputation for originality is to impugn the verdicts of the past,—to whitewash what is traditionally black or to blackwash what is traditionally white. Only the other day one of the English reviews published the "Blackwashing of Dante." A still better example is Renan's blackwashing of King David, which concludes as follows: "Pious souls, when they take delight in the sentiments filled with resignation and tender melancholy contained in the most beautiful of the liturgical books, will imagine that they are in communion with this bandit. Humanity will believe in final justice on the testimony of David, who never gave it a thought, and of the Sibyl, who never existed," etc. The whitewashings have been still more numerous. Rehabilitations have appeared of Tiberius, the Borgias, and Robespierre. A book has also been written to prove that the first Napoleon was a man of eminently peace-loving disposition. Mr. Stephen Phillips undertakes to throw a poetical glamour over the character of Nero, that amiable youth, who, as the versifier in "Punch" observes,—

"would have doubtless made his mark,
Had he not, in a mad, mad, boyish lark,
Murdered his mother!"

If this whitewashing and blackwashing goes on, the time will soon come when the only way left to be original will be to make a modest plea for the traditional good sense of the world. This traditional good sense was never treated with an easier contempt than at present. A writer named Bax, who recently published a volume rehabilitating the revolutionary monster Marat, says in his preface: 'It is in fact a fairly safe rule to ascertain for oneself what most people think on such questions'' (*i.e.* as the character of Marat), "and then assume the exact opposite to be true." Of most books of this kind we may say what FitzGerald said when Henry Irving made himself up in the role of Shylock to look like the Saviour: "It is an attempt to strike out an original idea in the teeth of common sense and tradition." Of course there are in every age and individual, as we have said elsewhere, elements that run counter to the main tendency. One of the regular recipes for writing German doctors' theses is to seize on one of these elements, exaggerate it, and take it as a point of departure for refuting the traditional view. Thus Rousseau says in one place that he has always detested political agitators. We may be sure in advance that some German will start from this to prove that Rousseau has been cruelly maligned in being looked on as a revolutionist.

Even our more serious scholars are finding it hard to resist that something in the spirit of the age which demands that their results be not only just, but novel. Even our older universities are becoming familiar with the professor who combines in about equal measure his love of research and his love of the limelight. In public opinion, the perfection of the type is the Chicago professor whose originality has become the jest of the cheap newspapers. Here are a few Chicago "discoveries," selected almost at random from the many that have been announced from time to time in the daily press:—

Kissing causes lockjaw.

The Pennsylvanians are turning into Indians.

A man does not need to take exercise after the age of thirty-five.

Music is antiseptic.

A dog will not follow an uneducated man.

Marriage is a form of insanity.

Americans are incapable of friendship.

Boccaccio was a Swede.

John D. Rockefeller is as great a man as Shakespeare.

Some day a wounded or even worn-out heart of a human being may be replaced by a healthy heart from a living monkey, etc.

The Chicago professors would say, and no doubt rightly, that they are misrepresented by these newspaper statements.[1] But we are only giving the general impression. Even the utterance of Dr. Osler that at once gave him such a start over all his academic rivals in the race for notoriety becomes comparatively unsensational when read in its context. The professor with an itch for the limelight has only to pattern himself on Rousseau, the great master of paradox. Rousseau's method has been compared to that of a man who fires off a pistol in the street to attract a crowd. When Rousseau has once drawn his crowd, he may proceed to attenuate his paradox, until sometimes it is in danger of dwindling into a commonplace.

Most good observers would probably agree that contemporary scholarship and literature are becoming too eccentric and centrifugal; they would agree that some unifying principle is needed to counteract this excessive striving after originality. For example, Professor Gummere, who is one of the most distinguished representatives of the scholarly tradition that ultimately goes back to Herder and the Grimm brothers, diagnoses our present malady with great clearness in a recent article on "Originality and Convention in Literature."[2] The higher forms of poetry and creative art, he says, are being made impossible by the disintegrating influences at work in modern life, and by an excess of analysis. He suggests as remedy that we jettison this intellectual and analytical element, and seek to restore once more the bond of communal sympathy. This remedy betrays at

1. Chicago instructors have told me that the University is the victim of a sort of conspiracy on the part of certain newspapers.

2. *Quarterly Review*, January, 1906.

once its romantic origin. It is only one form of Rousseau's assumption that an unaided sympathy will do more to draw men together than the naked forces of egoism and self-assertion will do to drive them asunder. Even in his studies of the beginnings of poetry Professor Gummere should, perhaps, have insisted more on communal discipline as a needful preliminary to communal sympathy. However that may be, our present hope does not seem to lie in the romanticist's attempt to revert to the unity of instinct and feeling that he supposes to have existed in primitive life. We need to commune and unite in what is above rather than in what is below our ordinary selves, and the pathway to this higher unity is not through sympathy, communal or otherwise, but through restraint. If we have got so far apart, it is because of the lack, not of sympathy, but of humane standards.

Without trying to enter fully into so large a topic as the impressionism of our modern society, its loss of traditional standards, and its failure as yet to find new, we may at least point out that education should be less infected than it is with a pedantic straining after originality. In general, education should represent the conservative and unifying element in our national life. The college especially must maintain humane standards, if it is to have any reason at all for existing as something distinct from university and preparatory school. Its function is not, as is so often assumed, merely to help its students to self-expression, but even more to help them to become humane. In the words of Cardinal Newman, the college is "the great ordinary means to a great but ordinary end;" this end is to supply principles of taste and judgment and train in sanity and centrality of view; to give background and perspective, and inspire, if not the spirit of conformity, at least a proper respect for the past experience of the world. Most of us have heard of Mrs. Shelley's reply when advised to send her boy to a school where he would be taught to think for himself: "My God! teach him rather to think like other people." Mrs. Shelley had lived with a man who was not only a real genius, but also an original genius in the German sense, and knew whereof she spoke. Now the college should not necessarily teach its students to think like other people, but it should teach them to distinguish between what is original and what is merely odd and eccentric, both in themselves and others. According to Lowell, this is a distinction that Wordsworth could never make, and Wordsworth is not alone in this respect among the romantic leaders. We must insist, at the risk of causing scandal, that the college is not primarily intended to encourage originality and independence of thought as these terms are often understood. The story is told of a professor in one of our Eastern colleges that he invariably gave a high mark to the undergraduates who contradicted the received opinions in his subject; but the highest mark he reserved for the undergraduate who in addition to contradicting the traditional view set up a new view of his own. As this fact became known, the professor was gratified by a rapid growth among his students of independent and original thinking.

The college should guard against an undue stress on self-expression and an insufficient stress on humane assimilation. This danger is especially plain in the teaching of English composition. A father once said to me of a "daily theme" course that it had at least set his son's wits to working. But what if it set them to working in the void? The most that can be expected of youths who are put to writing with little or no background of humane assimilation is a clever impressionism. They will be fitted, not to render serious service to literature, but at most to shine in the more superficial kinds of journalism. It is still an open question whether any direct method of teaching English really takes the place of the drill in the niceties of style that can be derived from translation, especially the translation of Latin; whether a student, for example, who rendered Cicero with due regard for the delicate shades of meaning would not gain more mastery of English (to say nothing of Latin) than a student who devoted the same amount of time to daily themes and original composition. We must, however, be fair to our departments of English. They have to cope with conditions not entirely of their own making, of which the most serious is something approaching illiteracy in many of the students that are forced upon them from the preparatory schools. In practice they have to devote most of their time to imparting not the elegancies, but the simplest decencies of the English language. Ultimately a great deal of what goes on in the more elementary college courses in English may well be relegated to the lower schools, — and the home, — and the work that is done in the advanced courses in composition will probably either be omitted entirely, or else done, as it is in France, in connection with the reading and detailed study of great writers. Assimilation will then keep pace as it should with expression.

Spinoza says that a man should constantly keep before his eyes a sort of exemplar of human nature (*idea hominis, tamquam naturae humanae exemplar*). He should, in other words, have a humane standard to which he may defer, and which will not proscribe originality, but will help him to discriminate between what is original and what is merely freakish and abnormal in himself and others. Now this humane standard may be gained by a few through philosophic insight, but in most cases it will be attained, if at all, by a knowledge of good literature — by a familiarity with that golden chain of masterpieces which links together into a single tradition the more permanent experience of the race; books which so agree in essentials that they seem, as Emerson puts it, to be the work of one all-seeing, all-hearing gentleman. In short, the most practical way of promoting humanism is to work for a revival of the almost lost art of reading. As a general rule, the humane man will be the one who has a memory richly stored with what is best in literature, with the sound sense perfectly expressed that is found only in the masters. Conversely, the decline of humanism and the growth of Rousseauism has been marked by a steady decay in the higher uses of the memory. For the Greeks, the Muses were not the daughters of Inspiration or of Genius, as they would be for a modern, but the daughters of Memory. Sainte-Beuve says that "from time to time we should raise our eyes to the hill-tops, to the group of revered mortals, and ask ourselves: What would they say of us?" No one whose memory is not enriched in the way we have described can profit by this advice. Sainte-Beuve himself in giving it was probably only remembering Longinus.[3]

3. See *On the Sublime*, section xiv.

IX

Academic Leisure

UNDER PRESENT CONDITIONS there is almost a touch of irony in associating the words "academic" and "leisure." A prominent physician has said that the two classes of persons most subject to nervous breakdown are Wall Street speculators and college professors. Nervous breakdown, as is well known, draws its victims from both those who have too much and those who have not enough to do; and the business man would no doubt add that the college teacher belongs among the latter. In spite of the gibe of the business man, however, the college teacher not only has enough and more than enough to do, but his work would seem to involve an unusual degree of strain and high pressure. At the present rate a college will soon come to suggest not the "quiet and still air of delightful studies," but a place from which one needs to retire occasionally to recuperate in a sanitarium. With the increase of Baconian strenuousness there has come into existence that strangest of all anomalies, the hustling scholar,—that is, if we render "scholar" according to its Greek derivation, the hustling man of leisure.

A great deal of the hustling that is either encouraged or imposed in academic circles is unintelligent, even from a strictly

Baconian standpoint. For if it is not important in the eyes of the Baconian that a man should have time to meditate, it is important that he should have time to do his own work to the best advantage. In Europe, for example, a man who is deemed capable of productive scholarship is not usually expected to spend more than three hours a week in lecturing. In this country the productive scholar often has to teach or lecture from nine to eighteen hours a week; in addition he is likely to be burdened with administrative duties, not to speak of the pot-boiling devices to which he sometimes resorts to eke out an insufficient salary. This state of affairs is contrary not only to sound Baconian principles, but to common sense, and will no doubt gradually be remedied.

The problem of relieving our scholars of unnecessary drudgery is one that touches the problem of leisure at a number of points, but is entirely distinct from it at others. We can imagine a company of productive scholars, each distinguished in his own subject and free to pursue it, and yet among them all not a single man of leisure. When the scholar of to-day complains of lack of leisure he nearly always means lack of time to do his own work. This failure to attach any further meaning to the word leisure simply expresses the change that has taken place in our whole conception of scholarship. Formerly the scholar was esteemed not so much for what he did as for what he was. In the words of Ecclesiasticus: "The wisdom of a learned man cometh by opportunity of leisure, and he that hath little business shall become wise." The Baconian tendency, on the other hand, is to measure the scholar's achievement almost entirely in terms of work. For example, President Harper, in an address delivered a short time before his death, enumerated what he conceived to be the qualifications of the perfect professor, and ended by saying that "he should be willing to work hard eleven months in the year." There is something in these words that reminds one involuntarily of the late Russell Sage and his celebrated article on the "Injustice of Vacations" (with portrait of the author at the age of eighty-eight in the benign attitude of leaning over a stock-ticker). One is also reminded, by way of contrast, of a saying of Aristotle's: "We work in order that we may have leisure." If President Harper's model professor ever snatches a brief interval from his fierce activity, it is evidently not that he may have leisure, but merely that he may recuperate (in a sanitarium or elsewhere), and prepare for fresh labor. The hero of the hour is not the man of leisure, but the man who engages in what may be termed humanitarian hustling. It has been taken as self-evident for some time that the college president [1] and the minister of the gospel should chiefly distinguish themselves in this way, and of late we are beginning to hear the still stranger doctrine that the judge on the bench should also be a humanitarian hustler.

It is no ordinary phenomenon,—this universal glorification of work, not only by business men like Russell Sage, but by college presidents, who stand traditionally for the idea of leisure. "The joy in work," says President Eliot, "is the chief hope of an industrial democracy." Once more one is reminded of Aristotle, and his conclusion that the highest good is not the joy in work, but the joy in contemplation. Aristotle, it should be remembered, in his praises of leisure and the contemplative life does not speak as a quietist or mystic, but as the interpreter of what is ripest in Greek, and, we are tempted to add, in all culture. Mr. Bosanquet excellently says: "Leisure — the word from which our word "school" is derived—was for the Greek the expression of the highest moments of the mind. It was not labor; far less was it recreation. It was that employment of the mind in which by great thoughts, by art and poetry which lift us above ourselves, by the highest exertion of the intelligence, as we should add, by

---

1. The comic papers, however, are beginning to have their doubts. Here are two samples from a list of College Presidents, New Style, in a recent number of *Life*:—

"Philander Boggs, D.D., President of the University of Arkana, has just received the degree LL.D. from Yarvard. President Boggs, by his recent action in raising $250,000 in three weeks, has well merited this honor, and at the same time has placed his institution among the foremost of the land.

.   .   .   .

When that sterling educator, Boxall Webster, took charge of the Hilldale Seminary, there was scarcely a dollar in the treasury. Now there are five new buildings, and bequests have been streaming in so fast that it has been necessary to buy a new safe. President Webster is undoubtedly a leader in modern thought," etc.

religion, we obtain occasionally a sense of something that cannot be taken from us, a real oneness and centre in the universe; and which makes us feel that whatever happens to the present form of our little ephemeral personality, life is yet worth living because it has a real and sensible contact with something of eternal value.''

Some tradition of this scholarly leisure still lingers along with the old humanism in the English universities. But even at Oxford and Cambridge, and still more in our own college faculties, the humanist and man of leisure is being elbowed aside by the scientific specialist and the bustling humanitarian. The view of life that tends to prevail excludes the idea of repose. It looks upon man, not as having his goal in himself, but as an instrument for the attainment of certain outer ends; it therefore disregards the ways in which the activity and proper perfection of a human being differ from the activity and proper perfection of an instrument or machine; it neglects, in a word, all that the Greek epitomized in his idea of leisure, and sets up instead the worship of energy and mechanical efficiency. ''The stress and rush of life seems greater to-day in America than it ever was before,'' says Mr. Bryce. ''Everybody, from the workman to the millionaire, has a larger head of steam on than his father had.'' Man, as Mr. Bryce's metaphor suggests, is judged by much the same standard as a locomotive, and is considered inactive unless the wheels are visibly turning. Now, just as it has been found good economy when a locomotive begins to show signs of wear to consign it to the scrap heap and substitute a new one, so there is a tendency to prefer to even a middle-aged man a young man whose vital machinery is still unimpaired. There are not lacking academic Baconians, like Dr. Osler, who are ready to give a sort of scientific sanction to this drift toward a brutal naturalism in the world of business. After large deductions are made for humorous exaggeration, Dr. Osler's utterances still remain a curious example of the way in which certain minds are reverting, under the guise of scientific progress, to the ethics of the Stone Age.

Bacon himself would, no doubt, disapprove of much of our modern strenuousness. Yet the connection is plain between even the more exaggerated forms of this strenuousness and Bacon's exaltation of the active over the contemplative life. Up to the time of Bacon there had been a fairly consistent tradition in the world that the highest good is attained, not by action, but by meditation. In this one point, at least, Orient and Occident, Greek and Christian, Mohammedan and Buddhist and Hindu, were agreed. Faith in the benefits of an undisturbed meditation led to the founding of innumerable monasteries. Mediaeval theology appropriated Aristotle's doctrine of leisure, and used it to give additional sanction to the Christian doctrine that exalted the wisdom of Mary above the wisdom of Martha, and saw in the attainment of beatific vision the crown and fulfillment of the religious life. And so Bacon's attack on Aristotle and his conception of leisure was at once felt to imply an attack on one of the central tenets of traditional belief. The Baconian reaction against the contemplative life was aided by the discontent that had been growing for centuries with certain aspects of the organized attempts to encourage this life. Men have always felt the necessity of leisure and contemplation; and yet their efforts to promote what they assumed to be the highest good have often seemed to promote almost equally what is certainly one of the greatest of evils,—indolence (*corruptio optimi pessima*). For example, in theory the monastery was a place where the sage and saint were to use their release from secular affairs to engage in austere meditations. The reality was only too often the lazy friar, who, as Voltaire puts it, "had made a vow to God to live at our expense." Again, universities like Oxford and Cambridge were intended to be the homes of learned leisure. Instead, Oxford became the home of port and prejudice that Gibbon has described; and another eighteenth-century observer saw in Cambridge merely a place where a man might perfect himself in the art of lounging.[2] Lowell was in favor of establishing a few "lazyships" at Harvard, but the phrase is obviously unfortunate, since it obscures the all-important distinction between idleness and leisure.

The idea of leisure, then, has suffered not only from the

2. See *Spectator*, No. 54.

progress of Baconian principles, but from the unworthiness of many of those who have claimed to represent it. It has also suffered during the past hundred years or more from the influence of Rousseau and the Rousseauists. On either side of the entrance to the reading-room of the new Sorbonne at Paris are mural paintings of two female figures: one, of strenuous aspect, and with contracted brow, is entitled Science; the other, in floating draperies, and with vague, far-away eye, is entitled Rêve. The scientific analyst and romantic dreamer who are symbolized in this way have divided between them the nineteenth century, and in their very opposition have been hostile to leisure. If the Baconian denies leisure entirely as something distinct from rest or relaxation, the Rousseauist converts leisure into revery. He tends to efface the line between thinking and dreaming. He fails to feel sufficiently the difference between the "sessions of sweet silent thought" and a "wise passiveness." He is unwilling or unable, as Thiers said was the case with Louis Napoleon, to distinguish between the verbs *rêver* and *réfléchir*. Revery, as Sainte-Beuve remarks, was Rousseau's great discovery, his America (*son Amérique à lui*). The charms of plain loafing have been thoroughly appreciated since the beginning of the world. But in his practice of "le rêve" Rousseau attained to a sort of transcendental loafing—he invited his soul to loaf. He is the first of a long series of aesthetic vagabonds who have found solace in a world of luxurious dreams, and often sought refuge in this world from a reality disenchanted by scientific analysis. This confusing of the contemplative life with revery is doubtless destined to become a matter of curious study when we see the romantic movement more from the outside and are less inclined than we are at present to take the romantic leaders at their own estimate of themselves. "I am in no wise tempted by the active life," says Rousseau, and thus far he speaks like some sage or eremite; but as we read on we discover that he was a kind of hermit who, as Byron puts it, would have liked a "harem for a grot," and who entertained his solitude with the very images that St. Anthony sought to escape by leaping into the snow.

The confusion between revery and leisure is still more flagrant in Friedrich Schlegel's extraordinary Elegy on Idleness:

"O idleness, idleness! thou art the native element of innocence and poetry;... blessed the mortals who cherish thee, thou sacred gem, sole fragment of godlike being that is left to us from paradise.... Why are the gods gods if not because they consciously and purposely do nothing, because they understand this art and are masters in it? And oh, how the poets, the sages and saints are endeavoring to become like the gods in this respect! How they vie with each other in the praise of solitude, leisure, and a liberal carelessness and inactivity!... Through composure and gentleness only, in the sacred quietude of genuine passiveness, can we realize our whole self.... The right of idleness marks the distinction between the noble and the common, and is the true essence of aristocracy. To say it in a word: The more divine man is, the more fully does he resemble the plant." [3]

Revery is variously modified not only by individual but by national temperament. If it is voluptuous in Rousseau, and sentimental and pedantic in the Germans, in an Englishman like Wordsworth it tends to become austere and ethical. Wordsworth seeks to bestow moral seriousness and dignity on what is at bottom only a delicious epicureanism, a rapturous mingling of soul and sense. For example, Peter Bell "had a dozen wedded wives," and had committed other heinous offenses against God and man (the most heinous, of course, being his failure to transcendentalize "a primrose by a river's brim"). All might have been different with Peter Bell if he had only felt the "witchery of the soft blue sky."

We do not mean to make an indiscriminate attack on romantic revery. The humanist will not deny the uses of a "wise passiveness;" he will simply deny that a wise passiveness is a sufficient substitute for leisure. He will be grateful for those new faculties with which, according to his admirers, Rousseau enriched the human soul, though he will always regret that what is sound and valuable in Rousseau's message should be mixed up with so much that is morbid and pathological. The humanist will grant freely the good of Rousseauism in its proper place, but

3. *Lucinde*, in which the Elegy on Idleness appears, was published in 1799.

of Rousseauism out of its place he will say, with a recent French writer, that it is an "integral corruption of the higher parts of human nature." [4]

In general the humanist will not repudiate either sentimental or scientific naturalism; for this would be to attempt an impossible reaction. His aim is not to deny his age, but to complete it. Various modern tendencies have been freely criticized throughout these essays, especially the tendency to make utopian appeals to the principle of brotherhood when what is wanted is a submission to the discipline of common sense and humane standards. But because some sobering off is desirable after what one is tempted to call the romantic and naturalistic debauch of the nineteenth century, it does not follow that we should return to the point of view of the eighteenth century (though a greater respect for an eighteenth-century writer like Dr. Johnson, as compared with certain romanticists, would not be a bad symptom). The great expansion of the nineteenth century, its fullness of knowledge and sympathy, are excellent; but only in so far as they prepare the way for a juster judgment and a richer selection. Knowledge and sympathy alone will work out into ironical contradictions of themselves,[5] and at the same time prove impotent to save us from anarchy and impressionism. The pathway to the new synthesis that we need is not through the strenuousness of the Baconian; nor can we hope to escape the Baconian one-sidedness by resorting to the revery of the Rousseauist. The fruitful opposite of strenuousness is not revery, but leisure and reflection.

Plato, who, as Emerson remarks, makes sad havoc with our originalities, has discussed this whole question of the strenuous life toward the end of his dialogue called "The Statesman." [6] There are two types of character, according to Plato, each admirable in its own way; one of these may be described in

---

4. See P. Lasserre, *Le romantisme francais* (1907), p. 70. Lasserre's book is a keen analysis and arraignment of the French romantic movement, but is weak on the constructive side.

5. Cf. pp. 103ff.

6. See Jowett's *Plato*, iv, p. 429 and pp. 517, 518.

terms expressive of motion or energy, and the other in terms expressive of rest and quietness. Of the first we say, how manly! how vigorous! how ready! And of the second, how calm! how temperate! how dignified! The greatest triumph of statecraft is to see that the balance is maintained between these two types, and that neither unduly predominates. For strenuousness, when it gains excessive mastery, "may at first bloom and strengthen, but at last bursts forth into downright madness," and is especially likely, Plato adds elsewhere, to involve a state in wars with all its neighbors. On the other hand, "the strenuous character, inferior though it be to the temperate type in justice and caution, has the power of action in a remarkable degree, and where either of these two types is wanting, there cities cannot altogether prosper either in their public or in their private life." Therefore Plato imagines a perfect statesman, a sort of *deus ex machina*, whose business it is to weave together the strenuous and the temperate characters as the warp and woof of the perfect state.

Some of the duties that Plato assigns to his ideal ruler would seem to belong in our own day to the higher institutions of learning. Our colleges and universities could render no greater service than to oppose to the worship of energy and the frantic eagerness for action an atmosphere of leisure and reflection. It would seem that they might recognize the claims of the contemplative life without encouraging a cloistered seclusion or falling into the monastic abuses of the past. We should make large allowance in our lives for the "eventual element of calm," if they are not to degenerate into the furious and feverish pursuit of mechanical efficiency. The industrial democracy of which President Eliot speaks will need to temper its joy in work with the joy in leisure if it is to be a democracy in which a civilized person would care to live. The tendency of an industrial democracy that took joy in work alone would be to live in a perpetual devil's sabbath of whirling machinery, and call it progress. Progress, thus understood, will prove only a way of retrograding toward barbarism. It is well to attain to the secret of power, but not at the sacrifice of the secret of peace. What is wanted is neither Oriental quietism, nor again the inhuman strenuousness of a certain type of Occidental; neither pure action nor pure repose, but a blending of the two that will occupy all the space between them, — that activity in repose which has been defined as the humanistic ideal. The serious advantage of our modern machinery is that it lightens the drudgery of the world and opens up the opportunities of leisure to more people than has hitherto been possible. We should not allow ourselves to be persuaded that the purpose of this machinery is merely to serve as point of departure for a still intenser activity. The present situation especially is not one that will be saved—if it is to be saved at all—by what we have called humanitarian hustling. We have already quoted the federal judge who exhorts the American people to combine ten per cent of thought with ninety per cent of action. If we ourselves ventured on an exhortation to the American people, it would rather be that of Demosthenes to the Athenians: "In God's name, I beg of you to think." Of action we shall have plenty in any case; but it is only by a more humane reflection that we can escape the penalties sure to be exacted from any country that tries to dispense in its national life with the principle of leisure.

Index

212